KEY ISLAMIC POLITICAL THINKERS

KEY ISLAMIC POLITICAL THINKERS

KEY ISLAMIC
POLITICAL THINKERS

Edited by John L. Esposito

AND

Emad El-Din Shahin

OXFORD
UNIVERSITY PRESS

OXFORD
UNIVERSITY PRESS

Oxford University Press is a department of the University of Oxford.
It furthers the University's objective of excellence in research, scholarship,
and education by publishing worldwide. Oxford is a registered trade mark of
Oxford University Press in the UK and in certain other countries.

Published in the United States of America by Oxford University Press
198 Madison Avenue, New York, NY 10016, United States of America.

The essays in this volume were originally published in
The Oxford Handbook of Islam and Politics

Library of Congress Cataloging-in-Publication Data
Names: Esposito, John L., editor. | Shahin, Emad Eldin, 1957- editor.
Title: Key Islamic political thinkers / edited by John L. Esposito and Emad
El-Din Shahin.
Description: New York, NY : Oxford University Press, 2018. | Includes index.
Identifiers: LCCN 2018013406 (print) | LCCN 2018015122 (ebook) |
ISBN 9780190900366 (updf) | ISBN 9780190900373 (epub) | ISBN 9780190900359
(pbk.) | ISBN 9780190900342 (hardcover)
Subjects: LCSH: Political science-Islamic countries. | Political
science-Philosophy. | Islam and politics.
Classification: LCC JA84.I78 (ebook) | LCC JA84.I78 K49 2018 (print) | DDC
320.55/70922—dc23
LC record available at https://lccn.loc.gov/2018013406

1 3 5 7 9 8 6 4 2
Paperback printed by WebCom, Inc., Canada
Hardback printed by Bridgeport National Bindery, Inc.,
United States of America

CONTENTS

PART III
THE "INTELLECTUALS" OF POLITICAL ISLAM

CONTRIBUTORS

Shahrough Akhavi is Distinguished Professor Emeritus in the Department of Political Science at the University of South Carolina.

John L. Esposito is Professor of Religion and International Affairs and Founding Director of the Prince Alwaleed Bin Talal Center for Muslim-Christian Understanding in the Walsh School of Foreign Service at Georgetown University.

Behrooz Ghamari-Tabrizi is Professor of sociology and history at the University of Illinois, Urbana-Champaign.

Bettina Gräf is a Researcher of Arabic and Islamic studies at Ludwig-Maximilians-Universität in Munich.

Mojtaba Mahdavi is the Edmonton Council of Muslim Communities Chair in Islamic Studies and Associate Professor of political science at the University of Alberta.

Ahmad Moussalli is Professor of political studies at American University of Beirut.

Ahmad Sadri is Gorter Professor of Islamic World studies and Professor of Sociology at Lake Forest College.

Mahmoud Sadri is Professor of sociology at the Federation of North Texas Universities.

Emad El-Din Shahin is the Dean of the College of Islamic Studies, Hamad bin Khalifa University, Qatar Foundation, and a Senior Fellow at Georgetown University.

Niloufer Siddiqui is a postdoctoral fellow in the Department of Political Science at the Rockefeller College of Public Affairs and Policy, State University of New York at Albany.

CONTRIBUTORS

Azzam Tamimi is an academic and political activist and the former director of the
Institute of Islamic Political Thought.
Joshua T. White is Associate Professor of the Practice of South Asia studies and
Senior Fellow at the Edwin O. Reischauer Center for East Asia Studies at the
Paul H. Nitze School of Advanced International Studies at Johns Hopkins.
Peter Woodward is Professor of politics at the University of Reading.

NOTE ON TRANSLITERATION

Due to variance in usage, rather than attempt to impose a style of transliteration across the entire volume, we have allowed each author to transliterate foreign-language terms according to his or her stylistic preference.

KEY ISLAMIC POLITICAL THINKERS

Key Islamic Political Figures

JOHN L. ESPOSITO AND EMAD EL-DIN SHAHIN

INTRODUCTION

The purpose of this book is to help readers understand the different streams within contemporary Muslim political thought. Each essay in this book explores the work of a key twentieth-century Islamic thinker whose influence stretches beyond his home country. Many of these figures are still active, and their thought continues to affect thousands of Muslims. The choice of a specific time frame should not indicate any discontinuity in the intellectual stream within Muslim societies. In fact, we see the evolution of Muslim political thought as a continuous process that in a few cases manifests a clear organic connection. For example, one can trace a continuous path from the Islamic reformer Jamal al-Din al-Afghani (1838–1879) to Muhammad ʿAbduh (1849–1905), Muhammad Rashid Rida (1865–1935), Hassan al-Banna (1906–1949), and today's Muslim Brothers. Similar connections can be easily traced between generations of intellectuals in other parts of the Muslim world, not only chronologically but also across borders as certain intellectuals or movements in one country see themselves as the heirs of reformers in another.

Obviously, the context in which this discourse evolved has been extremely important. The last two centuries have been vibrant yet turbulent and unsettling. Three transformative developments had the greatest bearing on Islamic political thought: the decline of the old order and eventual collapse of the caliphate; colonial occupation and the continuation of external hegemony; and the rise of secular Muslim intellectuals and secular movements. They were accompanied by the demise of the old legal and social structures (the old order); the emergence of nation-states; increased westernization and modernization; the creation of Israel and repeated defeats and humiliations of Muslims; the rise of Islamic revival movements; globalization; and the rise of nonstate actors and resistance.

FOUNDERS OF POLITICAL ISLAM

This book focuses on key Muslim intellectual figures from various schools of contemporary political Islam. "Political Islam" here refers to attempts by individuals, groups, and movements to reconstruct the political, economic, and social dimensions of their societies along Islamic lines, including an orientation toward *shari'a* and an approach to the questions of whether and how to establish an Islamic state. Given the countless number of Muslim intellectuals who have emerged over the past century and a half seeking to reform Islam from within, no single volume could hope to offer an exhaustive survey of Islamic political thought. Instead, we have chosen a selection of thinkers that is, we think, representative of the main streams in contemporary Muslim political thought and of its principal themes. We have divided those thinkers into three main categories: the founders of political Islam, revolutionary ideologues, and the "intellectuals" of political Islam. Hassan al-Banna and Abu al-A'la al-Mawdudi are rightly considered the forefathers of contemporary political Islam. Both reinterpreted the faith to make religion a vehicle for social and political action. This understanding became a common feature of political Islam. For al-Banna and Mawdudi the fulfillment of *tawhid*—the unity of God—is manifest in political unity under *shari'a* as a comprehensive way of life, central government, and an Islamic caliphate. After the collapse of the caliphate, which for centuries had acted as the symbol of the political unity of the *umma* (the global community of Muslims), al-Banna and Mawdudi proposed *shari'a* as an alternative unifying concept. *Shari'a* engenders the submission of the Muslim community not to an unsalvageable and bygone caliphate and central caliph but to a superior yet abstract and immutable notion that also can act as a unifying bond. *Shari'a* becomes a new source of legitimacy for the state, constitutional guidelines, and political authority. In brief, both al-Banna and Mawdudi succeeded in reproducing *shari'a* as a comprehensive body of laws, a way of life, guidelines for Muslims, divine legislation, a source of unity and stability for the Muslim community, and a shared worldview.

Al-Banna and Mawdudi also succeeded in producing a coherent blueprint for a revivalist Islam that consists of an ideology, organization (the avant-garde party), and activism. They emphasized individual activism and individual engagement in community affairs as a religious duty. As the chapters on al-Banna and Mawdudi show, both men provided intellectual blueprints that attempted to explain the reasons for the decline of Muslim society and the ways to revive it. Al-Banna and Mawdudi also institutionalized two major Islamic organizations in their respective countries that survived beyond their lifetimes. Another lasting impact of these two founders has been the centrality of the state to political Islam and Islamic activism. Al-Banna sees Islam as *din wa dawla* (both religion and state), while for Mawdudi, *shari'a* cannot function without the agency of the state. An Islamic political system is critical for Mawdudi. If a government discards the revealed laws it becomes illegitimate, and its authority will not be binding. As for al-Banna, despite his recognition of the need to "form" the Muslim individual, the Muslim family, the Muslim society as the bases for establishing an Islamic state, he viewed the centrality and supremacy of the state as necessary for keeping the balance and well-being of the *umma* and creating an all-encompassing Muslim way of life.

Finally, with regard to their perceptions of the West, both al-Banna and Mawdudi believed that there is not much the West could offer Islam. Islam contained all the necessary values for progress, and only via a Muslim revival could Muslim societies achieve modernity. Unlike the Westernized elite, they wanted to subordinate modernity to Islam, not the other way around.

In his analysis of the intellectual thought of Hassan al-Banna, Ahmad Moussalli focuses on al-Banna's religious and political discourse. He discusses al-Banna's intellectual framework under three central principles: Islam and politics, the Islamic state and *shari'a*, and democracy and *shura* (consultation). In this chapter, Moussalli traces the connection al-Banna makes between a metaphysical *tawhid* and its political articulations. According to Moussalli, al-Banna demonstrated the possibility of synthesizing Western political thought and contemporary Islamic political frameworks (similar to his predecessors Afghani and 'Abduh). For example, he believed that it was possible to assimilate democracy with the Islamic concept of *shura* and comprehensive governance. Moussalli shows how this central concept has evolved within Islamic movements to become a source of legitimation (or delegitimation) of regimes and a reason for their seizure of power in the name of the people.

In their chapter on Mawdudi and his intellectual framework, Joshua T. White and Niloufer Siddiqui highlight the significance of context in shaping his ideas, starting with the collapse of the caliphate, which forced Muslims to live within the boundaries of a nation-state, not a universal Islamic one. For them, "Mawdudi delivered a message that spoke to his age and provided a template for those engaged in constitutional experimentation in a newly established Pakistani state." Indeed, the impact of Mawdudi's ideas and thought was felt well beyond Pakistan. White and Siddiqui maintain that Mawdudi's ideas helped in shaping "the contours of modern Islamic discourse."

REVOLUTIONARY IDEOLOGUES

The revolutionary ideologues of political Islam reject the prevailing order in their respective societies and advocate a radical and comprehensive change of the existing systems. The revolutionary ideas of Sayyid Qutb, Ali Shari`ati, and Ayatollah Khomeini were the product of their postcolonial context. This context was dominated by increasing secularization and westernization as a state-adopted model of development, the emergence of a bipolar system and the entanglements of the Cold War, and the growing state repression and suppression of Islamic movements. Turkey's Ataturk model was a source of inspiration for leaders such as Reza Khan of Iran, Zahir Shah of Afghanistan, Nasser of Egypt, and Bourguiba of Tunisia, who all acknowledged Ataturk's influence on them and attempted to emulate his style of rule. Instead of adopting systems that took Islam seriously, a Kemalist model that rested on one-man rule, a single party, populism, statism, demagoguery, secularization, and central planning prevailed.

Qutb, Shari'ati, and Khomeini share common features as revolutionary ideologues. They all tried to achieve a total break with the Kemalist model and the existing order. They vehemently rejected the secular postindependence framework and advocated severing any ties with it. While focusing on the "delegitimation" of that framework, they were also critical of the traditional religious establishment. Their criticism (to a lesser degree with Khomeini) was aimed at the members of society who either followed these *jahili* (un-Islamic) regimes or accepted submission to "black" Shiism (the type of distorted Islam promoted by the monarchy and its co-opted religious scholars). All were revolutionaries in the true sense, as they called for bringing about a radical change in their respective societies. For Qutb, all existing systems were *jahili* (un-Islamic) and had to be replaced by an Islamic one. Shari'ati envisioned a totally new system following the footsteps and exemplar of the imam. He reinterpreted the imamate to mean "a committed and revolutionary leadership, responsible for the movement and growth of society on the basis of its worldview and ideology, and for the realization of the divine destiny of man in the plan of creation."[1] Imam Khomeini provided that leadership, the "formula" that mobilized the entire Iranian people toward the fulfillment of Shari'ati's dream. That formula was the rule of the jurist, *wilayat al-faqih*, and the Islamic government.

Another feature common to Qutb, Shari'ati, and Khomeini is that all had a strong faith in Islam as an alternative to capitalism and socialism. For them the West had become ideologically bankrupt in both its capitalist and socialist iterations. Decades before Samuel Huntington, they believed that the conflict between Islam and the West was religious and cultural in essence. For Sayyid Qutb, the West's racism and moral promiscuity epitomized modern-day *jahiliyyah.* Sharia`ti was critical of capitalism for its enslavement of the human being and socialism for its vulgarity. For Khomeini, the West was toxic and entirely irrelevant to his model.

Despite these similarities, some differences stand out. Khomeini had a clearer vision of the type of government he wanted to build (theocratic-populist) and the way to achieve it. Shari`ati was most original in thought, particularly in carving new meanings that had a profound practical impact on the Shi`a community. Qutb broadened the concept of *jahiliyyah,* or "disbelief/un-Islamic," to include the West and the Muslim societies, thus reenhancing a severe state of polarization, an irreconcilable one, between Islam and the West.

Sharough Akhavi's chapters on Ali Shari`ati and Sayyid Qutb tread the different contours of their lives and ideas. He sees Shari`ati's greatest contribution in the practical impact of his ideas more than their ideological coherence. Akhavi describes Shari`ati as a tragic figure who held a strong belief and a deep sense of mission to change his society and the world, a will to induce collective change and mobilize nations, and unwavering determination to confront not only local tyrants but also international hegemons. In fact, these traits apply to Qutb as well, indeed to many of the key figures in this book. Some wrote their memoirs while in their midthirties, in anticipation of their premature deaths; others met their fates in a tragic way by execution or assassination.

In his chapter on Ayatollah Khomeini, Mojtaba Mahdavi traces the evolution of Khomeini's thinking through five distinct stages, beginning with political quietism and concluding with political absolutism. Mahdavi contends that Khomeini's transition from quietism to activism was a result of his fear of increasing secularization and the need to institutionalize the revolution. Mahdavi considers the postrevolution Iranian regime Khomeini's most significant legacy.

THE INTELLECTUALS OF POLITICAL ISLAM

Those whom we have termed the "intellectuals" of political Islam make an excellent case for the diversity and complexity of contemporary Muslim discourse. Their intellectual interests may seem similar (renewal of religion, modernizing Islam, views on women, views on the West), but their approaches and ways of thinking can be quite different. What distinguishes them from other intellectuals who have concerned themselves with political Islam is the fact that they maintain a critical view of Islamic heritage as well as of secularism. They advocate a realistic (a historic) view of Muslim history and the Muslim experience. Their intellectual discourse reflects a deep concern with the renewal of Islamic thought and practices *from within* and with engaging in meaningful debates about modern intellectual challenges in their societies. Unlike most of the Muslim thinkers in our first two categories (the founders of political Islam and the revolutionary ideologues), their views are often controversial and seek to end the polarization between Islam and the West. Most do not recognize the "state" as a central requisite for the fulfillment of the Islamic way of life. In fact, they call for a noninterventionist state. *Shari`a* is not the main determinant of the legitimacy of a regime. For Rashid al-Ghannushi, for example, a regime is neither Islamic nor legitimate if it does not permit the people to express their freedom and will in society.

Each thinker's context and education played a major role in shaping this synthesizing orientation. Most are well-grounded in both traditional and modern education, bilingual, and well-exposed to Western philosophies and debates (either educated in the West or thoroughly studied or taught Western philosophy). All are in opposition to authoritarian and autocratic regimes, strongly advocate freedoms and democracy, and seek to engage positively with global intellectual currents and philosophical ideals. In this regard, they have contributed to steering the Islamic intellectual discourse away from Qutb's and Mawdudi's defiant approaches to the West.

Peter Woodward explores Hassan al-Turabi's efforts to forge connections among the Islamic state, democracy, and popular sovereignty. The innovative ideas of most of the intellectuals in this category are rejected by conservatives and hardliners in their countries; outsiders view their attempts at synthesis with skepticism as well. Woodward highlights this dilemma this way: "Turabi's approach to democracy, which appeared to be that of liberalism in an Islamic context, led to criticisms of him for a series of steps that seemed opportunistic." In his chapter on Ghannushi, Azzam Tamimi argues that among contemporary Islamic thinkers and activists, "Rashid al-Ghannushi is distinguished by his daring and innovative endeavors to introduce new dimensions in contemporary Islamic thought." Indeed Ghannushi has provided fresh ideas on public freedoms in the Islamic state, citizenship, civil society, women, democracy, and the need for specialization within the Islamic movements and separation between political practice and Islamic *da'wa* (call to Islam).

Bettina Gräf demonstrates the wide scope of issues that shaykh Yusuf al-Qaradawi—a highly prolific writer who produced more than 160 books—has dealt with. Graff discusses Qaradawi's contributions on the issues of *tajdid* or renewal, the "Islamic Solution," the moderation of the middle way (*wasatiya*), the Islamic Awakening, Muslim minorities, gender relations, democracy and pluralism, and the use of violence, among many other topics.

Mahmoud Sadri and Ahmad Sadri analyze Mohammad Khatami's intellectual discourse and assess his place in the reformist movement in Iran. They highlight his distinguished contribution on the issues of cultural openness, human rights, political participation, and civic liberties. According to the Sadris, "Khatami's sustained belief in the compatibility of Islam, democracy, and modernity and his natural tendency toward civility and respect has thus engendered nothing short of a cognitive shift on the Iranian political discourse."

Behrooz Ghamari-Tabrizi examines the intellectual discourse of Abdolkarim Soroush, tracing the various steps in Soroush's intellectual journey. Ghamari-Tabrizi makes a brief comparison between Ali Shari'ati, the ideologue of the Iranian Revolution and Soroush, considering Soroush to represent the paradigmatic intellectual of the post-revolutionary era. He sees Soroush's main contribution in the progress of Islamic theology and political philosophy.

DYNAMIC AND EVOLVING

As the chapters in this book show, Muslim intellectual discourse is a dynamic and evolving construct. Over more than a century, this discourse has developed on many issues. To mention but a few examples, the perception of Muslim weakness and decay it was originally attributed to external causes, but later to internal authoritarianism, despotism and lack of freedoms. A glorified and holistic view of Islamic history has given space to realistic and historicized perspectives of Islamic experiences, and in the case of Soroush, a historicized divine text. While early generations of Muslim political thinkers consider the adoption of *shari'a* as the basis on which to judge the legitimacy of a regime, later Muslim intellectuals viewed the regime's respect of public freedoms as the source of its legitimacy. Perceptions of the Islamic state, its nature and role, have been evolving. The pioneers of contemporary political Islam portrayed the state as necessary to deliver society, fulfill *shari'a*, and achieve a comprehensive Islamic way of life. For later intellectuals, the state is still necessary, but it is the *umma* (society) that is truly central. The Islamic state is the manifestation of the popular will. It should be noninterventionist and should not interfere in the personal choices of individuals. Civil society should be enhanced and should limit the power of the state. Khatami maintains that "the people must believe that they have the right to determine their own destiny and that the power of the state is bound by limits and constraints set by law. State authority cannot be attained through coercion and dictatorship" (chapter 9 here). These intellectuals present Islam not as self-contained but as open to benefiting from Western concepts and practices. Thus, they clearly contribute to ending the polarization between Islam and the West that characterized the thought of the founders of political Islam as well as the revolutionary ideologues.

We hope that this book shows these nuances and contributes to providing a better understanding of contemporary Muslim intellectual discourse.

NOTE

1. Ali Shariati, *On the Sociology of Islam*, trans. H. Algar (Berkeley, CA: Mizan Press, 1979), pp. 119–120.

PART I

FOUNDERS OF POLITICAL ISLAM

Chapter 1

Hassan Al-Banna

AHMAD MOUSSALLI

This essay focuses on Hassan al-Banna's religious and political discourse, which still provides substantive ideological foundations for the Muslim Brotherhood in Egypt and elsewhere as well as for many other Islamist movements throughout the Islamic world. This discourse is discussed under three central and general principles that constitute the essence of political Islam: first, Islam and politics; second, the Islamic state and the *Shari'ah*; and third, democracy and *shūrā*. An assessment of al-Banna's views on these matters follows in the conclusion.

The agreement of most Islamists over these issues at a theoretical level does not mean that an agreement over a practical discourse or praxis is reached. On the contrary, a spectrum of discourses has spread. For instance, the discourses of Sayyid Qutb, Abu al-A'la al-Mawdudi, and Ayatollah Khomeini are more radical than those of al-Banna, Hassan al-Turabi, and Rashid al-Ghannushi. The first three discourses have no notion of gradual change or possible compromise and emphasize the need to overthrow secular governments as a nonnegotiable religious duty. They hold tightly and uncompromisingly to both divine governance and universal paganism. However, al-Banna's discourse is more open and less particular about a forceful overthrow of un-Islamic regimes.[1] In fact, his discourse shows readiness to compromise, both practically and theoretically, and relegates ultimate earthly authority to the community. Social agreement is in itself an embodiment of divine will. If a community is not willing to adopt an Islamic state, then its imposition does not reflect the nature of Islam. The focus is here on discussing al-Banna's discourse, which is elaborated under three main principles. But we start first with a brief of his life.

THE BEGINNINGS

Hassan al-Banna was born in October 1906, in al-Buhayra, one of Egypt's northern Nile delta provinces, to a religious father. He was educated first at a traditional Islamic Kuttab (religious school) and, then at the age of twelve, joined a primary school. During the early part of his life, al-Banna became involved with Sufism and continued that association for most of his life. At the age of fourteen, he joined a primary teachers' school and two years later enrolled in *Dar al-'Ulum* College from which he graduated as a teacher.[2]

In Cairo, during his student years, al-Banna joined religious societies involved in Islamic education. However, he soon realized that this type of religious activity was inadequate to bring the Islamic faith back to its status in the public life of Egypt. He felt that more activism was needed, so he organized students from al-Azhar University and *Dar al-'Ulum* and started to preach in mosques and popular meeting places. During this period, al-Banna came to be influenced by the writings of Muhammad 'Abduh, Rashid Rida, and Ahmad Taymur Pasha (Brynjar 1998; Moussalli 1999).

When he graduated in 1927, he was appointed as a teacher of Arabic in a primary school in al-Isma`iliya, a new small town with a semi-European character. It hosted the headquarters of the Suez Canal Company and a sizable foreign community. In Isma`iliya, al-Banna started to preach his ideas to poor Muslim workers, small merchants, and civil servants. He kept warning his audience against the liberal lifestyle of the Europeans in the town and the dangers of emulating it, thus cultivating strong feelings of fear and anxiety in them.

In March 1928, he founded the Muslim Brotherhood or, actually, Brethren. In the first four years of its existence, al-Banna's primary goal was to recruit membership, establishing branches along the eastern and western edge of the delta. The quick and remarkable spread of the Brethren engendered governmental resistance, especially during the cabinet of Isma`il Sidqi Pasha.

In 1932–1933, al-Banna was transferred to Cairo, and his group merged with the Society for Islamic Culture, forming the first branch of the Muslim Brothers, which then became the headquarters of the society. During this period, the number of branches went from 1,500 to 2,000; most of which ran schools, clinics, and other welfare institutions. Not only that, but branches in Sudan, Syria, and Iraq were established, and the society's publications were distributed throughout Islamic countries.

At the beginning of his political career, al-Banna did not have an elaborate program and his message focused on the centrality of Islam. Gradually, he developed the notion of Islam as a religion that embraces all aspects of human life and conduct. He declared that the objective of the Muslim Brotherhood was to create a new generation capable of understanding the essence of Islam and of acting in accordance. He believed that Islam was the solution to the problem of Egypt and the Islamic world. However, following World War II, al-Banna assumed a greater political role. He started to call for the replacement of secular institutions by Islamic-oriented ones and asked for major reforms. However, al-Banna did not advocate violent political action as the means toward achieving political goals.

In fact, several members of his organization and he ran for parliamentary elections more than once and lost. For al-Banna accepted the legitimacy of the Egyptian regime and tried to work from within the system. His condemnation of Egyptian parties was not based on rejecting the idea of multiparty systems but more on the rejection of corruption and manipulation. This is why the Egyptian Brethren today have been able to theoretically introduce the legitimacy of pluralism, human rights, and democracy as respectively *ikhtilaf* (difference of opinion), *al-huquq al-shar'iyyah* (legal rights), and *shūrā* (consultation).

By the end of World War II, al-Banna had become an acknowledged political figure, and the Muslim Brethren emerged as a strong force presenting itself as a political alternative. As was the case with other parties, the society established a military wing, which assassinated a number of its adversaries. The Brethren reached its apogee during the Arab-Israel War (1948), in which the Muslim Brothers participated through their paramilitary organs. However, the expansion of the society, its growing influence, and its development of a strong military force brought it into a clash with the government. In February 1949, al-Banna was assassinated by police agents. Today, his ideology still informs most of the moderate Islamic movements across the entire Islamic world, and his movement is still the leading ideological power behind the expansion of Islamism.

THE DISCOURSE: THREE PRINCIPLES

The Islamic state and Shari`ah

The Muslim Brotherhood in Egypt focused more on the political aspect of Islam as the cornerstone in promoting a modern Islamic revival. It called for the urgent need of establishing an Islamic state as the first step in implementing the *Shari`ah.* While the Brotherhood centered its intellectual reinterpretation on going back to the fundamentals, they selectively accepted major Western political concepts such as constitutional rule and democracy as necessary tools for overhauling the doctrine of an Islamic state. However, the Brotherhood's extremely antagonistic dealing with the Egyptian government of Gamal Abd al-Nasser led some Brothers to rally under the leadership of Sayyid Qutb. While Qutb upheld the need for establishing an Islamic state, he rejected any openness to the West or others. He made the existence of an Islamic state an essential part of creed. It represented to him and his followers the communal submission to God on the basis of *Shari`ah.* It became, as well, the representation of political and legal abidance to the *Shari`ah* that was the basis of both legal rules and the constitution. The absence of *Shari`ah* would remove any shred of legitimacy that the state may enjoy and bring it into *jahiliyyah.* On yet another level, Ayatollah Khomeini restricted further his concept of a legitimate Islamic government. Although *Shari`ah* was the basis of government, it was only through the rule of the jurist that its existence was legally actualized.

Within the Islamic world today, the demands of the mainstream Islamist movements in Algeria, Tunisia, Jordan, and Egypt follow mostly al-Banna's discourse. However, radical Sunni movements follow mostly the discourse of Sayyid Qutb, and Shiite political movements follow that of Khoemini.

A prerequisite for understanding the demand of the majority of Islamists requires an in-depth study of al-Banna's doctrine of Islamic state. However, this cannot be even entertained—although people, including scholars, do so anyway—without an analysis of al-Banna's political discourse. Again, this in turn requires an understanding of al-Banna's philosophy of life as well as his religious discourse, which are derived from the basic sources of the Qur'an and the *sunnah* and the historical role of religion in the life of Muslims. He not only was concerned with political rule but also believed that the impurity of politics resulted from the unethical exercise of power as well as from mishandling multilayered social, economic, and educational crises. A mere change of government did not seem to be what was required or desired for the revival of the ethical spirit of the community. The state was an agency that organized people's affairs and transcended such a description to be morally involved in protecting creed and religion's supremacy so that a human regeneration was affected and humankind's lifestyle was amended in accordance with the spirit of religion. The state's function, though limited, must help the people to live a virtuous life by, for example, redirecting the course of education toward God. A view of life that was accepted by the people became the conditioning ground for establishing the desired state. The legitimate exercise of authority or the withdrawal of legitimacy depended then on the same conditions, and, once the Islamic state was established, the state could not nullify the original contract between the people and the ruler.

Of course, reestablishing the Islamic caliphate has been generally entertained by al-Banna and most Islamic movements as the highest political institution. As was the case historically, it is still viewed as the cornerstone for theoretical political discourses on government and politics. It represents politically the highest goal for Islamic movements and constitutes the symbol of Islamic unity and power.

Because it brings together religion and politics, its field of study is not restricted to jurisprudence but includes also theology and the science of the principles of religion (*usul al-din*).

In the history of Islam, great theoreticians, such as al-Mawardi in *Al-Ahkam al-Sultaniyya*, Ibn Taymiyya in *Al-Siyasa al-Shar'iyyah*, Abu Yusuf in *Kitab al-Kharaj*, al-Ghazali in *Al-Iqtisad fi al-I'tiqad*, Ibn Jama'a in *Tahrir al-Ahkam*, and Ibn Khaldun in the *Muqaddima*, started tying the caliphate's functions and qualifications to political and economic development. In this sense, it must therefore shoulder the responsibility of tuning the community with the ups and downs of history and represent the realities of a given age. However, when it was al-Banna's turn to discuss the caliphate, it had then already been abolished by Ataturk. Thus, the symbol of Islamic unity in al-Banna's eyes was gone, and this was why the existence of the caliphate was to him a nostalgic affinity with glory and power as well as the supremacy of Islam. Because the caliphate was a historical event, its regeneration required an awesome task. For it represented nothing less than the unification of Muslims again in an international state, the achievement of which was a task whose difficulties al-Banna knew. For its revival must be preceded by a total program of reforming the Muslims of his day and must include issues such as preparations of complete educational, social, and economic cooperation between Muslim peoples; the formation of alliances and conferences among these peoples; and finally, founding a league of nations responsible for the caliph's choice (al-Banna 1984b, 70–71). Such issues, however, were not much easier than establishing the caliphate itself and this was why an alternative institution was called for that seemed more practical and achievable. As an indispensable step for establishing the caliphate the concept of an Islamic state became as important, both theoretically and practically, as the caliphate itself.

The Muslim Brotherhood, according to al-Banna, believes that the caliphate is the symbol of Islamic unity and the sign of commitment to Islam. It is a rite that the Muslims must be concerned about achieving. It is the caliph who is in charge of applying numerous divine legal commands. Al-Banna shows the importance of the caliphate by describing a major event surrounding the Prophet's death. This event is that the Muslims discussed and resolved the issue of political succession even before the Prophet's burial. But, because the caliphate does not exist anymore, al-Banna calls for some rethinking about the issue of political rule, since it is the center of political contract between the people and their unifying agency. This is why the Muslim Brotherhood makes the revival of Islam dependent on establishing an Islamic system of government. However, the flourishing of Islam cannot take place without spreading the Qur'an and its language as well as achieving a comprehensive political unity among Muslims. At the same time, a modern Islamic government to al-Banna can take many forms, with new military, economic, and political organizations (al-Banna 1984, 70–71; 1984a, 95–96).

The scriptural Qur'anic references to political rule constitute the legitimacy of Islamic rule and its function: the spiritual, political, and economic well-being and defense of the community. Furthermore, its function is extended worldwide, especially since geographical limitations are not, in al-Banna's view, applicable to the Islamic call and therefore to the state that universalizes that call. Therefore, the well-being of humankind as a concern of the Islamic call makes the role of the Islamic state moral and universal (al-Banna, 194?).[3] In turn, the universality of the call (the message is fine but the call is more general) makes the existence of a universal caliphate a necessity, since it is the institution that transcends localities, borders, and the like. However, and for the time being, al-Banna looks at the geographic Islamic entity, or the state, as more pivotal for instituting the

Islamic system. Practically speaking, it is more possible to achieve the Islamic state than the caliphate (al-Banna n.d., 63, 72, 347; *Minbar*).

To al-Banna, an Islamic state is the essential first step for achieving the good Islamic society. Without the state, the society would rather find many difficulties in voluntarily organizing itself on an Islamic basis. For the nature of many basic Islamic doctrines requires an organizing agency of the first rate. Within modern geographic realities, that agency is the Islamic state (al-Banna n.d., 317).

To al-Banna, it is only the state that can function as both an executive agency that remedies all problems and an institution that develops Islamic laws suitable for this age. His perception of Islam as "as a complete system regulating all aspects of life and including a system of social norms, government, legislation, law, and education" cannot be realized without the state. Furthermore, because a great substance of reform is of political nature, the state must be involved as well. Al-Banna finds that mere religiosity without solid commitment to political, social, and economic activism is useless to the community of Muslims (al-Banna 1984b, 53–5; n.d., 101, 104).

More importantly, not committing to political Islam is *jahiliyyah* to al-Banna. He subordinates the legitimacy of the state to fulfilling basic Islamic goals. Because these goals include a commitment to apply the Islamic law and the spread of the Islamic call, religious commitment is linked to political legitimacy. Thus, the call to Islam is a moral and religious duty that must be carried out privately by the community and officially by the Islamic government. But it is the government that must carry out the broader essentials of the Islamic call, that is, addressing the general moral or spiritual atmosphere within the *ummah* and curbing moral and political degeneration and atheistic orientations (al-Banna 1974, 15–17). In this sense, the government becomes the executive arm of the virtuous society, and, by trust, it performs the society's moral, religious, and political objectives. Only through following such an attitude does an Islamic government receive legitimate recognition from Hassan al-Banna (al-Banna 1984, 55). Thus, an Islamic government could not be conceptually and functionally compartmentalized, that is, to function at one time as a secular agency, at another, as religious. By following the demands of a virtuous society, the state does not produce conflicting claims but becomes the popular guiding social executive power in charge of executing just laws. Only through such a role could the necessary conditions for the legitimacy of government be fulfilled (*Minbar*, 24–45).

This conclusion about the state's function and attitude is entertained by al-Banna because he builds his political discourse on a reinterpretation of the doctrine of God's *rububiyyah* (lordship) and *hakimiyyah* (sovereignty). God's universal *rububiyyah* makes Islamic revelation the basic text in matters relating to both politics and political philosophy. To him, the history of Islam shows testimonies to Muslims' subordination of politics to religion; for instance, all political expansions were made in the name of Islam (al-Banna n.d., 36–37, 317). And insofar as Muslims did that, they were victorious, but when they disassociated politics from true religion and lost their religious zeal, they became losers. Consequently, Islam lost the role it had played throughout history (al-Banna 1984b, 56).

In line with al-Ghazali's thought, al-Banna still does not give the government the upper hand in all domains of life but views it as only an appendix to the *Shari'ah* and constrained by it. The government cannot then change the *Shari'ah* under the guise of its development. It can, however, rework its principles in accordance with the changing needs and demands of society. The government's policies should not, therefore, neglect the general and guiding principles of the *Shari'ah*.

For instance, universal principles as the necessity of Islamic unity cannot forever be replaced by narrow bonds of patriotism and nationalism, though the two can be used to strengthen the universal principle. For such an act of replacement distorts the true spirit of the Qur'anic discourse, which aims at unity, not disunity. To al-Banna, denying God's *uluhiyyah* (divinity) over this life and the concomitant disavowal of universal unity lead simply to unbelief (al-Banna 1984a, 317; n.d., 347). Therefore, al-Banna believes that a major function of the Islamic state is not to yield to those ideologies and philosophies that disrupt the unity of humankind and the Muslims in particular. In fact, the state must counterattack the political and philosophical endeavors to limit the scope of Islam through imposing humanly developed systems over God's system. If the Islamic state yields to such an act, it would be solidifying *jahiliyyah* and contributing to the disunity of humankind, and thus breaking the postulates of the *ah* (al-Banna 1984a, 317; n.d., 54).

ISLAM AND POLITICS

Al-Banna links his political discourse to developing a religiously derived Qu'ranic discourse that includes both creed and action. The testimony that there is "no god but God" is to al-Banna a call to establish divine governance on earth. The perfection of a Muslim's creed must lead him to act on behalf of society (al-Banna, 178–179).[4] Furthermore, Islam's comprehensiveness makes it fit for human *fitra* (innate constitution) and capable of influencing not only the majority of people but elites as well. Because Islam to al-Banna provides the worldliest just principles and the straightest of divine legal codes, it uplifts the human soul and sanctifies universal brotherhood. It also gives practical ways to achieve all of this in people's daily life, social living, education, and political aspirations. It is also on these bases that Islam sets its state and establishes its universal call to humankind. For while Islam asks humans to satisfy themselves spiritually and materially, it provides them with regulations that prevent extreme behaviors and arrive at balanced fulfillment. Such a balance is important to al-Banna because humans do not live in isolation but are members of a community. The community has, however, its "collective reason," which differs from the individual's. Thus, diverse Islamic regulations satisfy different needs: the economic, for material well-being; the political, for unity, justice, and freedom; and the social, for equality. To al-Banna, all these regulations are only fractions of the authentic Islamic method. Only this method can lead humankind to remove itself from its miserable existence (al-Banna 1974, 65–66).

Al-Banna adds that what distinguishes Islam from most other religions is its concern with not only worship but also a social system. To al-Banna, Islam is thus composed of creed, worship, and governance and is a collective and state religion. Muslims must then derive their general principles from it. Islam as a social system deals with all social phenomena, and as such the Qur'an and the *sunnah* must represent the highest fundamental authority and point of reference. But their interpretations must be conducted through analogical deduction and consensus. In brief, to al-Banna, Islam is concerned with all aspects of life and postulates precise methods, fundamentals, and foundations for humankind. It is simply a general code for all races, peoples, and nations (al-Banna 1974, 66–67, 38–39).

Activism is to al-Banna the sign of good belief, and political action should be in line with Islamic teachings. In fact, separating Islam from politics is not Islamic. Theoretically, Islam is more comprehensive than politics and absorbs it. Individual perfection requires politicizing Islam. In this sense, Islam is a complete active religion that must relate to all aspects of life. For instance, al-Banna believes that one of the main religious objectives is to provide society with laws of organization. From al-Banna's perspective, Islam must act as a regulator of behavior of both Muslim communities and all human societies. Its general goals are designed to fit all societies, and this can be done through reinterpretations of texts to suit different times and ages (al-Banna 1984a, 157–159, 119–121; 1974, 71–83).

Islam, then, aims at setting up a good nation with a message of unity and sacrifice. It also aims at establishing a just Islamic government without tyranny or authoritarianism and in the service of the people. A government like this helps in establishing a virtuous society (al-Banna 1969, 112–115). The function of Islam is based on four foundations: first, pure creed that brings humans closer to God; second, correct worship and good religious deeds such as praying and fasting that add meaning to life; third, unity, which completes the faith and reduces the tension between sects and political tendencies; and fourth, just legislation and good laws that are derived from the Qur'an and the *sunnah* (al-Banna 1969, 192–194; 1970, 23–29).

As for other revealed religions, al-Banna argues that Islam is the last of them and their complete manifestation. Islam does not negate their ethics and ways of worship and life because it contains most of the teachings of other religions. What constitutes good religion is good behavior toward the self, the other, the community, and God, and not necessarily better argumentations (al-Banna 1970, 62).

Creed to al-Banna is the soul's tranquil acceptance of a notion without any doubt. Thus, in matters of belief no force can have its way on people's heart. Furthermore, because the source of Islamic creed is God's divine text and the Prophet's *sunnah*, it is not opposed to but supported by reason. The Qur'anic discourse speaks of reason as the source of responsibility and makes its existence a requirement for applying the *Shari'ah*. The Qur'anic discourse exhorts also the human being to think, search, and contemplate and asks its opponents to produce their evidence. Thus, Islam does not call for limiting the function of reason but makes it the instrument of knowledge by providing it with a framework to prevent its aimlessness (al-Banna 1984a, 379–381). God's essence, to al-Banna, is beyond the comprehension of human reason. Being limited in time and space, reason precludes its understanding of the essences of things. This does not mean that Islam is against the freedom of thought or the search for truth. To al-Banna, it is a warning to the human being against falling into falsehood and total dependence on reason. It cannot provide everlasting truths but rather partial interpretations that depend on human conditions and the power of an individual's reason. A Muslim must still exert his reason, but such an action cannot constitute a categorical understanding. To al-Banna, when humans disagree they must always fall back to the basic religious texts that are the ultimate source of justification. Because the metaphysical realm is beyond human understanding, the Qur'anic discourse gives humans few basic metaphysical ideas (al-Banna 1984a, 357–359, 382–390).

Thus, the role of religion to al-Banna is not to set forth a detailed discourse on metaphysics but to aim at specific existential outcomes. It aims at, first, the revival of conscious awareness of the self's powers; second, cultivation of virtues to uplift the self; third, sacrifice in quest of truth and guidance toward God; fourth, removal of humans from ephemeral material happiness and providing ways for achieving real happiness; fifth, making God the ultimate goal of the soul; sixth, making religion the source of unity and the resolution of conflicts; seventh, the encouragement of sacrifice for humankind's sake; and eighth, making Islam the focus of development of individuals, societies, nations, and the world (al-Banna 1984a, 71–73).

The issues of renaissance, knowledge, and the good society require, according to al-Banna, establishing an Islamic state. Otherwise, religion becomes separated from politics, and politics become outside the realm of religion. The Islamic state cannot be established except by a general religious message, or else its attainment becomes unattractive. The separation of religion from politics is now in practice and has made politics equivalent to corruption. Furthermore, al-Banna argues that when a Muslim community is ruled by laws other than its own, a clash is bound to erupt between it and the ruling power, thus posing difficulties for believers to accept a secular ruler. Furthermore, most Egyptian laws, which are derivatives of European ones, are contrary to the divine law and shed doubts on the integrity of Islam in the modern world. The laws of a nation should not contradict its system of beliefs, especially that the divine law is not opposed to modernity or change (al-Banna 1984a, 317; 1970, 37–45).

DEMOCRACY AND *SHŪRĀ*

The *shūrā's* assimilation of, and not subordination to, democracy is an example of not yielding to other philosophies and systems. The modern *shūrā* as advocated by al-Banna and others postulates the necessity of people's involvement not only in political matters but also in all issues concerning the community. *Shūrā* denies the legitimacy of authoritarian rule or political monopoly over the community and makes the community the source of executive power. Al-Banna argues that the ruler, regardless of his social or religious position, must not single-handedly regulate state affairs: in the final analysis, he must resort and yield to people's choices (al-Banna 1974, 99–100). Further, employing *shūrā* makes the ruler sensitive to, or at least accommodating of, popular demands. From an Islamic point of view, the supremacy of God's law must be maintained in all aspects: political, social, economic, and personal. Current laws are, however, against people's consciousness (al-Banna 1970, 37–39). The authority of Islamic law over society and people is grounded, according to al-Banna, in the following verses (al-Banna 1970, 40–41):[5]

> And this (He commands): Judge thou between them by what God hath revealed, and follow not their vain desires, but beware of them lest they beguile thee from any of that (teaching) which God hath sent down to thee. And if they turn away, be assured that for some of their crimes it is God's purpose to punish them. And truly most men are rebellious. (V: 49)
>
> But no, by thy Lord, they can have no (real) Faith, until they make thee judge in all disputes between them, and find in their souls no resistance against thy decisions, but accept them with the fullest conviction. (IV: 65)

These verses not only indicate the supremacy of Islamic law but also provide most Islalmists, starting with Hassan al-Banna, with textual references to political *hakimiyyah* as the major political doctrine of Islamist ideologies. These verses are now interpreted by the Islamists in general and the radicals in particular to indicate the non-Islamicity of contemporary states. For nonadherence to this political *hakimiyyah* has been viewed by the radicals as *kufr* (disbelief) and *shirk* (polytheism). However, the possibility of such a charge has arisen because the Islamists have removed these verses from their social and political contexts and have universalized their use metahistorically to include every age and every country. While decontextualizing many verses may be liberating such as is the case concerning verses related to knowledge and *shūrā*, yet at times this process may lead to the opposite, that is, to hardening and narrowing the meaning of the verses within a specific context. Harsh contexts pave the way for harsh interpretations, while favorable conditions lead to accommodating interpretations.

The disavowal of any legitimate theoretical possibility of legislation and political action without proper grounding in the comprehensive flexible and total Islamic legislation leads al-Banna to ground the appropriateness of actions in correct doctrines. This is why he calls for the derivation of all civil, criminal, commercial, and international affairs from Islamic law. To al-Banna, it is Islamically self-defeating to ground laws for Muslims in non-Islamic laws that deal with foreign cultural particularities, not to mention their possible contradiction to Islam. This becomes more acute since Islamic law, along with its eternal and comprehensive principles, has not precluded the possibilities of individual and collective reformulations (al-Banna 1970, 40–45). In fact, when Islam was the dominant ideology in the life of the government and the people, the history of Islam shows that the development of Islamic law was comprehensive and flexible (al-Banna 1984a, 61–62).

Because of the flexible nature of Islamic law, al-Banna argues that its development does not lead to reactionary thinking. He adds that the nature of Islam cannot be reactionary since Islamic law itself allows progressive individual and collective adaptations to meet the needs of changing living conditions (al-Banna 1984a, 165). While Islam postulates specific eternal doctrines and ordinances, this does not mean that everything considered Islamic is divine and, thus, not subject to change. Every philosophy or ideology includes basic unchanging doctrines, but this does not make it reactionary. In this sense, al-Banna feels that labeling Islam in this way exemplifies ignorance of the nature of both divine law and Islamic jurisprudence (al-Banna 1974, 95). Focusing only on a juristic fraction of Islamic law and neglecting the overall organizing religious roots lead to misinterpreting Islam. The truth of the matter is to understand Islam, one has to see the multiple functions of Islam as a religious, social, and political system. It includes codes of worship and behavior. Religious beliefs constitute only one part of the Islamic system, and Islam regulates both religion, in the narrow sense, and life, in a general sense. True Muslims to al-Banna could not but subject all aspects of their life to Islam (al-Banna n.d., 304).

In order to get over the problem of the priority of implementing the Islamic law over establishing the Islamic government or vice versa, al-Banna specifies no particular method for implementing the law. What is important is its implementation, whether carried out by a secular or religious government. Al-Banna posits no problem with Western-style constitutional rule because it maintains, in accordance with Islam, personal freedom; upholds *shūrā*; postulates people's authority over government; specifies the responsibilities and accountability of rulers before their people; and delineates the responsibilities of the executive, the legislative, and the judiciary. Constitutional rule to al-Banna is thus harmonious with the *Shari'ah* (al-Banna 1984b, 56–58; n.d., 355–357).

However, al-Banna's adoption of constitutional rule is not a matter of exact copying of a particular Western constitution. The concept is Islamized through a process of philosophical reformulation on religious grounds and is applied through objective institutions. Thus, when al-Banna criticized Egypt's experimentation with constitutional rule, he was calling for its reorientation toward Islamic law and was condemning its failure to perform objectively in the Egyptian political life (al-Banna 1984b, 58–60).

On the theoretical level, al-Banna grounds constitutional rule in *shūrā* by claiming that the former is the closest form of government to the nature of Islamic politics. More importantly, al-Banna finds textual justifications for adopting constitutional rule as *shūrā* and grounds its necessity in a Qur'anic text: "and consult them in affairs (of moment). Then, when thou hast taken a decision, put thy trust in God . . ." (III: 159). Such a derivation is possible to al-Banna because this Qur'anic revelation is interpreted as "the basic principle of rule of government and exercise of authority." The Qur'anic power is employed by al-Banna to highlight the power of the community in making and unmaking of political systems, governments, forms of government, and political behavior. It provides the community with further powers vis-a-vis the state that must act in conformity with the ambitions and needs of people.

Because to al-Banna the Islamic government represents the central organ of an Islamic system of government, it derives its legitimacy to exercise power from the people. The responsibility of the government is twofold: religious before God and political before the people. Furthermore, it is morally and politically responsible for the community's unity and therefore must be responsive and defer to communal preferences and wishes. The ruler's power over and responsibility before his people derives from the fact that Islam views the setting up of governments as a social contract between the ruler and the ruled so that the interests of the latter are taken care of. The ruler's reward and punishment must hinge on people's opinions. People enjoy moral supremacy over the ruler in matters of general and particular concerns. Therefore, a legitimate ruler or government must always refer to consultation with the community and yield to its will. Political forms may change from time to time and from one locality to another, but the basic rules of Islam must always be adhered to (al-Banna 1984b, 318–319).

While the role of reason is not denied in political matters, it is employed more at the theoretical level to extract political rights and duties. Equality among human beings is postulated by the Qur'an. That this equality means equal political rights and duties is only a rational derivation. Again, this means that no individual or group can claim privileged positions, whether political or religious. Al-Banna does not refer equality to any natural quality such as reason but refers it to Qur'anic texts as a means to prove the necessity of people's rule within divine *hakimiyyah* (al-Banna 1984a, 160–161; 1974, 99; Qur'an V: 48–50).

Another reason for al-Banna's democratization of *shūrā* is related to his ability to distinguish divine *hakimiyyah* from human *hakimiyyah*. The first one can never be properly represented; consequently no individual, group, or institution can properly claim to represent a specific mandate or a divine right to rule. However, the legitimacy of representing human *hakimiyyah* must be sought in fulfilling and adhering to Qur'anic instructions (or, in al-Banna's words, "the Islamic constitution") and on the proper conditions for carrying out *shūrā*. This theoretical principle, applying the Islamic constitution, defines to the *ummah* at large the kind of *nizam* (system) to be upheld. However, the practical principles that lead to applying *shūrā* make the *ummah* the sole legitimate *sultah* (authority) for government. Al-Banna converts *al-amr bi-l-ma'ruf wa-l-nahi 'an al-munkar* (enjoining the good and forbidding evil) from an ethical concept into a formulation of public, legal, and political right to watch over the government. Moreover, the ruler is made accountable not only to God but to the *ummah* as well. By believing that the exercise of authority requires the continuous ratification and approval of the *ummah*, governance is transformed into nothing more than a contract between the ruled and the ruler. In this sense, Muslim politics is democratized (al-Banna 1984a, 317–318; n.d., 63, 332–337).

Two central doctrines are needed however for legitimacy, namely, justice and equality. They are to al-Banna the philosophical and religious guidelines that both the ruler and the ruled must adhere to and take into consideration while legislating or exercising power (*Minbar*, 78–9; al-Ikhwan 1979, 9). *Tawhīd* then manifests itself politically and morally in equity and justice (*Minbar*, 79, 136; al-Ikhwan 1979, 9).

Furthermore, al-Banna argues that a more apparent manifestation of *tawhīd* is political unity. It centers on the Qur'an and its language under one central government. This unity does not exclude however the existence of the *ummah* in many states, if *tawhīd* constitutes the ideological framework and if *Sharīʿah* is the law of the land (al-Banna 1984a, 95–96, 317). That many legitimate Islamic states can co-exist is to al-Banna possible under the practical orientations of modern Islamic thought and due to the conditions of modern existence. Al-Banna stands, however, against any ideological religious disunity and internal division, which he equates with *kufr* (unbelief). From this perspective, ideologically based multiparty politics and opposed political fundamentals cannot be justified. Hence, once ideological unity becomes the basis of multiparty politics, policy differences and programs are acceptable. Al-Banna does not accept the notion that parties represent opposed doctrinal views, since all parties must adhere to *tawhīd* and *wahda* (unity; al-Banna 1984a, 165–167).

More specifically, political partisanship to al-Banna does not function properly in Egypt since it is exploited by foreign powers to interfere in the affairs of Egypt, and the Egyptians have suffered regardless of the party that is ruling. Before a party system can function properly, Egypt must be delivered from the occupiers, the British. Furthermore, Egyptian parties are not real parties but reflect personal ambitions and foreign affiliations. Their role has exhorted itself. As an example he mentions the *Wafd* party, which started by demanding independence only to splinter later on into the party of free constitutionalists. The *Itihad* party was the result of a deal between many parties and the king (al-Banna 1984a, 166–167). Notwithstanding this, the rejection of this kind of party politics does not lead al-Banna to impose a ban on multiparty politics or to restrict the freedom of expression. The freedom of expression must aim at showing the truth that both the majority and the minority must adhere to it (al-Banna 1984a, 167–169). To him, political opposition finds justification only when political authorities neither adhere to nor apply the rules of Islam. The Muslim Brothers, according to al-Banna, are neither advocates of revolution nor believers in its utility. In fact, their belief in the capacity of Qur'anic principles to stand against any ideological creed allows the *ummah* through either the process of Arabization or Islamization of political doctrines, like multiparty politics, to transcend any danger to its social and political unity (al-Banna 1984b, 53; 1984a, 96–97, 161–162).

On the international level, the legitimacy of any world power must stem, to al-Banna, from its adherence to Islam. But such a situation cannot be brought about except by an Islamic state that positions itself as a guide to other nations (al-Banna 1984a, 162–163). Islam has postulated the superiority of Islamic sovereignty and the necessity of power building so that the just nation should hold power. Al-Banna grounds this view in the Qur'anic injunction that calls on Muslims to enjoin what is right and to forbid what is evil (al-Banna 1984a, 163).[6]

In order to bring out the full context of this call, al-Banna hastens to provide an *aya* (verse) that guarantees the rights of non-Muslims and quells their fears about an Islamic state or an international Islamic order: "God forbids you not, with regard to those who fight you not for (your) Faith nor drive you out of your homes, from dealing kindly and justly with them: For God loveth those who are just" (LX: 8). In fact, al-Banna believes in the duty of the governing authority to liberate and guide other nations into Islam: "We, the Muslims, are neither communists nor democrats nor anything similar to what they claim; we are, by God's grace, Muslims, which is our road to salvation from Western colonialism" (al-Banna 1984a, 304–307; n.d., 53).

CONCLUSION

Al-Banna's political discourse is grounded in his view of metaphysical *tawhīd* and its political articulation, divine *hakimiyyah*. While al-Banna could have theoretically stressed not compromising and denial of the other, he did not—an act that was taken up later by others. Al-Banna opened during his time the theoretical possibility of harmonizing Western political thought with the Islamic. Unlike al-Mawdudi and Sayyid Qutb, who radicalized the doctrine of *hakimiyyah*, he transformed it into a human act. To him the divine governance might at times co-exist with the worldly *jahiliyyah*. "No governance (*hukm*) except God's" becomes to al-Banna a linchpin that could be employed by the people to claim certain rights and powers that have been historically denied to the Muslims by their rulers. Governance is an all-comprehensive doctrine that could be used morally, legally, politically, and internationally. Because its power is originally textual and its exercise is basically communal, it has become a powerful tool used by most Islamists to evaluate political rules on scriptural bases. But the reality of the matter is that they were judging political governments in terms of the actual exercise of power. Whenever *hakimiyyah* is mentioned nowadays, it means this kind of rule based on scriptural Qur'anic precepts extracted from their social, economic, political, and historical contexts. This is why all Islamists, whether radical or not, advocate the fulfillment of God's order, the minimum of which is replacing existing governments with Islamic ones. But it does not mean by necessity closing up on oneself and rejecting any dealing with the community. In fact, al-Banna dealt openly with and tried to practically influence Egyptian politics.

Although divine governance has become to al-Banna an absolute political doctrine, so has the doctrine of *shūrā*. In fact, the good realization of the former becomes dependent on the good exercise of the latter. What al-Banna's development of *shūrā* has done is to absorb democracy within Islamic political thought and, consequently, to take the initiative from its secular advocates. It has also provided legitimate religious means toward the control of government since legitimacy is linked to popular approval. By denying any contradiction between democracy and constitutional rule with *shūrā* and divine law, al-Banna became capable of postulating their correspondence. This view has become a part of his and the Islamists' nonhistorical discourses that transform Islam into a system capable of absorbing what is best in philosophy, politics, economics, science, and history without the need to deny the validity of Islam. On the contrary, this shows to the Islamists the true nonhistorical and metaphysical power of the Islamic revelation as an eternal message capable of meeting the needs that arise from development.

Shūrā has become to al-Banna and almost all of the Islamist movements the source of legitimation of any authority, while the continuation of legitimacy hinges on the application of the *Shari'ah* and the approval of the people. While great political thinkers such as al-Mawardi, al-Ghazali, and Ibn Taymiyya have justified the seizure of power if the ruler, the sultan, or the prince upheld nominally the superiority of *Shari'ah*, one wonders what prevents contemporary Islamic movements from seizing power in the name of Islam! If people do not want an Islamic state and if an Islamic movement succeeds in setting up an Islamic state, could such a state be legitimate from an Islamist point of view? In other words, if the ultimate organizing principle is *shūrā*, then the Islamists should accept a secular government if chosen by people; but if the ultimate government stands on its own then there is no need to postulate *shūrā* as being the ultimate organizing principle. One could get around this theoretical difficulty only when the people are devout Muslims and employ *shūrā*. The historical experience of Muslims shows that by giving the state the power to employ and to execute *Shari'ah* in the name of the *ummah* more substantial doctrines of *Shari'ah* were overlooked in favor of a political interpretation of Islam. What is needed seems more than just an overhauling of doctrines that might ultimately be used by political authority.

NOTES

1. Numerous studies have attempted to focus on his political arguments. Older references include al-Husayni 1956; Heyworth-Dunne 1950; Harris; Adams 1968; Mitchell 1964. Ishaq Musa al-Husayni, Moslem Brethren (Beirut: Khayat's College Book, 1956); James Heyworth-Dunne, Religious and Political Trends in Modern Egypt (Washington, D.C., 1950); Christina Harris, Nationalism and Revolution in Egypt; Charles Adams, *Islam and Modernism in Egypt* (New York: Russell and Russell, 1968); Richard Mitchell, *The Society of the Muslim Brothers* (London: Oxford University Press, 1964). Recent references to him occur throughout the literature on modern Islamic thought and fundamentalism; see, for instance, Marsot 1–9; Lapidus 1983, 23–29; Taheri 1987, 37–49; Munson, 29–37; Warburg, 4–9, 24–27, 46–47; GommaGomaa 143–147; and Carre, 262–280; Hussain, 117–121, 174–177; Mortimer, 250–257; Hiro, 60–69. Ira Lapidus, *Contemporary Islamic Movements in Historical Perspective, Policy Papers in International Affairs*, 18 (Berkeley and Los Angeles: University of California Press, 1983), pp. 23–29; Amir Taheri, *The Holy Terror: The Inside Story of Islamic Terrorism* (Johannesburg: Hutchinson, 1987), pp. 37–49.

2. For biographical information see Shaikh 1981; Muru Qarqar 1980; al-Sa'id 1980; Shaikh 1981. See also Harris 1964, chaps. IV–V by M. N. Shaikh (Karachi: International Islamic Publishers, 1981); Muhammad Muru Qarqar, *Dawr al-Haraka al-Islamiyya fi Tasfiyat al-Iqta'* (Kuwait: Dar al-Buhuth al-Iqlimiyya, 1980); Rif'at al-Sa'id, Hassan al-Banna, *Mu'assis Harakat al-Ikhwan al-Muslimin* (Beirut: Dar al-Tali'a, 1980); M. N. Shaikh, *Hassan al-Banna Shahid: A Brief Life Sketch* (Karachi: International Islamic Publishers, 1981). See also Christina Harris, *Nationalism and Revolution in Egypt* (The Hague: Mouton, 1964), chs. IV–V.

3. Hassan al-Banna, *Nazarat fi Islah al-Nafs* (Cairo: Matba'at al-I'tisam, 1969), 194.

4. Ibid., 178–179.

5. See also *Sura* V: 44, 45, 47 where the Qur'an describes those who do not rule by what God has revealed as unbelievers, unjust and infidel.

6. See the verses III: 110, II: 143, LXIII: 8, and VIII: 60.

REFERENCES

Adams, Charles. 1968. *Islam and Modernism in Egypt*. New York: Russell and Russell.

al-Banna, Hassan. 1969. *Nazarat fi Islah wa-l-Mujtama*'. Cairo: Maktabat al-I'tisam.

al-Banna, Hassan. 1970. *Din wa Siyasa*. Beirut: Maktabat Huttin.

al-Banna, Hassan. 1972. *Kalimat Khalida*. Beirut.

al-Banna, Hassan. 1974. *Al-Imam al-Shahid Yatahaddath*. Beirut: Dar al-Qalam.

al-Banna, Hassan. 1978. *Minbar al-Jum*'a. Alexandria: Dar al-Da'wa. (hereafter cited as *Minbar*).

al-Banna, Hassan. 1984a. *Majmu*'at Ras'il al-Shahid Hassan al-Banna. 4th ed. Beirut: al-Mu'assasa al-Islamiyya.

al-Banna, Hassan. 1984b. *Rasa'il al-Imam al-Shahid Hassan al-Banna*. Beirut: Dar al-Qur'an al-Karim.

al-Banna, Hassan. n.d. *Majmu*'at Rasa'il al-Imam al-Shahid, Hassan al-Banna. Beirut: Dar al-Qalam.

al-Banna, Hassan. 1969. *Nazarat fi Islah al-Nafs*. Cairo: Matba'at al-I'tisam.

al-Banna, Hassan. 1971. *Al-Salam fi al-Islam*. 2nd ed. Beirut: Manshurat al-'Asr al-Hadith. 1979. *Al-Da*'wa, no. 7.

al-Sa'id, Rif'at, and Hassan al-Banna. 1980. *Mu'assis Harakat al-Ikhwan al-Muslimin*. Beirut: Dar al-Tali'a.

Brynjar, Liya. 1998. *The Society of Muslim Brothers in Egypt: The Rise of an Islamic Mass Movement, 1928–1942*. Reading, UK: Ithaca Press.

Carre, Oliver. 1983. "The Impact of the Egyptian Muslim Brotherhood's Political Islam since the 1950s." In *Islam, Nationalism and Radicalism in Egypt and Sudan*, ed. Gabriel Warburg and Uri Kumpferschmidt. New York: Praeger; 262–280.

Gomma, Gomaa Ahmed. 1983. "Islamic Fundamentalism in Egypt during the 1930s and 1970s: Comparative Notes." In *Islam, Nationalism and Radicalism*, ed. Warburg and Kumpferschmidt. ed. Gabriel Warburg and Uri Kumpferschmidt. New York: Praeger; 140–150.

Harris, Christina. 1964. *Nationalism and Revolution in Egypt*. The Hague: Mouton.

Heyworth-Dunne, James. 1950. *Religious and Political Trends in Modern Egypt*. Washington, DC.

Hiro, Dilip. 1989. *The Rise of Islamic Fundamentalism*. New York: Routledge.

Hussain, Asaf. 1984. *Political Perspectives*. New York: St. Martin's Press.

Lapidus, Ira. 1983. *Contemporary Islamic Movements in Historical Perspective*. Policy Papers in International Affairs, 18. Berkeley: University of California Press.

Marsot, Afaf Lutfi al-Sayyid. 1984. *Protest Movements and Religious Undercurrents in Egypt, Past and Present*. Washington, DC: Georgetown University.

Mitchell, Richard. 1964. *The Society of the Muslim Brothers*. London: Oxford University Press.

Mortimer, Edward. 1982. *Faith and Power*. London: Faber and Faber.

Moussalli, Ahmad. 1999. *Moderate and Radical Islamic Fundamentalism: The Quest for Modernity, Legitimacy, and the Islamic State.* Gainesville: University Press of Florida.

Munson, Henry. 1988. *Islam and Revolution.* New Haven: Yale University Press.

Musa al-Husayni, Ishaq. 1956. *Moslem Brethren.* Beirut: Khayat's College Book.

Qarqar, Muhammad Muru. 1980. *Dawr al-Haraka al-Islamiyya fi Tasfiyat al-Iqta'.* Kuwait: Dar al-Buhuth al-Iqlimiyya.

Shaikh, M. N. 1981. *Hassan al-Banna Shahid: A Brief Life Sketch.* Karachi: International Islamic Publishers.

Shaikh, M. N, trans. 1981. *Memoirs of Hassan al-Banna Shahid.* Karachi: International Islamic Publishers.

Taheri, Amir. 1987. *The Holy Terror: The Inside Story of Islamic Terrorism.* Johannesburg: Hutchinson.

Warburg, Gabriel. 1983. "Introduction." In *Islam, Nationalism and Radicalism in Egypt and Sudan,* ed. Warburg and Kumpferschmidt. New York: Praeger; 4–9, 24–27, 46–47.

Chapter 2

Mawlana Mawdudi

JOSHUA T. WHITE AND NILOUFER SIDDIQUI

Mawlana SAYYID ABU AL-ʿALA MAWDUDI stands as one of the leading Islamic figures of the twentieth century. His political and religious vision of Islam and the Islamic state have gained widespread currency within his adoptive country of Pakistan, as well as in the broader Middle East, North Africa, and throughout Central, South, and Southeast Asia. Mawdudi's expansive influence is due in large part to his dual role as a scholar and an advocate. Not only a political theorist, he was also a well-known translator and commentator of the Qur'an; a best-selling author; a frequently jailed political activist; and the founder of South Asia's leading Islamic party, the Jamaʿat-i Islami.

Born in 1903 to a religious family in Hyderabad Deccan, India, Mawdudi began his career as a journalist, ascending in his early twenties to the editorship of *al-Jamiah*, the newspaper of India's leading Muslim clerical organization. He went on to assume the editorship of *Tarjuman al-Qur'an* (Interpreter of the *Qur'an*), which he used as a platform from which to advocate for a systematic and uniquely Islamic way of life and against the influences of the West, which he believed had captivated the Muslims of India. Mawdudi's emphasis became increasingly political following the landmark Indian elections in 1937 and the growing agitation against British rule by Hindu and

Muslim leaders. He remained pointedly opposed to the political visions of both the Indian National Congress and the Muslim League, declaring that Muslims had little in common with the Hindus of India, while at the same time decrying the Muslim League's nationalist vision as an un-Islamic substitute for true religious devotion. In 1941 he founded the Jama'at-i Islami, a party he would lead for the next three decades (Nasr 1994).[1] Although Mawdudi rejected the League's "two nation" theory and opposed the formation of Pakistan, following the partition of 1947 he quickly became the leading advocate for the Islamization of the Pakistani state, thrusting his party into debates over the nature of the constitution and participating actively in electoral politics until his death in 1979.

Mawlana Mawdudi's ideas were deeply grounded in the historical context in which he wrote. First the dismantling of the Mughal empire in 1857 and then the formal abolishment of the Ottoman caliphate after World War I fueled feelings of powerlessness among the Muslims of India. Stripped of the formal symbols of their political rule, Muslims viewed themselves as doubly isolated, first as colonial subjects of the British and second as a subservient class to the increasingly confident and politically aware Hindu majority. At the same time, new ideologies were gaining currency, imported from Europe and from other anticolonial movements. The early successes of communism and fascism appeared to demonstrate the power of mobilizing small, ideological cadres for social and political revolution. It was in this milieu that Mawdudi's ideas found a warm reception. By borrowing aspects of the 'ulamas traditionalism, joining them with the social mobilization theories of the modernist narrative, and appealing all the while to the sense of profound political disenfranchisement felt by the Muslims of the subcontinent, Mawdudi delivered a message that spoke to his age and provided a template for those engaged in constitutional experimentation in a newly established Pakistani state.

Inasmuch as Mawdudi's worldview was a product of his times, his ideas and impact have far transcended the South Asian context of the early twentieth century.[2] Countless scholars and ideologues have drawn on Mawdudi's writings on subjects as diverse as Islamic economics, war, gender roles, the Islamic state, and international relations. Indeed, his ideas have widely shaped the discourse of modern political Islam, often contributing concepts and vocabulary that today are so ubiquitous as to seem ordinary and unremarkable.

In the discussion that follows, we highlight four particular areas in which Mawdudi's ideas have shaped Islamic discourse in Pakistan and the wider Muslim world[3] : first, his expansive vision of Islam as a worldview but also as a complete way of life for which the Qur'an and Sunnah provide an infallible guide; second, his compelling (if overly abstract) rationale for an Islamic state, led by righteous rulers and tasked with the goal of purifying society; third, his efforts to describe the prerequisites for political participation by non-Muslims in a modern Islamic polity; and finally, his simple (if simplistic) framing of the relationship between Islam and the West as a choice between religious submission and utter godlessness. Mawdudi's contribution on each of these subjects varied. But in each case, both his writings and his political activities served to shape the contours of modern Islamic discourse and frame the ways in which debates on religion and politics have been conducted by scholars and activists alike.

ISLAM AS A WAY OF LIFE

One of Mawdudi's most fundamental contributions to public discourse about religion was his championing of the idea that Islam constitutes a *nizam-i zindagi*—a complete system of life that is simultaneously an ideology, a civilization, and a legal-political order. Much of his teachings revolved around this seemingly elementary concept.

Islam, for Mawdudi, was not merely a collection of disconnected rituals, rites, and practices. Nor was it an abstract set of identities and allegiances. It was, instead, a totalizing ideology that allowed no distinction between the public and private spheres and was structured as "an all-embracing social order where nothing is superfluous, and nothing is lacking" (Maududi 2005, 52). Analyzing the Qur'anic use of the Arabic word *din* (commonly translated as "religion"), Mawdudi declared that it referred broadly to "law, code, the Shari`ah, method, and system of thought and a praxis by which humans live their collective existence" (Mawdudi 2006, 157).

This systemic view of Islam can be understood, in part, as a natural response to the social and political milieu of the day; the early twentieth century had seen the promulgation of numerous conflicting ideologies and metanarratives. If Islam were to compete vigorously with alternative worldviews, it needed to frame its agenda in a similar vein. Thus Mawdudi insisted that Muslims constituted "an ideological society," that is, a social enterprise based upon a contract between man and God. Once members of this society, Muslims could not adopt any other way of life without becoming un-Islamic.

Mawdudi made tangible his view of the "ideological society" by invoking the authority of the Shari`ah. In essence, he claimed that the Shari`ah, based on the Qur'an and Sunnah, contains directives that are necessary and sufficient to "fulfil the needs of human society in every age and in every country," and in every possible sphere: religious, personal, moral, familial, social, economic, judicial, international, etc (Maududi 2005, 58). Moreover, he insisted that one had to accept or reject this "system of life" in its entirety; there could be no half-measures.

If this vision of an expansive Shari`ah sounds banal to modern ears, it must be remembered that, in the context of the early twentieth century, it was anything but ordinary. Muslim intellectuals at the time were grappling with the political powerlessness of their communities, while simultaneously being confronted with new ideologies and the solidification of the modern state system—a system from which they were largely excluded. Mawdudi's claim that the Shari`ah spoke clearly to every aspect of social and political life not only stretched the traditional scope of Islamic law, which historically had restricted itself to personal and family matters rather than affairs of state, but also appealed to an Islamic community that was yearning for a broader political profile.[4]

The impact of Mawdudi's insistence on Islam as a *nizam-i zindagi* has been widespread. It has, in one sense, allowed Islamic political thinkers to drive a wedge between "true believers" and *kafir*, the infidels. Mawdudi's analysis left no room for individuals or societies to accept certain tenants of Islam while rejecting others; he regularly mocked those who privatized Islamic law and adopted their own interpretations of its scope. Challenging the applicability of the Shari`ah over any area of life was thus framed as a denial of true Islam.

Mawdudi's logic has thus been used to justify the relentless expansion of the scope of the Islamic reform agenda. Not only did it provide, as described below, an integral part of Mawdudi's rationale for the Islamic state, but it also afforded a basic conceptual template for religious parties such as the Jama`at-i Islami and others who have pursued the systematic Islamization of legal and economic sectors. In Pakistan, for example, the gradual acceptance of Mawdudi's expansive rhetoric led to the establishment of independent Shari`ah courts and Shari`ah review mechanisms within the existing civil courts—developments that have become almost impossible to challenge without appearing to reject Islam itself. Many of Mawdudi's disciples, most notably Khurshid Ahmad, undertook efforts to extend Shari'ah to the finance sector with "Islamic banking." Although this movement largely failed in its efforts to change the fundamental structures of finance, it has nonetheless legitimized the notion that the Shari'ah is naturally applicable to every field of human endeavor.

Few intellectuals, particularly in Pakistan, have bothered to challenge Mawdudi's totalizing rhetoric of the *nizam-i zindagi*. Some, most prominently Javed Ahmed Ghamidi, have argued that Mawdudi gave too much weight to the legal-political aspects of Islam at the expense of its philosophical and ethical dimensions and inexplicably judged the narrowly scoped Shari'ah to be a sourcebook for every possible sphere of life. Such criticisms, powerful as they may be, have nonetheless failed to seriously diminish the impact of Mawdudi's discourse. Even critics from traditions that opposed him have frequently mimicked his language; witness the Barelvi '*ulama*s advocacy for *nizam-i mustafa* (system of the Prophet) and the Deobandis' regular use of *nifaz-i* Shari'ah (enforcement of the Shari'ah). Muslims around the world have been shaped by Mawdudi's insistence that Islam cannot be confined to the sphere of personal devotion, or even community life, but must by necessity spill over into law and statecraft. This insistence was guided by his radical belief that *din* "actually means the same thing as state and government" and that a life of Islamic devotion is inadequate absent a drive for political influence (Mawdudi 2008, 295).

THE ISLAMIC STATE

Mawdudi's political theology culminated in a simple imperative: Islam, he argued, craves a state, led by the righteous, for the purpose of establishing a social and political order consistent with the Qur'an and Sunnah.[5] Adopting a deeply state-centric perspective, he insisted that Islam necessitated the acquisition of political power and the creation of ideologically pure states through which to realize an all-encompassing Islamic way of life. This vision sat at the heart of Mawdudi's writings and his creation of the Jama'at-i Islami as a vehicle for political transformation.

Mawdudi's privileging of political power and the state must be understood, nonetheless, as the culmination and not the origin of his political theology. His argument began instead with the idea of *hakimiyyah*, or sovereignty. For Mawdudi, sovereignty represented the fundamental link between the creator and His creation. As he reminded his readers again and again, God is the ultimate sovereign. A life of true submission begins with this stark recognition. Moreover, since God is fully sovereign, man cannot be. At best, he can—and is called to—exercise *khilafat*, or vice regency, over the created world and over his fellowman. It was through the lens of sovereignty that Mawdudi critiqued the modern world and Muslim leaders of his era. Both, he insisted, had ignored God's sovereignty in place of their own and in doing so had committed *kufr*, or infidelity. It was for this reason that much of the world remained in *jahili-yyah*, the ignorance that characterized the pre-Islamic era.

In the face of this endemic infidelity, Mawdudi provided a simple and appealing prescription. Both in his political writings and in his widely read *Tahfim al-Qur'an*, he built his argument not from the top down—the need for an Islamic state—but from the bottom up—the need for the submitted Muslim to channel his devotions into a broader revolutionary agenda in the cause of righteousness.

Since, in Mawdudi's vision, Islam is a complete way of life and organic whole, every Islamic practice from prayer, to fasting, to almsgiving, to pilgrimage must prepare Muslims for the ultimate devotion, which is *jihad*. Mawdudi's writings on *jihad* are voluminous and complex and evolved over the course of his lifetime. On the whole, though, he was less concerned with defining *jihad* as a form of "just war" theory for Muslims (and was, indeed, often dismissive of the distinction between defensive and offensive *jihads*) than he was in defining it as a gradual social and political revolution whereby devout Muslims gain political power for the purposes of establishing an Islamic order.

Thus by connecting a foundational insight about sovereignty with a particular definition of *jihad*, Mawdudi made the necessity of an Islamic state, as an expression of the *hukumat-i ilahiyah*—the divine government—appear almost self-evident. His conclusion rested on two arguments. First, he advanced, in remarkably facile terms, an elite-oriented view that "corrupt rule is the root of all the evils you find in the world" (Mawdudi 2008, 286). And second, he read the Qur'an—in interpretations that have widely been contested by his both contemporaries and later scholars—to say that the believers must therefore possess state power to enjoin the good and forbid the evil.[6] True Islam, at its root, could not be fully practiced without "the coercive powers and authority of the state" (Maududi 2005, 56).

Although Mawdudi was disparaging of Western democracy as an expression of the false sovereignty of the collective, he believed that the Qur'an favored consultative decision making. Joined with his concept of *khilafat*, he proposed what he dubbed an Islamic democracy, or "theo-democracy," which would elect righteous leaders as God's vice-regents on earth (Maududi 2005, 139). Muslims were therefore to join Islamic parties that held to this vision and aspired to state leadership, stand for elections, and agitate for Islamic constitutional language that properly framed the philosophical and legal bases of the state.[7]

Mawdudi's overall line of argument—from sovereignty, to *jihad*, and finally to the Islamic state—proved to be innovative and influential. While his rhetoric of *hakimiyyah* has not been picked up as a common feature of everyday Islamic political language, the very idea of the compulsion for an Islamic state, constitution, and Shari`ah is now so widespread among many Muslims as to seem prosaic. In Pakistan, for example, even relatively liberal parties blithely accept the premise that Muslims ought to live in an Islamic state whose laws, by constitutional design, must accord with the Qur'an and Sunnah and that seeking such a state constitutes a religious obligation. (This assumption about Islam's fundamental objectives, ironically enough, has also been adopted by many commentators in the West.) While Mawdudi by no means invented his notion of the Islamic state from whole cloth—he drew heavily on Islamic history, and particularly historical interpretations of the Medinan state—he did play a major role in reframing for the modern age the idea that political power ought to be the central aspiration of the Islamic community.

Second, Mawdudi gave great currency to the idea that rule by the righteous constitutes a fundamental solution to vice. He argued passionately that if only one could make the state good, people would become good as well.[8] This "outside-in" view of social and personal transformation—deeply at odds with both much of the revivalist Islamic thinking of the nineteenth century and traditional Christian theological narratives—provided a theological basis for Islamic political advocacy in a number of spheres. It influenced Ayatollah Khomeini and his fellow Iranian revolutionaries in 1979. And it continues to shape the development of Islamic legal systems throughout the world, in which calls for powerful religious judges, police, and administrators often clash with Western conceptions of the rule of law that expressly limit the powers of any one government functionary.

Third, it is arguable that the very concept of religious-political parties has its modern origin in Mawdudi's advocacy and his logic of social transformation. It was he who brought together a robust view of the Islamic state with the belief that democratic processes are not a priori un-Islamic. The idea of an Islamic democracy, led by a political party that forms the vanguard of a gradual revolution, found a natural constituency among the middle classes and has become a commonplace feature of political Islam. While scholars in countries from Egypt to Indonesia to Turkey continue to question the extent to which Islamic political parties are truly invested in the democratic process and committed to respecting constitutional bounds, it is notable that these parties are increasingly an accepted part of the global political landscape.

Lastly, Mawdudi's reintroduction and adaptation of the concept of *jahiliyyah* for the modern age has markedly shaped the discourse of many Islamic movements, including some of the most radical organizations. Drawing on Taqi al-Din Ahmad ibn Taymiyyah (1263–1328), Mawdudi critiqued leaders and societies that were ostensibly Muslim, calling them to account for their infidelity. Although he was careful to say that Muslims who do not live according to the sovereignty of God are not *kafir* as such (with the exception of the Ahmadis, against whom he agitated intensely), others who later drew upon his ideas were not so generous.[9] Sayyid Qutb, influenced by Mawdudi, took this logic further, condemning much of the Muslim world as *jahiliyyah*.[10] Similarly, al-Qaeda and modern Taliban groups in Afghanistan and Pakistan have regularly targeted the state and its institutions for being insufficiently Islamic. This theological turn— the willingness to declare other Muslims as *kafir*—did not begin or end with Mawdudi. But it was given succor by his powerful political theology and will likely play out for a long time to come as Muslims grapple with the definition of a "true" Muslim and that of a "pure" Islamic state.

THE ROLE OF NON-MUSLIMS

One of Mawdudi's most significant legacies was the reintroduction into the modern world—and into modern language—of an idealized vision of the Islamic community. This vision demanded, in turn, an ideologically homogenous and exclusive state in which participation by non-Muslims in public life must be circumscribed so that true religious leadership could thrive. While the Qur'an itself, and generations of Muslim jurists after it, had taken up the question of minority rights in Islam, Mawdudi adapted this tradition and applied it to Pakistan—the first ideological religious state of the modern era.

He began with the premise that religious minorities were bound to be treated better under an Islamic system than under a Western pluralistic system. By comparing the most egregious examples of majority domination in Western countries with that of an idealized Islamic state that gave minorities limited but guaranteed rights, he concluded that Islam was more beneficent. While he did indeed grant that non-Muslims should be protected insofar as their basic rights, given equality in the criminal and civil law, and guaranteed that their personal (i.e., family) law would "remain immune from state interference," he also outlined a number of restrictions (Maududi 2005, 274).

Non-Muslims in the Muslim state would be categorized, in classical terms, as *dhimmis*, a protected class; would be restricted from holding high political office; would have to pay the *jizyah* poll tax; would face restrictions on public religious practice in "purely Muslim habitations"; could serve in parliament only so long as they accepted the Qur'an and Sunnah as the chief source of public law; and would be forbidden from practices deemed detrimental to the public interest. In addition, following many Muslim jurists before him, Mawdudi affirmed that conversion from Islam to any other faith amounted to apostasy and was punishable as a capital crime. His view, in short, was that the participation of non-Muslims should not interfere with the compulsions of a true *hukumat-i ilahiyah*; it was, he wrote, "not fair for the minorities to ask us to throw our ideology overboard and introduce laws that are against our convictions merely for the sake of appeasing them" (Maududi 2005, 69).

By themselves, these were not radically new ideas. But Mawdudi did not view them as simply ideas; he sought to integrate them in practice into the architecture of a modern Islamic state. He successfully advocated for constitutional provisions in Pakistan that sought to guarantee Muslim leadership in key posts and declare that no law could contravene the Qur'an or Sunnah. These actions, at least within Pakistan, had an ideational impact that far outstripped their practical legal significance. They propagated the idea that minority religious groups were less than full citizens of the state and that their communities were to be, at best, self-replacing but not permitted to grow by expansion or conversion. They also had the effect of framing laws ostensibly derived from the Qur'an and Sunnah as virtually unimpeachable. As a result it has become almost impossible to challenge laws on blasphemy or apostasy in Muslim countries around the world, even if those laws are of questionable theological merit.

Mawdudi's pernicious impact on religious minority rights was also a function of his political activism. Beginning in the early 1950s, he emerged as one of the most outspoken voices denouncing the Ahmadi sect (the followers of the prophet Mirza Ghulam Ahmad, also known as the Qadianis) as a "constant menace," claiming that they amounted to a fifth column within Pakistan and demanding that they be declared non-Muslims (Maududi 2006, 18). His writings against the Ahmadis contributed indirectly to riots in 1953 against the sect in Punjab province, and it was due to his efforts and those of the Jama'at over the subsequent two decades that the

Ahmadis were eventually disenfranchised of their full rights in 1974 and declared non-Muslims.[11]

MODERNITY AND THE WEST

Mawdudi's writings demonstrate a preoccupation with Western civilization and with those Muslims who seek to emulate the West. The centuries-long political and intellectual decline of the Islamic world, he believed, induced two different responses among Muslims, neither of which could provide a sustainable answer to the problems of the *ummah*, Islam's global community. The first response, conservatism, would inevitably fail because it relies on the rigid and unrealistic ways of the orthodox *'ulama'* who, "still living in the eighteenth century," refuse to adapt religious practice in the face of new problems and challenges.[12] The second response, modernism, would fail because it represents a departure from Islam rather than a genuine attempt to respect it and reform it. Of the two, Mawdudi saw modernism as clearly the greater evil.

By equating modernity with the West and deeming the West irreconcilable with true Muslim devotion, Mawdudi left no room for modernity within the ambit of Islam; Islam and the West, he wrote, "are like two boats sailing in totally opposite directions. Any attempt to sail in both the boats at a time shall split the adventurer into two pieces" (Maududi 2006, 13–14). What modern, educated Muslims paraded as rationalism, he argued, was little more than a thinly veiled attempt at disguising their own confusion: "their minds have embraced apostasy while their hearts are anchored in Islam" (Mawdudi 2004, 59). Modernity, in other words, subjected Muslims to a form of demeaning servitude.

Closely linked in Mawdudi's thinking to the dangers of modernity were those of secularism, which he viewed as a false, irrational, Western paradigm that violated the basic tenants of *hakimiyyah*. If God was all-sovereign, he reasoned, why would one allow him space in the private sphere of life while excluding him from the public domain? Along with denying the true sovereignty of God, secularism also exposed a state to class- or ethnic-based internal schisms. Without a public faith, the community would be riven by competing identities. This dark view of secularism as God denying and politically risky has gained remarkable traction among Muslims in South Asia, in part because of Mawdudi's success in promulgating his translation of secularism in Urdu as *ladiniyat*, literally, "godlessness." This translation has become so widely accepted in Pakistan that discussion of secularism is almost by definition precluded; who, after all, could possibly favor godlessness?

Mawdudi applied the same stark dichotomy of modernity and religiosity to his analysis of gender norms. He held a number of so-called conservative attitudes regarding women—for example, that segregation of the sexes is essential for men to successfully carry out their jobs without distraction.[13] Going beyond traditional arguments, however, he accused those who oppose *purdah* of adopting a Western worldview and suggested that they were outside of the legitimate Islamic tradition. Citing the West's "moral decrepitude" as the "logical consequence" of the emancipation movement that began in the nineteenth century, he lamented that women had become the "victim[s] of a vicious process of de-womanization" masquerading as a movement for women's empowerment (Mawdudi 2004, 58, 29). By framing legitimate differences of interpretation—in this case, on issues of gender—as examples of the Muslim elite's "mental servitude" to the West, Mawdudi positioned himself and the Jama`at-i Islami as the legitimate guardians of Islamic tradition and sought to dis-credit those who saw a via media between tradition and modernity.

In his writings and speeches, Mawdudi consistently railed against modern liberalism, impugning its values by making use of his own religious concepts and vocabulary. Even as he did so, however, he and his acolytes often pursued a parallel approach, trying to co-opt the rhetorical categories of the West. They did this, to some extent, by defining their *hukumat-i ilahiyah* as an idealized form of democracy. And they did it with respect to human rights discourse as well, framing Islam as the true fulfillment of ideals—such as women's rights, rational thought, and progressive social policy—which were poorly realized in the West. The precise definitions of these terms are, of course, hotly contested. But their continued use by the Jama'at-i Islami and other Islamic movements represents, in many respects, a striking picture of Mawdudi's complicated but enduring relation-ship with the rhetoric of modern politics. His ability to critique the West, while at the very same time embracing a great many aspects of modernity—human rights rhetoric, the idea of the ideological nation-state, party-based political mobilization, new media, etc.—helped to establish a template for modern Islamic activism. In this sense, Mawdudi can be seen as a precursor of those groups—from responsible Islamic political parties to extremist organizations like al-Qaeda—which today posit a "clash of civilizations" yet go about their activism borrowing liberally from both the political concepts and technologies of the West.

CONCLUSION

Throughout his lifetime and in the years since his death, Mawdudi has come under withering criticism. One easy target has been his purported lack of ideological consistency. Although Jama`at-i Islami cadres are quick to portray Mawdudi's ideology as internally consistent and essentially unchanging, his views on the political imperatives of Islam were in fact evolutionary, as his polemical early writings gave way to more practical and applied discussions of state power. Believing that the Jama`at had a chance to succeed under Pakistan's new constitutional framework, for example, he shifted gears in the late 1950s to become more accommodating of the democratic process.[14] Contravening his early writings on women in politics, he supported on grounds of political expediency Fatima Jinnah's bid for the presidency in 1965. And he gradually backed away from his emphasis on the centrality of a powerful executive, highlighting instead the values of a strong and accountable parliament.[15]

Critics have also challenged the religious foundations of Mawdudi's political ideology. Here the most trenchant criticisms have come from two of his former followers and members of the Jama`at-i Islami, Wahiduddin Khan and Javed Ahmed Ghamidi, both of whom disputed Mawdudi's core vision of *hakimiyyah* and argued that he fundamentally misread verses in the Qur'an pertaining to political power.[16] Other scholars have questioned the ease with which Mawdudi reconciled his vision of the "pure" Islamic state with democratic norms, contending that his theories left little room for true democratic dissent and placed unrealistic weight on the character of leaders.[17] On a host of other issues he has received criticism from Muslims and non-Muslims alike, most notably on account of his willingness to so harshly criticize other Muslims, his writings on religious minorities and women, his simplistic views of the West, and his inability to recognize his debts to modernity.

As these debates attest, Mawdudi's legacy remains very much disputed. On the one hand, his activism plainly failed to bring about the Islamic revolution that he desired. The Jama`at-i Islami is today an influential but niche player in the politics of South Asia, and neither the party nor other disciples of Mawdudi have succeeded in restructuring the basis of the modern state. On the other hand, Mawdudi has been quite successful in shaping the discourse of Islamic politics. His acolytes see this success as the fruit of his careful restoration of a long-lost "pure" Islam. His critics, particularly in the years since September 11, 2001, have framed it in more sinister terms, drawing an intellectual genealogy from his ideas, to the writings of Sayyid Qutb, and finally to the violent *takfirist* ideology of al-Qaeda.

Neither reading of Mawdudi's legacy captures his most lasting effect on Islamic political discourse, which was to convince middle classes throughout South Asia and the broader Islamic world that Islam is and ought to be an all-encompassing life system and that advocacy for an Islamic state constitutes a fundamentally religious obligation. These ideas gained currency well beyond the scholarly or activist fringes, and they did so because Mawdudi provided Muslims with a political and religious vision that resonated with their sense of disenfranchisement vis-à-vis the West. To the extent that his ideas continue to have currency, it is due in no small part to that enduring malaise.

Mawdudi's ideological contributions have made him a towering figure in modern Islamic thought. Less appreciated, but perhaps no less significant, has been his concurrent role in shifting the locus of debate on Islam and politics away from the `ulama' and toward a new generation of ideologues and activists. For all of his emphasis on law and political power, Mawdudi himself devoted remarkably little attention to traditional Islamic jurisprudence and instead privileged innovative readings of the Qur'an that most clerics considered to be unmoored from Islamic tradition. By doing so, and by channeling his energies into the formation of a technocratic, disciplined, middle-class Islamic party, Mawdudi contributed to the gradual marginalization of the *'ulama'* within Pakistan and created space for other nonclerical voices who declared themselves equally competent to interpret Islam for the modern age. This model of middle-class activism did not go unnoticed and has been emulated widely throughout the Muslim world. And as it has spread, coming into dialogue and confrontation with existing state systems in places as diverse as North Africa, Western Europe, and Southeast Asia, it has continued to do so largely on Mawdudi's own terms—silently borrowing from him a rich lexicon, a simple and compelling ideology of the state, and a religious vision wedded to the pursuit of political power.

NOTES

1. For the history of Mawdudi's leadership of the Jama'at, see Nasr 1994.
2. Scholars continue to debate the degree to which Mawdudi's ideology should be situated in the particular interwar, communal context of the subcontinent. Vali Nasr's definitive biography of Mawdudi has sometimes been criticized on this count for overly contextualizing his ideas and downplaying their wider role in Islamic political discourse.
3. The discussion that follows draws upon the authors' interviews with a number of scholars and contemporaries of Mawdudi, conducted in July 2009 in Pakistan, including Mumtaz Ahmad, Zafar Ishaq Ansari, Javed Ahmed Ghamidi, Rafi-ud-Din Hashmi, Muhammad Ibrahim, Khalid Masud, Salman Raja, Khalid Rehman, and Chaudhry Aslam Salimi.
4. On Mawdudi's move beyond the traditional scope of Islamic law see, e.g., Adams 1966, 395.
5. This phrase, "Islam craves a state," has been attributed to Javid Iqbal.
6. Mawdudi drew particularly from Qur'an 4:59, arguing that the command to obey "those invested with authority among you" constitutes "the cornerstone of the entire religious, social and political structure of Islam and the very first clause of the constitution of an Islamic state" (Mawdudi 2006, 171).
7. For more on the ways in which Mawdudi "presented as true democracy what the West regarded as theocracy," see Nasr 1996, 88.

8. See Mawdudi 2008, 285ff; and Maududi 1970.

9. For Mawdudi's views on this subject see, e.g., Mawdudi 2008, 58, 130–131.

10. For comparisons between the ideologies of Mawdudi and Qutb, see Sivan 1990.

11. For a report on Mawdudi's role in the 1953 riots and debates within Pakistan over the nature of Islamic politics, see Munir and Kayani 1954. For a cogent and sharply written Ahmadi critique of Mawdudi and his views of minority religious groups, see Ahmad 1989.

12. Maududi 1992, 42. Mawdudi was condemned frequently by traditionalist `ulama`, who were suspicious of his lack of formal theological training, his pointed criticism of several of the companions of the Prophet, and his willingness to question the authority of the hadith as a reliable guide for Islamic practice.

13. See, e.g., Maudoodi 1998.

14. See, e.g., Adams 1966, 378; Nasr 1996, 73ff.

15. Mumtaz Ahmad has suggested that this shift was due in part to Mawdudi's own treatment at the hands of various regimes in Pakistan (Ahmad 1991, 489).

16. For more on Khan's criticisms, see Omar, "Islam and the Other." More recently, American Muslim scholars such as Muqtedar Khan and Khaled Abou El Fadl have also challenged Mawdudi's concept of hakimiyyah.

17. See, e.g., Adams 1983, 118ff.

REFERENCES

Abbott, Freeland. 1968. *Islam and Pakistan*. Ithaca, NY: Cornell University Press.

Adams, Charles J. 1966. "The Ideology of Mawlana Mawdudi." In *South Asian Politics and Religion*, ed. Donald Eugene Smith, 71–397. Princeton, NJ: Princeton University Press.

Adams, Charles J. 1983. "Mawdudi and the Islamic State." In *Voices of Resurgent Islam*, ed. John L. Esposito, 99–133. New York: Oxford University Press.

Ahmad, Hazrat Mirza Tahir. 1989. *Murder in the Name of Allah*. Trans. Syed Barakat Ahmad. Cambridge, UK: Lutterworth Press.

Ahmad, Irfan. 2009. Genealogy of the Islamic State: Reflections on Maududi's Political Thought and Islamism. *Journal of the Royal Anthropological Institute* 15, no. s1: S145–S162.

Ahmad, Khurshid, and Zafar Ishaq Ansari. 1979. *Mawlānā Mawdūdī: An Introduction to His Life and Thought*. Leicester, UK: Islamic Foundation.

Ahmad, Mumtaz. 1991. "Islamic Fundamentalism in South Asia: The Jama`at-i Islami and the Tablighi Jama`at of South Asia." In *Fundamentalisms Observed*, ed. Martin E. Marty and R. Scott Appleby, 457–530. Chicago: University of Chicago Press.

Ahmad, Sayed Riaz. 1976. *Maulana Maududi and the Islamic State*. Lahore: People's Publishing House.

Binder, Leonard. 1961. *Religion and Politics in Pakistan*. Berkeley: University of California Press.

Hassan, Masudul. 1984. *Sayyid Abul A`la Maududi and His Thought*. 2 vols. Lahore: Islamic Publications.

Hassan, M. Kamal. 2003. The Influence of Mawdudi's Thought on Muslims in Southeast Asia: A Brief Survey. *The Muslim World* 93, no. 3–4: 429–464.

Maudoodi, Syed Abul A`la. 1998. *Purdah and the Status of Woman in Islam*. Trans. al-Ash'ari. 16th ed. Lahore: Islamic Publications, 1998.

Maudūdī, Abūl A`la. 1970. "The Moral Foundations of the Islamic Movement." In *Muslim Self-Statement in India and Pakistan 1857–1968*, ed. Aziz Ahmad and Gustave E. Von Grunebaum, trans. Charles J. Adams, 158–166. Wiesbaden: Otto Harrassowitz.

Maududi, Sayyid Abul A`la. 2005. *Islamic Law and Constitution*. Trans. Khurshid Ahmad. 13th ed. Lahore: Islamic Publications.

Maududi, Sayyid Abul A`la. 2006. *The Qadiani Problem*. 4th ed. Lahore: Islamic Publications.

Maududi, Syed Abul A`la. 1992. *West Versus Islam*. Trans. S. Waqar Ahmad Gardezi and Abdul Waheed Khan. 2nd ed. Lahore: Islamic Publications.

Mawdudi, Sayyid Abul A`la. 1995. *Jihad in Islam*. Ed. Huda Khattab, Trans. Khurshid Ahmad. Birmingham, UK: UKIM Dawah Centre.

Mawdudi, Sayyid Abul A`la. 2004. *Islam and the Secular Mind*. Ed. and trans. Tarik Jan. Markfield, UK: Islamic Foundation.

Mawdudi, Sayyid Abul A`la. 2006. *Four Key Concepts of the Qur'ān*. Ed. and trans. Tarik Jan. Leicestershire, UK: Islamic Foundation.

Mawdudi, Sayyid Abul A`la. 2006. *Towards Understanding the Qur'ān: Abridged Version of Tahfīm al-Qur'ān*. Ed. Zafar Ishaq Ansari. Leicester, UK: Islamic Foundation.

Mawdudi, Sayyid Abul A`la. 2008. *Let Us Be Muslims*. Ed. Khurram Murad. Leicestershire, UK: Islamic Foundation.

Munir, M., and M. R. Kayani. 1954. *Report of the Court of Inquiry Constituted Under Punjab Act II of 1954 to Enquire Into the Punjab Disturbances of 1953*. Lahore: Superintendent, Government Printing, Punjab.

Nasr, Seyyed Vali Reza. 1994. *The Vanguard of the Islamic Revolution: The Jama`at-i Islami of Pakistan*. Berkeley: University of California Press.

Nasr, Seyyed Vali Reza. 1996. *Mawdudi and the Making of Islamic Revivalism*. Oxford: Oxford University Press.

Omar, Irfan A. 1999. Islam and the Other: The Ideal Vision of Mawlana Wahiduddin Khan. *Journal of Ecumenical Studies* 36, no. 3/4: 423–438.

Osman, Fathi. 2003. Mawdudi's Contribution to the Development of Modern Islamic Thinking in the Arabic-Speaking World. *The Muslim World* 93, no. 3–4: 465–485.

Sivan, Emmanuel. 1990. *Radical Islam: Medieval Theology and Modern Politics*. Enlarged edition. New Haven: Yale University Press.

PART II

REVOLUTIONARY IDEOLOGUES

Chapter 3

Sayyid Qutb

SHAHROUGH AKHAVI

INTRODUCTION

SAYYID QUTB's name has achieved near iconic status in the realm of
what has come to be called "political Islam" (*al-islam al-siyasi*). He
never viewed himself as a leader of this movement[1] but simply as a
passionate missionary urging people to recognize Islam as a total
system of life. "Political Islam"—a phrase also captured by the expression, "Islamism," from the French, *Islamisme*—stresses the full and
immediate application of Islamic law in all areas of human existence.
Qutb's worry was that Muslims had forgotten the essentials of their
faith and in a facile manner increasingly tended to relegate their religion to the private sphere. Doing so was, in his opinion, not only
absurd—because Islam was indivisible—but a mortal existential
threat, since it undermined the necessary and sufficient vehicle for
the well-being of Muslims. Given its integral nature, he felt, it was
essential to remind believers of the ultimate validity of Islam as
"religion and the world" (*din wa dunya*). Any other understanding
was tantamount to the destruction of the faith and therefore the
believers.

Qutb did not in principle advocate violence to bring about the
immediate application of Islamic law to all arenas of life. However,

he did ultimately conclude that if the state resorted to violence against the advocates of *din wa dunya*, then it was legitimate for Islamists also to resort to violence to protect the true religion.

Sayyid Qutb, or, in full, Ibrahim Husayn Shadhili Sayyid Qutb, was born in the largest village of Asyut Province, Musha, into a relatively well-known family of peasants whose fortunes had declined. He was frail in health and not very prepossessing in mien, with large, droopy eyes and stooped shoulders. Though personally a pious youth, Qutb did not attend religious schools but instead matriculated and graduated from public school and then the Dar al-ʿUlum in Cairo (a teachers' training school established in 1871 with a Western-style curriculum). Upon his graduation in 1933 with a BA in education, Qutb was employed by the Ministry of Education as a schoolteacher. He was attracted to literature and wrote various works of poetry, short stories, and literary criticism, including an autobiography. These writings were secular and contained little hint of his future turn to Islamism. The one exception was a book he published on artistic imagery in the Qur'an, which was published in 1945, prior to his turn to Islamism. Also, it may be noted that he considered himself a protégé of the conservative author ʿAbbas al-ʿAqqad (d. 1964) and advocated in newspaper columns on behalf of ʿAqqad's literary works, which were significantly informed by Islamic themes.

Qutb also had been a member of the nationalist party, the Wafd, but he became disillusioned with what he saw as the opportunistic behavior of its politicians. He abandoned his membership in the Wafd and renounced the party system in 1945, believing that the nationalism of Saʿd Zaghlul, the Wafd's founder, had been unable to resolve Egypt's accumulating problems. In other words, Qutb, as so many Egyptians, gravitated to nationalism but eventually abandoned it in favor of Islamism.

Ultimately, he became so convinced of the moral bankruptcy of the ruling elites and the scandalous economic, political, and social disparities between the wealthy and the poor that he had to take some action in protest. He had as early as his village days become sympathetic to the cause of the *tarahil,* or seasonal workers on the land, because of their desperate economic conditions. Why he began to drift toward Islamism in the late 1940s rather than earlier is not certain. However, we know that when he and some like-minded individuals founded a short-lived magazine entitled *al-Fikr al-Jadid,* which published articles on Islam and Egyptian society from January to April 1948, he had finally and unequivocally turned his back on his literary career and secular perspectives. The magazine was eventually closed down by the government, which considered it to be subversive. He would have lost his job in the Ministry of Education, but apparently someone put in a good word for him, and so instead he was sent to America in September 1948 to learn about its educational system as well as to study for an advanced degree. He actually attended Columbia University Teacher's College for a while and also Colorado State College (currently the University of Northern Colorado) in Greeley.

This trip proved an epiphany for him. Already repelled by the exploitation of Egypt's poor by the wealthy landowners and their allies in the state apparatus, he found in America confirmation of his mounting hostility to capitalism, or at least to that version of capitalism that insisted on the unfettered operation of the market. In addition, he was revolted by the racial discrimination he found in this country and outraged by the unquestioning support for Zionism and the state of Israel in American public opinion and public policy. In America when the founder of the Muslim Brotherhood, Hassan al-Banna, was assassinated by the Egyptian government, he was embittered by the approval he saw in the American reaction to this event.

Even before leaving for America, Qutb had basically completed the draft of his first "religious" work, *Social Justice in Islam*, which was published in 1949. With this work, Qutb turned his back on his previous life as a secular writer and bureaucrat and launched a career that, little did he suspect, would make him an international figure for whom even the Pope would intercede. Upon his return to Egypt in 1951, he promptly joined the Muslim Brotherhood and eventually became director of its propaganda office. One source quotes him as saying, "I was born in 1951" (Kepel 2003, 41).

After the military coup of July 1952 that overthrew the pro-British monarchy, all political organizations were abolished, but the new rulers exempted the Muslim Brotherhood (technically, not an organization but rather a social movement whose support from the masses the new regime feared) from this proscription. Qutb in particular attended early sessions of the Revolutionary Command Council (RCC) and served as the Brotherhood's liaison with the junta leaders. He chaired a major conference in Cairo in August 1952 on the theme of Islam as an emancipating religion and was praised by both Nasser and General Naguib (the nominal leader of the junta) for a job well done.

But Qutb became disillusioned when the regime rejected the Brotherhood's demand for the application of *sharī'ah* throughout society. He was arrested in January 1954 for supporting this cause and served a three-month sentence. The Brotherhood strongly criticized the deal, announced in June 1954, between the government and the British for their withdrawal from Egypt, an agreement that permitted them to reintroduce troops into the Canal Zone over the next seven years should they determine the security situation required it. With this criticism, the die was cast. Matters stood at this pass when, as a result of an incident (to this day it is uncertain whether it was actual or staged) in October 1954 involving an assassination attempt against Nasser, he was caught up in the sweep of arrests that drove the Brotherhood underground, where it stayed until the early 1970s.

He was subjected to a show trial that found him guilty of charges and sentenced to twenty-five years of hard labor. During both his detention and then his incarceration after this trial, he was subjected to atrocious torture. Due to his frail health, he was transferred to the prison hospital, where conditions were somewhat better. It is there that he wrote most of the works for which he has become famous. Released in late 1964, due to the intercession of then President `Abd al-Salam `Arif of Iraq, he was rearrested for the publication of his book *Milestones*—no doubt the work for which he is best known and which was immediately placed on the blacklist. Ironically, President Nasser is said to have ordered its removal from censorship, but when it went through several printings, demonstrating its public appeal, it was replaced on that list, and he was arrested again. Though, as in 1954, the government cast its arrest net widely, Qutb was unquestionably its most notable victim. He was again subjected to torture, tried in a kangaroo court in August 1965, found guilty, and sentenced to death. Although international efforts arose to save his life, including by the Vatican, he was executed a year later, thus becoming a martyr and symbol of Islamist resistance.

SOCIAL THOUGHT

Qutb's writings contain a strong strain of didacticism, perhaps revealing the influence of his earlier turn in teaching. It is also driven by passionate commitment to the "true faith." At the same time, he never tires of speaking about Islam as a "practical" or "realistic" (*waqi`i*) faith. This leads some scholars, such as Leonard Binder, to consider him as a "non-scripturalist fundamentalist" (Binder 1988, 170). By this, he means that Qutb was perfectly willing to infuse his teachings with "modern" concepts, such as social justice and egalitarianism, something scripturalists avoid because of their conviction that the sacred texts "speak for themselves" and have no need for modern analytical constructs. As to "fundamentalist," this refers to the desire to renew Islam by reverting to its roots, meanwhile eliminating reprehensible accretions that have distorted it.

Yet scripturalism does seem apposite when considering the thought of Sayyid Qutb, because the modern concepts that he deploys are basically reifications whose roots are embedded in the holy scriptures. Thus, even if Qutb stresses that Islam is a practical religion and has reference to such modernist terminology as "mutual responsibility" (*al-takaful al-ijtima'i*), he is nevertheless eviscerating that terminology of any secular meaning and merely materializing it in the purely divine discursive formations of the holy texts. It is as though he is saying to himself, "I live at a time that privileges certain expressions, such as freedom, equality, and justice. It is imperative to address these. But I will reject their anthropocentric roots. Instead, I will materialize them in the holy texts as a way of showing how wrong it is for people to regulate their lives not by those texts but by human constructions. Such constructions by their very nature cause human beings to deviate from God's path and must be defeated." What we have, here, is professions of the practicality of Islam and, in fact, ahistorical attempts to anchor that practicality in Islamic scriptures.

The subtext for all of Qutb's works consisted of his conviction that human beings cannot understand truth by unique recourse to unconstrained rational endeavor; still less, he believed, could they understand it by empirical inquiry. This does not mean he opposed rational discourse. But as is the case with many pious thinkers, the discursive logic that he upheld was one that was at the outset premised upon divine axioms that restricted the scope of inquiry within the bounds of transcendental faith. Accordingly, he totally rejected philosophical inquiry, because in his view it began from premises that could lead the thinker into serious error and, indeed, defiance of God.

Qutb, then, believes that reason is a valuable asset, but it has its limits. In his worldview, God endowed human beings with reason as a gift of His grace. Without reason, human beings cannot carry out their functions as the vice-gerants of God on earth. Qutb notes that several verses of the Qur'an refer to human beings as God's vicar or deputy on earth (Qur'an 6:165, 27:62, 35:39). God's motive in endowing the individual with reason was so that he could be a faithful follower of His commands and also a loyal steward of the earth's resources, made available to mankind and womankind to enjoy in moderation. But, he believes that Western thinkers have taken this gift and shorn it of its carefully constructed restrictions. The result is licentious and wanton application of reason without any moral guidelines. Any exercise of human reason without awareness of the limitations that confine it is nothing less than arrogance, sure to lead its users astray.

The following passage makes Qutb's points:

Human thought is . . . a great and valuable tool that grasps the features . . . of [the Islamic conception]. But thought is not the only thing. . . . A hallmark of this conception . . . is that it responds to human existence in its entirety. That which [human thought] does not comprehend of [the Islamic conception] is the understanding of essence and truth, the understanding of causality, a situation to which it is possible to [i.e., one must] surrender calmly. (Qutb 1962, 52–53)

These ideas drive Qutb to reject all philosophy, whether ancient Greek, medieval Islamic, or contemporary analytical. Outstanding figures in the Muslim philosophical tradition, such as Ibn Rushd (d. 1198) are denounced for their efforts to reconcile revelation and reason. The ground for doing so is Qutb's belief that their systems of thought are embedded in Platonic and Aristotelian philosophy, both of them alien to Islamic thought because they are purely human constructions. Such constructions, he insisted, amount to word play, or as he puts it, "mere abstract knowledge that traffics with minds." He even accuses Muslim theologians (*mutakallimun*) for edging over into the domain of philosophy. Seeking to decode the nature of God, they depend on Aristotelian logic, he claims, and he sees that logic as reducible to mentalism. And he does not spare the towering figure of Islamic modernism, the former Grand Mufti of Egypt, Muhammad ʿAbduh (d. 1905) for his efforts to reconcile revelation with reason (Qutb 1962, 8–10).

It is true that Qutb clearly *was* offering a different choice to the Muslims of the 1950s and 1960s as well as to those of the decades after his death. Once Qutb came on the scene, Muslims no longer had to choose either to support the unreconstructed clergy, the guardians of a tradition that had for centuries been in decline, or to embrace foreign ways, thereby undermining their own religious heritage. For pious Egyptians hoping to steer a course between stultifying emulation of tradition and arrant embrace of "Western" culture, Qutb seemed to offer something new. On this point, it is worth emphasizing that Qutb was to a great degree working out his own personal understandings of what it means to be a Muslim in modern society. He did not, seemingly, view himself as a leader who was impelled to promote his views in the public arena or even among those who sympathized with his orientation. Of course, he hoped

that those who read his works would be won over. But he was at the
same time trying to resolve issues affecting his own identity and so
he was involved in a very personal journey. Thus, the fact that later
activists embraced his substantive ideas concerning the relationship
between faith and politics is less an outcome of his own conceits and
more the result of such historical conjunctures as the Arab defeat in
the June War of 1967, the poor performance of the Egyptian economy, and the parasitic quality of elite political rule and the bureau-
cratic administration of society.

As he was feeling his way toward a new synthesis of faith and
human action, Qutb came across the writings of the Indian Muslim
scholar, Abu al-A'la al-Mawdudi (Maudoodi; d. 1979). They had been
translated into Arabic, and Qutb was struck by the way Mawdudi
crystallized understandings of Islam that were to a significant degree
still inchoate in his own mind.

One may examine Qutb's thought by reference to certain concepts
that were central to his writings. These include

- God's unicity (*tawhid*)
- God's sovereignty (*hakimiyyah Allah*)
- praxis (*al-waqi'iyyah*)
- the Islamic way (*al-minhaj al-islami*)
- divine immanence (*al-kaynunah al-rabbaniya*)
- living in a state of ignorance of God commands (*al-jahiliyyah*)
- religious call (*al-da'wah*)
- exertion for God's sake (*al-jihad*)
- organic dynamic concrescence (*al-tajammu' al-haraki al-'udwi*)
- consultation (*shura*)
- mutual responsibility (*al-takaful al-ijtima'i*)
- social justice (*al-'adalah al-ijtima'iyyah*).

Qutb borrowed from Mawdudi the two critical notions that positive law cannot be the basis for human well-being and prosperity and that any system that rested upon human beings' subservience to other human beings was bound to fail. Put another way, only God's law could vouchsafe the well-being of the human race, and submission to God alone was the path to human happiness. Both of these principles were, in Mawdudi's and Qutb's views, a violation of the foundational principle in Islam of God's unicity.

The moment these two principles are asserted, however, they beg certain questions. God has already stopped legislating, and some of his commands are difficult to construe. Indeed, the Qur'an itself declares this to be so (3:7). Turning to experts for their meaning does not solve the problem, because this raises these experts into positions of superiority, in violation of the principle that human beings must not be made subordinate to other human beings. Furthermore, there is the problem of situations for which God's legislation has no answer because those situations have arisen as a consequence of the interplay of historical forces and pressures since the end of the revelation. If it is rejoindered that nevertheless human beings, by following the rulings of the religious experts— the *ulama*—on what constitutes God's law, will be walking on the righteous path, this again ignores that these religious experts are being placed in a position of superordination over others. Qutb might answer that these experts can be counted upon simply to interpret the law. But this is an idealistic assumption that may not bear any relationship to reality. In other words, it is one thing to maintain God's unicity (with its corollary that God must not be associated with others, the cardinal sin (*shirk*) in the Islamic tradition. But it is quite another to hold that only God should rule, since it will always be human beings, prone to error, who will decide how to operationalize this proposition. Qutb, who did not have a very favorable view of the *'ulama'* in any case, seems unaware of this contradiction in his enthusiasm to declare that God alone is master.

Another paradox in Qutb's thought is that his theistic (as opposed to deistic) position on God as sovereign and ruler is not easily reconciled with his perspective that Islam is a practical religion. What he means by its practicality, one supposes, is that Islam is a system that is equipped to deal with the hard realities of daily life and, one supposes, that it, as it were, bids the believers to utilize its assets to that end. One would imagine that if this were the case, then Qutb's unit of analysis would be human beings acting toward practical ends. But in fact Qutb's thought is thoroughly suffused with reifications. It is not Muslims who act in his worldview. Instead, he holds that "Islam" believes, "Islam" maintains, "Islam" establishes, "Islam" generates—in a word, that "Islam" is the actor. Human agency is assumed somehow to operate, but in fact, his theory cannot accommodate human agency. Accordingly, whenever he writes about the quotidian problems human beings face as a consequence of their religion being a practical religion, he is forced simply to assert in ad hoc fashion that they act. We never see Qutb problematizing human action. It is within the bounds of his theory, elided. Accordingly, if we follow him we must just assume that it somehow happens. Meanwhile, what is directing all the traffic, as it were, is a reified "Islam."[2]

Such, then, was the "Islamic way" (*minhaj islami*) in Qutb's writing. Taking his cue from Mawdudi, he invoked the classic scripturalist concept of *jahiliyyah*. This word originally referred to the historical era prior to the rise of Islam, a period known as the age of ignorance because people were deprived of the enlightenment provided by Islam. Its antonym, of course, was divine immanence (*al-kaynunah al-rabbaniyyah*). As utilized by Mawdudi and Qutb, however, it referred to the wanton or perhaps unwitting disobedience of modern-day Muslims (not to mention non-Muslims) of God's commands. Under this scenario, it was imperative to call the people (*da'wah*) back to Islam, just as the Prophet had originally called them away from their pagan practices to the new faith.

One of the ways this call would succeed was to remind the people of the admonitions of sacred scripture. Qutb utilized as a vehicle of persuasion innovative interpretations of key Qur'anic verses (5:44, 45, 47; 12:47, 60) containing the warning that those who do not "rule" according to God's revelation are apostates (the traditional rendering of the infinitive in these verses by Qur'anic commentators was "judge," not "rule"). With this innovative rendering, Qutb was sanctioning the anathematizing of contemporary Muslim rulers who were ruling according to secular models of authority. It was imperative to act against such rulers, in his view, invoking the classic principle of exertion for the sake of God (*jihad*).

In adopting this position, Qutb incurred the opposition of Hassan al-Hudaybi (d. 1977), who had become the Supreme Guide of the Muslim Brotherhood after the murder of its founder, Hassan al-Banna, in 1949. Apparently the Nasserist regime, which had earlier allowed Qutb to attend some sessions of the RCC, gave him an opportunity to distance himself from the Brotherhood at the time of the alleged assassination attempt against Nasser in October 1954. But Qutb refused, in effecting siding with Hudaybi. But after the publication of *Milestones* Hudaybi upbraided Qutb for his heretical interpretation of the Qur'anic versions discussed in the previous paragraph. Defiant, Qutb rejoindered:

Islam is servitude to God alone and assigning divine characteristics to Him, the foremost of which is sovereignty (al-hakimiyyah). . . . "And those who do not rule according to what God has revealed are unbelievers." What we have said about Islam is not a heretical innovation that we have thought up. (Qutb 1983, 12)[3]

Fifteen years after his execution, Islamists motivated by the need to restore to its rightful place the "forgotten precept" (that is, *jihad*) assassinated Egyptian President Anwar Sadat in the belief that he was not ruling according to God's revelation.

Altogether, Sayyid Qutb embraced organic conceptions of Islamic society, conceptions that dovetail with his ahistorical ideas of change. Rather than examining concrete junctures of Islamic history and inspecting the instances of conflict and cooperation among specific social forces and groups at specific junctures in time, Qutb preferred to paint his canvas with broad brushstrokes, identifying Islam as a quiddity that unfolds dynamically and rhythmically, according to a pattern of movement (*harakah*), vitality (*hayawiyyah*), evolution (*tatawwur*), and growth (*nama'*). Islam, in his opinion, is an organism, and it is characterized by the central trait of all organisms—a whole with interdependent parts. This whole he labeled an "organic, dynamic concrescence" (*tajammu' haraki 'udwi*; Qutb 1964, 37). It appears that this whole is the *ummah*, or community of believers. The individuals who comprise this community are, as in classic organic theories, parts of the whole, but that whole is greater than the sum of the individual parts.

To make sure we understand the organicism of this outlook, Qutb cites Leopold Weiss, an Austrian convert to Islam who adopted the name Muhammad Asad. The latter wrote, "History tells us that all human cultures and civilizations are organic bodies resembling living creatures that pass through all the organic stages of life . . ." (Qutb 1962, 102). But, aware of the full implications of such a statement, Qutb quickly adds, "Of course, we could never say that, like other civilizations, [Islam] is subject to the passage of time and limited by the organic laws of life" (Qutb 1962, 103). Qutb appears to want to have things both ways. Islam is at bottom a residuum that he calls an organic dynamic concrescence governed by the usual patterns of organisms, but he then wants to limit these patterns to those of growth only. Presumably, its predilection for continued growth is a function of mechanisms of renewal that are immanent in it, such as *tajdid* (renewal). But if this is the case, the operation of this *tajdid* is left unexamined. A disembodied "Islam" is said to be in some mysterious manner subject to this renewal. Qutb, that is, is again reaffirming that it is not specific actors or social groups living at concrete junctures of historical time who act as agents of that renewal. They are merely the bystander beneficiaries of developments that seem to occur over their heads, beyond their reach, and clear of any actual engagement on their part.

CONCLUSIONS

Sayyid Qutb's influence on later generations would likely have remained somewhat marginal had not events on the ground transpired in the way they did. Of all these events, the critical ones were Israel's victory in the Six Day War of June 1967, the death of President Nasser in 1970, and the accession of Anwar Sadat (whose narrow base of support forced him to turn to the Muslim Brotherhood). These events drove certain activist-minded Muslims who came after him to utilize Qutb's ideas to vindicate their demand for the immediate application of *sharī'ah* in all areas of life. In 1971 the state responded to a degree to these demands by offering to the people in a plebiscite a draft of a new constitution that stated in its Article Two that "Islam is the state religion" and in an amendment in 1980 added that "Islamic law is the principal source of legislation." The previous "provisional" constitutions of 1956 and 1964 made no such references to Islam.

However, Qutb certainly would not have accepted these 1971 and 1980 changes in the country's constitution as sufficient warrants for his objective of an exclusively integral Islamic system, since in practice they have been interpreted in ways that permit non-Islamic sources of law to figure prominently, even to enjoy priority. Thus, the notion that "Islamic law is the principal source of legislation" has been operationalized by an interpretation that non-Islamic sources of law are acceptable, even preferable, as long as they do not directly contravene the *shari'ah*. Ruling elites could always define the *shari'ah* so elastically as to distort it beyond all recognition. Qutb would have totally rejected this kind of interpretation as legerdemain, a recipe bound to perpetuate the supremacy of manmade law and hence a guarantee of the continuing triumph of *jahiliyyah*.

For this reason, Qutb's ideas continue to carry currency. In Egypt, where the official religious establishment is under state authority, the regime has managed to obtain rulings from the *'ulama'* that depict Qutb as a puritanical extremist in the tradition of Islam's original "puritans"—the Khawarij. But this hardly puts the matter to rest, as many Muslims regard the judgments and rulings of the official religious establishment in Egypt with a great degree of cynicism. Even non-violence-prone Islamists have been influenced by Qutb's ideas in important ways. More worrying to ruling circles in Muslim-majority (or even Muslim-minority) countries is the continuing influence of Qutb's ideas on violence-prone groups, such as some elements of the FIS in Algeria and of the Taliban in Afghanistan.

It is, at the time of this writing, unclear whether the star of Sayyid Qutb is waxing or waning. But one thing seems certain: that influence will mainly exert itself in circles where emotional commitment trumps analytical argumentation. For Sayyid Qutb's logical and empirical persuasiveness is less at issue for an assessment of his enduring impact than is the passion that drove his understandings about the real world, the practical world, and the implications of those understandings for Islamic praxis.

NOTES

1. Indeed, the expression did not exist in his lifetime, even though the tendency associated with it that characterized a movement demanding immediate application of Islamic law in all areas of life certainly did.
2. We must, however, not lose sight of the fact that Qutb wrote most of his "Islamist" works while he was in the prison hospital, conditions that were—to say the least—far more conducive to writing with emotion and passion than with analytical clarity.
3. The first edition of this work was published in 1949, obviously at a time when Qutb had not engaged in his commentary on the Qur'an. Later editions of this work, however, came to include material that was new, including this riposte against Hudaybi's criticisms, which came after Qutb had come to a new understanding of the verses mentioned, now frequently glossed under the rubric of the *hakimiyyah* verses.

REFERENCE

Abu-Rabi`, Ibrahim. 1991. Discourse, Power, and Ideology in Modern Islamic Revivalist Thought: Sayyid Qutb. *The Muslim World* 81:3–4.

Abu-Rabi`, Ibrahim. 1996. *Intellectual Origins of Islamic Resurgence in the Modern Arab World*. Albany: State University of New York Press.

Akhavi, Shahrough. 1994. Sayyid Qutb: The Poverty of Philosophy and the Vindication of Islamic Tradition. In *Cultural Transitions in the Middle East*, ed. Serif Mardin, 130–152. Leiden: E. J. Bill.

Akhavi, Shahrough. 1997. The Dialectic in Contemporary Egyptian Social Thought: The Scripturalist and Modernist Discourses of Sayyid Qutb and Hassan Hanafi. *International Journal of Middle East Studies* 29: 377–401.

Akhavi, Shahrough. 2009. *The Middle East: The Politics of the Sacred and Secular*. London: Zed Books.

Binder, Leonard. 1988. *Islamic Liberalism*. Chicago: University of Chicago Press.

Diyab, Muhammad Hafiz. 1987. *Sayyid Qutb: al-Khitab wa al-Idiyulujiya*. Cairo: Dar al-Thaqafah al-Jadidah.

Euben, Roxanne. 1999. *Enemy in the Mirror: Islamic Fundamentalism and the Limits of Modern Rationalism*. Princeton: Princeton University Press.

Haddad, Yvonne Y. 1982. *Contemporary Islam and the Challenge of History*. Albany: State University of New York Press.

Haddad, Yvonne Y. 1983. The Qur'anic Justification for an Islamic Revolution: The View of Sayyid Qutb. *The Middle East Journal* 37:14–29.

Haddad, Yvonne Y. 1983. Sayyid Qutb: Ideologue of Islamic Revival. In *Voices of Resurgent Islam*, ed. John Esposito, 67–98. New York: Oxford University Press.

Kepel, Gilles. 2003. *Muslim Extremism in Egypt*. 2nd ed. Berkeley: University of California Press.

Khatab, Sayed. 2002. *Hakimiyyah* and *Jahiliyyah* in the Thought of Sayyid Qutb. *Middle Eastern Studies* 38: 145–178.

Khatab, Sayed. 2008 *The Political Thought of Sayyid Qutb: The Theory of Jahiliyyah*. London: Routledge.

Lee, Robert D. 1997. *Overcoming Tradition and Modernity: The Search for Islamic Authenticity*. Boulder: Westview, 83–116.

Moussalli, Ahmad S. 1990. Sayyid Qutb: the Ideologist of Islamic Fundamentalism. *Al-Abhath* 38: 42–73.

Moussalli, Ahmad S_.1993. *Radical Islamic Fundamentalism: The Ideological and Political Discourse of Sayyid Qutb*. Syracuse: Syracuse University Press.

Musallam, Adnan. 1993. Sayyid Qutb and Social Justice, 1945–1948. *Journal of Islamic Studies* 4: 52–70.

Musallam, Adnan. 2005. *From Secularism to Jihad: Sayyid Qutb and the Foundations of Islamic Radicalism*. New York: Praeger.

Muruwwah, Husayn. 1978. *Al-Naza`at al-Maddiyyah fi al-Falsafah al-`Arabiyyah al-Islamiyyah*. Beirut: Dar al-Farabi.

Qutb, Sayyid. 1949. *Al-`Adalah al-Ijtima`iyyah fi al-Islam*. Cairo: Dar al-Kitab al-`Arabi.

Qutb, Sayyid. 1951. *Al-Salam al-`Alami wa al-Islam*. Cairo: Dar al-Kitab al-`Arabi.

Qutb, Sayyid. 1951. *Ma`rakah al-Islam wa al-Ra'smaliyyah*. Cairo: Dar al-Kitab al-`Arabi.

Qutb, Sayyid. 1952–1957. *Fi al-Zilal al-Qur'an*. Cairo: Dar Ihya' al-Kutub al-`Arabiyyah.

Qutb, Sayyid. 1953. *Dirasat Islamiyyah*. Cairo: Maktabah Lajnat al-Shabab al-Muslim.

Qutb, Sayyid. 1962. *Khasa'is al-Tasawwur al-Islami wa Muqawwimatuhu*. Cairo: Dar Ihya' al-Kutub al-Islamiyyah.

Qutb, Sayyid. 1964. *Ma`alim fi al-Tariq*. Cairo: Maktabah Wahbah.

Qutb, Sayyid. n.d. *Al-Mustaqbal li Hadha al-Din*. Cairo: Maktabah Wahbah.

Qutb, Sayyid. n.d. *Hadha al-Din*. Cairo: Dar al-Qalam.

Qutb, Sayyid. 1983. *Al-'Adalah Al-Ijtima'iyyah fi al-Islam*. 9th edition. Cairo: Al-Shuruq, 1983.

Shehadeh, Lamia Rustum. 2000. Women in the Discourse of Sayyid Qutb. *Arab Studies Quarterly* 90: 45–55.

Shepard, William E. 1989. Islam as a System in the Later Writings of Sayyid Qutb. *Middle Eastern Studies* 25: 31–50.

Shepard, William E. 1996. *Sayyid Qutb and Islamic Activism: A Translation and Critical Analysis of Social Justice in Islam.* Leiden: E. J. Brill.

Shepard, William E. 1997. The Myth of Progress in the Writings of Sayyid Qutb (Egyptian Writer and Activist). *Religion* 27: 255–256.

Shepard, William E. 2003. Sayyid Qutb's Doctrine of *Jahiliyya. International Journal of Middle East Studies* 35: 521–545.

Sivan, Emmanuel. 1985. *Radical Islam.* New Haven: Yale University Press.

Chapter 4

Ali Shari`ati

SHAHROUGH AKHAVI

INTRODUCTION

ALI SHARI`ATI (1933–1977), an Iranian political activist and intellectual, emerged into the public eye in his own country around 1967, a mere decade before his death in mysterious circumstances in a suburb of London. His father, Muhammad Taqi Shari`ati, was an independent-minded cleric in Mazinan, a town located in western Khurasan province, who encouraged his son to read avidly. Muhammad Taqi's library of works in the religious sciences served as nourishment for the young Shari`ati's inquisitive and restless mind. Additionally, the father had established a Center for the Propagation of Islamic Verities. The distinctive orientation of the Center was to reform Shi`ism and thus to make it more relevant to the conditions of the time, as opposed to remaining restricted to the narrower confines of ritual and pedagogy in the seminary and mosque. As a sign of his commitment to religious reformation, the father did not wear a turban—a symbol of those to whom the son was later to refer as the "hide-bound" clergy (`ulama'-yi qishri). Reform and social activism were to remain critical elements in Shari`ati's own thinking and action, but putting himself so explicitly in the public eye could not have been easy for him. For, although he became a famous public figure as a result of his tremendously popular lectures in the Husayniyyah-yi Irshad in northern Tehran and his invited presentations at many universities throughout the country, he in fact was very much of a loner who craved solitude.

Shari'ati and his father both had been supporters of the nationalist prime minister, Muhammad Musaddiq, whose overthrow in a royalist coup d'etat engineered by the British, the Americans, and Iranian royalists in August 1953 marked their turn to oppositional activity against the Shah. They were both arrested and briefly imprisoned after the coup. The two were associated with the movement known as the God-Worshipping Socialists, and the son's idol was Abu Dharr al-Ghifari (d. 652), an early Muslim and companion of the Prophet who had distinguished himself for his piety, inclination toward justice, and unflinching support for the Prophet's cousin and son-in-law, 'Ali ibn Abi Talib (d. 661), the founder of Shi'ite Islam.

In 1959, Shari'ati was awarded a government stipend to pursue higher education at the Sorbonne in Paris. He was initially active in the anti-Shah Iranian Student Confederation in Europe during his years of study in Paris in the years 1959–1963. But he apparently later became disillusioned with what he believed was the penchant within this organization for endless discussion and aversion to action. Though he was not a trained philosopher or social theorist, this did not deter him from writing works in these areas after his return to Iran in 1964.

In the French university system at the time, one could pursue the *doctorat d'etat*, a rigorous course of study culminating in a dissertation requiring basic research, or a *doctorat d'universite* (sometimes also referred to as *doctorat de troisieme cycle*), whose requirements were more modest and required a minimum amount of basic research and analysis. It was the latter track that Shari`ati was in, although, since French practice seemed to be to assign all foreign students to that track, it may be that Shari`ati had had no chance to opt for the more rigorous course of studies. At any rate, his supervisor, a philologist by the name of Gilbert Lazard, recalled that Shari`ati had shown a basic knowledge of the French language but otherwise was an average student.

Despite his attitude as a young lad in his father's library who revered learning as an end in itself, Shari`ati's formal work at the Sorbonne was driven by an apparently instrumental perspective—he wanted to get the degree as soon as possible so that he could qualify as a university professor in Iran. For his dissertation, he was not able to come up with a developed research question, much less a methodology of research. So Lazard recommended that he edit for corrections in the original text and translate into French an obscure manuscript in Paris's National Library by an equally obscure four-teenth-century writer, Safi al-Din Abu Bakr `Abdullah ibn `Umar al-Balkhi, a work called *Faza'il-i Balkh* [The Moral Excellences of (the City of) Balkh]. This manuscript was itself a Persian translation of an Arabic work. To the editorial emendations and the translation into French, Shari`ati added a nine-page introduction. This thesis was submitted in 1963 and awarded a "pass," the lowest category possible for earning the degree (Rahnema 1998, 117–118).

By contrast, in his informal studies in Paris, Shari`ati was greatly influenced by the orientalist Louis Massignon, the sociologist Georges Gurvitch, the historian Jacques Berque, and the philosopher Jean Paul Sartre. The extent to which these major figures esteemed Shari`ati's intellectual prowess is uncertain, but he did interact with them and regarded their impact upon him as enormous. It is ironic that the Christian Massignon crystallized in Shari`ati his own Muslim faith; the Marxist Gurvitch reinforced Shari`ati's devotion to what he believed was Shi`ism's extraordinary commitment to social jus-tice; the agnostic Berque "taught me [Shari`ati] what religion was" (Rahnema 1998, 126); and the atheist Sartre buttressed Shari`ati's notions that Islam was a liberation theology that stressed the human being's responsibility for his or her actions in the world.

One source on Shari`ati somewhat hyperbolically asserts that "he wished to change, not interpret, lead, not argue, move, not con-vince, achieve, not rationalize" (Dabashi 1993, 104). I say hyperbolic because this characterization obscures Shari`ati's very real desire to interpret or, perhaps one should say, reinterpret, the Islamic verities; and he was a passionate polemicist for whom argument was highly important; he did seek to win over through persuasion; and he was not averse to rationalization—as can be seen by his determined effort to marry social thought with religious verities.

But it is true that Shari`ati was not a systematic thinker and scholar. He was in too much of a hurry for that. Accordingly, critiques of his writings that try to explore the ontological, epistemological, and the philosophically historical aspects of his thought may, at a certain level, be incomplete. For Shari`ati, a word can be made into an entire con-ceptual and analytical construct without having to embark on any disciplined, discursive, organized intellectual process for rendering this transformation.

According to Rahnema, Shari`ati learned this "truth" from the French orientalist historian Jacques Berque. Berque apparently impressed upon his students the notion of *degrée* [*sic*, i.e., *degré*] *de signification* (degree of signification). As Shari`ati understood it, this expression

meant that even though words had a unique and eternal mean-ing, their purpose and intent was subject to change within a given margin during different periods and under different circumstances. Words could thus be transformed from passive means for idle chatter and tools of stupefaction into instruments for socio-political change . . . [Shari`ati] took each commonly used term in the vocabulary of every Muslim and reinterpreted it until gentle lullabies became electric currents. Words and concepts resonating with resignation, fatalism and self-pity in the historical memory of Iranian Shi`i were suddenly transformed into forceful and dynamic concepts for action. (Rahnema 1998, 126)

We are, here, in the realm of ideology, rather than social theory. If Shari`ati could impregnate a word with a dynamic meant to mobilize large numbers of people, especially the younger generation, into action, then we should pay more attention to the ideological, rather than the purely intellectual, dimension of his efforts. By ideology, I mean a set of beliefs about politics and society that are utilized as metaphorical weapons to advance ideal and material interests in public arenas. Seen in this light, one can understand more clearly the testimonials of two major leaders of the Iranian revolution about Shari`ati: Ayatullah Mahmud Taliqani (d. 1979) and Ayatullah Muhammad Bihishti (d. 1981). According to Taliqani, "Shari`ati created a new *maktab* (doctrine). It was he who drew the youth of Iran into the revolutionary movement." And in Bihishti's assessment, "The works of Shari`ati were essential for the revolution. Those of Imam Khomeini were not exactly suitable for winning over the younger generation" (Abrahamian 1989, 105).

It is in this context that in Sharia`ati's hands Islam became transformed into a revolutionary world ideology. In saying this, I do not for one moment mean to imply that Shari`ati was an opportunist when it came to matters of faith. Quite the contrary, he was deeply pious. However, the measure of his piety was not to be found in the ritualistic aspects of the faith, enacted under the aegis of the mainstream clergy. Instead, it inhered in the manner in which one could work one's faith into service on behalf of social justice and liberation. The paradox lies in the fact that he was such an intensely private person, and yet he saw it his duty to be a voice for public causes, for the people—*al-nas*—one of his favorite expressions.

Shari'ati considered himself an "enlightened intellectual" (*rawshanfikr*) for whom the critical task was to deconstruct existing forms of Islamic knowledge and reconstitute the latter as socially relevant knowledge. "Islamology" is the nearest expression to the Persian word, *islamshinasi*. When he used the word, everyone knew that by it he did not mean knowledge of Islamic dogma, doctrine, and ritual. Rather, the meaning was knowledge of the ideological relevance of Islamic thought and its materialization in action to promote what he held to be the eternal objective of the faith: the achievement of true liberation and social justice.

Despite the fact that Shari'ati is more appropriately seen as an ideologist rather than a social theorist, it is hard to completely separate the two. Earlier, I defined ideology as a system of beliefs that one uses as metaphorical weapons to advance interests in public arenas. If this can be accepted, then social theory (defined here as systematic application of propositions from a variety of disciplines to generate knowledge about society) is the foundation for ideological discourses. In Shari'ati's case, the relevant social theory frameworks come from Marxist political economy and sociology, existential philosophy, liberation theology, and the sociology of religion.

One will not find a systematically integrated worldview in Shari'ati's oral and written discourse. His work is highly eclectic and lacks disciplined articulation and coherence. But the widespread support given to Shari`ati's thought by the younger generation is largely due, one supposes, to his vindication of equality and justice, values that this generation champions above many others. The following themes emerge from a study of Shari`ati's thinking: (1) history as a dialectical process, (2) the individual as a responsible actor who has the obligation to seek truth on his own and act to uphold it, (3) Shi`ism's true mission as the liberation of the human being, (4) the *ulama*'s claimed monopoly in regard to the interpretation and enunciation of the law as a certain recipe for injustice, and (5) contemporary international relations as a system that secures the domination of interventionist great powers pursuing their interests.

HISTORY AS A DIALECTICAL PROCESS

Let us take these motifs in the order that they have been listed. Shari`ati accepted the Marxist paradigm of social change, although he added his own ad hoc notions to it. In Marx's view, social change occurs as a consequence of contradictions and class conflict—not as a result of harmonious and consensual accommodations among groups in society. Shari`ati simply accepts this perspective without really problematizing and critiquing it, other than to fault it for leaving religion out of the picture. Doubtless the influence of the European left shaped his thinking in this area. While, as far as can be established, Shari`ati did not read the primary sources of Marxian thought, including Marx himself, Bernstein, Lenin, Trotsky, Lukacs, and Gramsci, he was introduced to Marxism by Georges Gurvitch's lectures at the Sorbonne, Sartre's existential philosophy, and, perhaps, Frantz Fanon's writings on the third world. Because he did not have the background, we can imagine Shari`ati listening to Gurvitch's lectures and focusing his mind on certain concepts and arguments that the latter made that seemed relevant for Shari`ati's own understanding of the contemporary world. Accordingly, he did not acquire an integral understanding of Marxist thought.

This led him to validate the Marxist view that change is dialectical, based on conflicts and contradictions. One of his favorite terms was *jabr-i tarikh*—historical determinism—(though this was not Marx's own phrase). But when it came to applying this framework to social change in a "genuine" Shi`i community, he simply elided its application in ad hoc fashion and thus implied that because the community was a "true" Shi`i community, historical laws that applied in all other circumstances did not apply for pious Shi`ites. The implication is that if people in a community believe they are living the lives that the Shi`i imams[1] enjoined upon them to live, the objective situation did not really matter in their case, since God, as it were, would absolve them of the universal pattern that change must occur dialectically and through conflict. In short, to apply the conflict paradigm for Shi`is seemed, to Shari`ati, to preempt God's role in guiding people to the truth by ensuring that they abided by the noble religious injunctions.

Liberated by his "Shi`i exceptionalism" thesis (if this expression may be permitted), Shari`ati is thus free to call upon all well-intentioned believers to rally to the standard of Imam Husayn b. `Ali (d. 680), the younger son of Shi`ism's founder, Imam `Ali b. Abi Talib (d. 661). Husayn is the central figure in classical Shi`ism's doctrine of martyrdom. That doctrine emphasizes this figure's sufferings on behalf of his faith and of those who espouse it. But Shari`ati goes far beyond this more limited characterization to convert Husayn into a *revolutionary*, whose paradigmatic act against Sunni impious tyranny centuries ago is dramatically relevant for contemporary politics.

THE INDIVIDUAL AS A RESPONSIBLE ACTOR

Historical determinism and the individual as a responsible actor seem to be two contending themes. On the one hand, we have a structuralist approach, according to which the causes of change lie in dynamics within macroentities, such as classes, states, and markets—all of which structuralists generally see as operating in some impersonal manner. On the other hand, we have an agency approach, according to which the causes of change reside in microlevel voluntary actions by individuals who, when faced with an actual situation, decide to throw the weight of their actions on this side or that side of an issue.

Shari`ati does not have the inclination to think about these antinomies. Nor would it serve his purpose to do so, which is to reach a broad audience and persuade its members to mobilize their energies to achieve freedom and justice. The principle that human beings are ultimately responsible for their actions and the corollary that they are free to choose among alternatives can be found in the thought of some earlier Muslim thinkers. Yet, Shari`ati seems to raise them not in the context of *their* thought but rather through his understanding of French existential notions, which he combines with his own private reconstruction of the motivations of Shi`ism's iconic figures, Imam `Ali and Imam Husayn. His message is that these imams devoted themselves to the masses, and one measure of this devotion was to urge that Shi`ites commit themselves wholeheartedly to the principles of responsibility and choice. Going one step beyond this, Shari`ati appeared to be arguing that if Shi`ites did not make this commitment, they would be betraying these leaders, a deeply wounding charge, of course, given the persistent belief among Shi`ites that they (that is, their ancestors) had betrayed them through abandonment.

SHI`ISM'S TRUE MISSION AS THE LIBERATION OF THE HUMAN BEING

Related to the above discussion is Shari`ati's navigation between the overt meanings of Islamic scripture and their latent, esoteric meanings. Feeling an affinity for the Muslim mystic Mansur al-Hallaj (d. 922), Shari`ati reasoned that exoteric and esoteric truths within the same message of the faith contend with one another in dialectical fashion. This dynamic process, he argued, was essential to maintain the resilience of Islamic thought, which, in their absence, would become stagnant, even sterile (Rahnema 1998, 135–137). He suggested that the clergy cherished the study of law to the detriment of the study of inherent meanings of symbols. He fully realized that his position would (and did) generate hostility from the `ulama' but convinced himself that such opposition would not matter once the broader masses freed themselves of the clergy's influence.

In this context, what mattered in Shi`i thought was not expert advice on the rituals of the faith (which he believed was the traditional preserve of the `ulama') but how the imams of Shi`ism exemplified struggle on behalf of both moral and revolutionary virtues. Shari`ati did not deny the seemliness of ritualistic obedience to the laws of Islam, and so the clergy had an important role to play in society. But he noted that their monopoly of interpretation of the faith had led to its stultification at best and the destruction of the revolutionary imperative at worst. Here, a paradox emerges. Shari`ati was never tired of upholding the cause of the masses (*al-nas*), which seems to be his unit of analysis and generator of change. But esoteric verities are often impervious to the efforts of common folks to understand. This necessitates that "enlightened thinkers" (*rawshanfikr/rawshanfikran*) take the leading role. Shari`ati seems to take it on faith that these enlightened thinkers will always see matters in the light of what best suits the ideal and material interests of the masses. Yet, what ensures that the former will act in ways to uphold the rights and interests of the latter? Another way of putting matters is that in spite of the democratic ethos of parts of Shari`ati's thought, an elitism may be found.

Of course, it is not surprising that a tension of this sort exists, since one could say much the same thing about many bodies of thought, including liberal or social democratic thought themselves. So the fact that Shari`ati wants the individual to think for himself or herself as a responsible actor who is free to make choices but also wants enlightened intellectuals to show the way does not cause his project to fall to the ground. But in eliding the process by which enlightened intellectuals, having led the way, then also facilitate the masses' actions on their own behalf, finally eventuating in Shi`ism's ultimate goal of liberation of the human being, Shari`ati seems to be begging the question of how this process unfolds.

THE `*ULAMA*''S ROLE AND INJUSTICE

Shari`ati had problems with the `*ulama*' for a number of reasons. The first was that his father was critical of them as a group because of their insularity and pedantry. To the degree that he was influenced by his father's teachings, Shari`ati himself adopted similar views. Note that his father had refused to wear the turban, as though by doffing this symbol he was freeing himself from constraints restricting the breadth of vision and depth of reformist thought of the traditional clerical sodality. Shari`ati never had it in mind to become a professional man of religion, although this did not prevent him from forming associations with them, such as Ayatullah Murtada Mutahhari (d. 1979). And, in the midst of campaigns by the clergy to deny him any credibility as a religious spokesman, Shari`ati expressed his appreciation for the fact that no clergyman had ever signed his name to a protocol, capitulatory agreement, or treaty that alienated a part of Iranian territory or resources to foreign powers or businessmen.

Yet, he blamed the *`ulama*' for two shortcomings: (1) they failed to make themselves relevant to the faithful—and especially to the younger generation—by wrapping themselves in a cocoon of scholasticism and casuistry; and (2) they unjustifiably tried to monopolize understandings of the faith and thus flaunted their elitism within a tradition that, to him, rested on egalitarian foundations. Shari`ati is not the only thinker whose efforts to vindicate the alleged egalitarianism of Shi`ism have foundered on the shoals of an inherently elitist juristic theory of rule. Following the Iranian revolution of 1978–1979, a number of *mujtahid*s have blithely argued that Shi`ism rests on the foundations of popular sovereignty, forgetting that its juristic theory of authority identifies the imams as the repositories of divine knowledge; and specially trained jurists as their deputies (Akhavi 1996). It is hard to see how these formulations lay the basis for the liberation of believers. They may do so, but these writers have failed to show how. Shari`ati believes that all believers have the right to engage in *ijtihad*—the utilization of independent judgment to adduce a legal ruling. This position directly conflicts with the *`ulama*'s unique control over this process. They have ridiculed his argument as ignorant, but their opposition tells us more about their fear of losing power than it does about the state of Shari`ati's knowledge of religious principles.

Yet, Shari`ati cannot simply assert Shi`ism's "natural" tendency to emancipate the human being. He needs to argue this in a sustained analytical process in which the connections are clear between creedal beliefs and human freedom. It is as though at the very point where he needs to substantiate his points he urges his listeners and his readers to "take it on faith" that Shi`ism does causally generate the liberation of humankind.

Clearly his impassioned pleas that Imam Husayn was the revolutionary model for all historical eras disturbed the Shi`i jurists and theologians, for whom that revered figure was the central figure in the faith's soteriological message. Shari`ati did not deny this traditional view of Imam Husayn. But he added to it the perspective of Imam Husayn as a charismatic political prototype of a modern political leader who devotes his efforts to recruiting members into a social movement and mobilizing resources on behalf of a political cause in the hurly burly of the contemporary political process. To the `ulama`, Shari`ati was debasing a revered religious icon by rendering him a political demagogue—by which I mean a popular leader espousing the cause of the masses, the hoi polloi—a category greatly distrusted by them. For Shari`ati, however, the `ulama`'s refusal to adapt to the world of mass politics was a guarantee of the continued exploitation of Shi`ite believers by powerful elites who benefited either by the clergy's political quietism or outright connivance. In either case, the outcome was injustice. To remedy this injustice necessitated that the `ulama` either become substantively and meaningfully politically engaged behind the masses or abandon the field to those who can place religious ideals in the service of the people.

INTERNATIONAL RELATIONS AS A SYSTEM OF DOMINATION BY THE GREAT POWERS

Shari`ati's understanding of international relations was significantly influenced by the writings of third world anticolonial writers, in particular Frantz Fanon (d. 1963) and Fanon's fellow Martiniquean

Aimé Césaire (d. 2008) and Che Guevara (d. 1967) as well as his interactions with writers for the Algerian newspaper published in Paris, *al-Mujahid* (*el-Moujahed*). Marxists among his contacts at the university and outside academia were also touchstones in the development of his worldview. In summary, Shari'ati accepted the Leninist and the neo-Marxist perspectives on world politics and the international economic system. But, as often happened, he lent to these leftist perspectives his own understanding of the role of religion as a liberating force. He could readily invoke examples of religiously based resistance movements that opposed colonialism and imperialism, including the Sufi-based movements in North Africa in the nineteenth and twentieth centuries, the Sudan in the 1880s–1890s, the Arab world from the 1870s to the 1950s, and Iran from the 1890s to the 1960s. Behind his rejection of the assumption by socialist and Marxist theorists that the sole product of religious allegiance was false consciousness lay his counterassumption that cultural (in this case, religious) authenticity was a—perhaps *the*—sine qua non of the successful revolutionary struggle of third world colonized peoples against their colonial and imperialist masters.[2]

As indicated in the previous sections, Shari'ati upheld the values of social justice, while holding that those values could not be ultimately vindicated without anticolonial revolutions on the international stage. Because of his idealized understanding of Islam (both Sunni and Shi'i, incidentally), it was axiomatic for him that the achievement of a genuinely just society was indicated by a fully integrated system of ideas and actions. In Islamic thought, going back to the earliest period of Islamic history, the discourse of the Prophet and the relators of the traditions (*ruwwat*), who were the precursors of the clergy, contained references to *tawhid*. This word, which translates as "unicity," originally referred to God's place in human understanding. It meant classically that God is one, and that He has no associates or compeers. But in later discourse, a system of *tawhid* referred not just to God's place in human understanding but also the ideal society, which was fully integrated around the principle of God's unicity and characterized by the noble values of exemplary levels of morality, fraternity, cooperation, and justice. These ideals could not be achieved in a society divided by class cleavages, and Shari`ati, showing the influence of Marxism upon him, was convinced that such distinctions would eventually be replaced by a fully egalitarian society. But the causal mechanism of this dynamic, that is, the transition from an inegalitarian to a fully egalitarian society, was elided in his thought.

I do not know whether Shari`ati was influenced by the thought of Antonio Gramsci, but it would not be surprising that he had heard about him from like-minded intellectuals with whom he associated in his Paris years. Gramsci's determined insistence that culture is exceptionally important for the successful construction of redoubtable revolutionary movements would have found powerful resonance in his own thinking. For in Gramsci's view such movements required the creation of "hegemonic blocs" that, over a long period of time, would incorporate intellectuals, nationalists, and members of the lower classes and integrate their thought and their action. Such blocs, he felt, were alone able to undertake breakthrough revolutions against ruling class systems on the way to the construction of the ideal, classless society. No amount of leadership (Gramsci has Lenin in mind here) can lead people to make revolution if these people are told that their traditional values are a hindrance to the achievement of that end and hence must be abandoned. On the other hand, Shari`ati closely followed the Leninist line that imperialism was "the highest stage of capitalism." This included Lenin's prescription for ending capitalist domination at the international level, that is, move against capitalism's entrenched positions in the colonies and semicolonies.

CONCLUSIONS

During his years in Paris, Shari`ati established himself as a strong critic of the Pahlavi state in Iran. Thus, upon his return to Iran in 1964, he was arrested at the Bazargan border crossing point. The government had concluded that he was a dangerous individual, an "Islamic Marxist." He was eventually released and tried to get a teaching job in the capital, but he had been blacklisted. Thus, he had to return to his native province and actually taught secondary school for a while. He did eventually find his way back to Tehran and, starting around 1967 until 1972, established a powerful reputation, especially among younger Iranians, as the indefatigable champion of the masses. In 1972, the government eventually closed down the institution where he was lecturing, the Husayniyyah-yi Irshad (literally, "place of guidance," after the model of Imam Husayn), arrested Shari`ati, and incarcerated him. He was released in 1975 and immediately sought permission to leave for Europe. The government tried to compromise his reputation by expurgating passages from a text called *Islam, the Human Being, and Marxism* in a bid to undermine his reputation by making it seem that he agreed with regime positions on Marxism.

Eventually, in 1977, he succeeded in gaining permission to leave, but his wife and son were not allowed to accompany him. Shortly after arriving in England, he died under mysterious circumstances. His followers suspected foul play by the Iranian intelligence services, but a British inquiry ruled he died of a heart attack. Speculation arose (and continued to the present day) about an alleged deal that he made with the Iranian authorities as the price for getting out of jail and eventually getting permission to leave for Europe. The broad outlines of this alleged deal are that he agreed to tone down his rhetoric and write material that would be subject to censorship prior to publication. Shari`ati was strongly opposed to both the traditional clergy, many of whom supported Ayatollah Ruhollah Khomeini or at least criticized the Shah's domestic policies, and the orthodox communists (Stalinists) of the Communist Party of Iran. The regime, so goes this line of thinking, felt it could use him against these two parties, while carefully undermining his popularity among his ardent youthful supporters.

In the end, Shari`ati was a tragic figure, though on a certain level this may have suited his temperament. He cherished his solitude and viewed it as a metaphor for heroic struggle. While never comparing himself to his early heroes in Islamic history (at least, not publicly), he nonetheless saw his task to be similar to theirs: to speak truth to power and to spread the message of justice, equality, and freedom. He was, it would seem, the nonpareil example of the true believer who had convinced himself that he had a special duty to perform. This duty was to sound the call to people to wake up and commit themselves to act against all those human failings that had made it possible for power holders to exercise their dominion over them and to unite to recapture the highest ideals with which human beings are capable of endowing their lives.

NOTES

1. The Imams are the leaders of the Shi`ite community. Twelver Shi`ites, who are politically the most influential of the Shi`ites in the world today, believe that they have been led by twelve Imams. The Prophet's paternal cousin and son-in-law, `Ali ibn Abi Talib, was the first Imam. His two sons, Hassan and Husayn, by his wife, Fatima, were the second and third imams. Later imams were descendants of these three. Imams were considered the proofs of God's existence and paragons of learning, inerrancy, and justice. Only the Imam is entitled to rule the Shi`i community. But the persecution of the Shi`a by the Sunnis led to the doctrinal mandate that they must disguise their true religious beliefs, lest all of their number be rounded up and the entire community massacred. Were that to have happened, in

Shi'i beliefs, it would have spelled the end of the religious injunctions. The twelfth imam, then a young boy, disappeared on God's command, for fear that his murder by the Sunnis would have extinguished the line of the imams. The Hidden Imam's return is expected, but until that day, Shi'ites must be cautious and were instructed to be politically quietist. This belief began to change beginning in 1970 when Ayatullah Khomeini declared the need for the Shi'a to emerge into the light of day and take matters into their own hands by establishing a government led by a supreme jurisconsult.

2. Abrahamian notes that Shari'ati specifically challenged Fanon on the latter's relegation of religious values to a secondary plane. See Abrahamian 1982, 25.

REFERENCES

Abrahamian, Ervand. "Shariati: The Ideologue of the Iranian Revolution," *MERIP Reports* (January 1982): 25–28.

Abrahamian, Ervand. 1989. *Radical Islam: The Iranian Mojahedin*. London: I.B. Tauris.

Akhavi, Shahrough. 1980. *Religion and Politics in Contemporary Iran: Clergy-State Relations in the Pahlavi Period*. Albany: SUNY Press. 143–158.

Abrahamian, Ervand. 1983. Shari'ati's Social Thought. In *Religion and Politics in Iran*, ed. Nikki Keddie, 125–144. New Haven: Yale University Press.

Abrahamian, Ervand. 1988. Islam, Politics and Society in the Thought of Ayatullah Khomeini, Ayatullah Taliqani and Ali Shariati. *Middle Eastern Studies* 24: 404–431.

Abrahamian, Ervand. 1996. Contending Discourses in Shi'ite Law on the Doctrine of *Wilayat al-Faqih*. *Iranian Studies* 29(3–4, Summer/Autumn): 229–268.

Algar, Hamid, ed. and trans. 1979. *On The Sociology of Islam*. Berkeley: Mizan Press.

Bayat-Philipp, Mangol. Shi'ism in Contemporary Iranian Politics: The Case of Ali Shari'ati. In *Towards a Modern Iran*, ed. Elie Kedourie and Sylvia Haim, 155–168. London: Frank Cass.

Dabashi, Hamid. 1993. *The Theology of Discontent*. New York: New York University Press. 102–146.

Keddie, Nikki. 1981. *Roots of Revolution*. New Haven: Yale University Press. 215–230.

Rahnema, Ali. 1998. *An Islamic Utopian: A Political Biography of Ali Shari'ati*. London: I. B. Tauris.

Sachedina, Abdulaziz. 1983. Ali Shariati: Ideologue of the Iranian Revolution. In *Voices of Resurgent Islam*, ed. John Esposito, 191–214. New York: Oxford University Press.

Shari'ati, Ali. 1347/1968. *Ravish-i Shinakht-i Islam* [Method for Knowing Islam]. Tehran: Husayniyyah-yi Irshad.

Shari'ati, Ali. 1349/1970. *Kavir* [Kavir]. Tehran: Husayniyyah-yi Irshad.

Shari'ati, Ali. 1350/1971. *Fatimah Fatimah Ast* [Fatimah Is Fatimah]. Tehran: Husayniyyah-yi Irshad.

Shari`ati, Ali. 1350/1971. *Hajj* [Pilgrimage to Mecca]. Tehran: Husayniyyah-yi Irshad.

Shari`ati, Ali. 1350/1971. *Intizar: Mazhab-i I`tiraz* [Waiting (for the Imam's Return): The Religion of Protest]. Tehran: Husayniyyah-yi Irshad.

Shari`ati, Ali. 1971. *Shahadat* [Martyrdom]. Tehran: Husayniyyah-yi Irshad.

Shari`ati, Ali. 1350/1971. *Tashayyu`-i `Alavi va Tashayyu`-i Safavi* [Ali's Shi`ism and the Shi`ism of the Safavids]. Tehran: Husayniyyah-yi Irshad.

Shari`ati, Ali. n.d. *Az Kuja Aghaz Kunim?* [Whence Shall We Begin?]. Tehran: Husayniyyah-yi Irshad.

Shari`ati, Ali. n.d. *Bazgasht bih Khishtan Bazgasht bih Kudum Khish?* [Return to Self, but to Which Self?]. Tehran: Husayniyyah-yi Irshad.

Shari`ati, Ali. n.d. *Chih Bayad Kard* [What Is to Be Done?]. Tehran: Husayniyyah-yi Irshad.

Shari`ati, Ali. n.d. *Islamshinasi* [The Sociology of Islam]. Tehran: Husayniyyah-yi Irshad.

Shari`ati, Ali. n.d. *Ummat va Imamat* [Ummah (The Islamic Community) and Imamate (Leadership and Rule of the Imams)]. Tehran: Husayniyyah-yi Irshad.

Chapter 5

Ayatollah Khomeini

MOJTABA MAHDAVI

Government can only be legitimate when it accepts the rule of God, and the rule of God means the implementation of the *sharī'ah*.

Ayatollah Khomeini

If we say that the government (*hokumat*) and guardianship (*velayat*) is today the task of the *fuqaha* (religious jurists), we do not mean that the *faqih* (jurist) should be the Shah, the minister, the soldier or even the dustman.

Ayatollah Khomeini

The government is empowered to unilaterally revoke any *sharī'ah* agreement that it has conducted with people when those agreements are contrary to the interests of the country or of Islam.

Ayatollah Khomeini

INTRODUCTION

THIS essay aims to contextualize the life and legacy of Ayatollah Khomeini (1902–1989). It suggests that the politics, perspective, and personality of Ayatollah Khomeini, Khomeinism, have been central in the making of Iran's postrevolutionary state. Ayatollah Khomeini's thinking, however, was almost half a century in the making: his thinking evolved over five distinct stages, beginning with political quietism and concluding with political absolutism. The essay is divided into three parts. First, it examines Ayatollah Khomeini's first and second stages of life. While the first and second stages of his politicointellectual journey—quietism and constitutionalism—did not directly contribute to Iranian politics, they remain significant in understanding Khomeinism. In the second section, we will examine the making of Khomeinism, that is the third, fourth, and fifth stages of his politicointellectual journey—Khomeini as the radical revolutionary, the *vali-ye faqih,* and the absolute *vali-ye faqih.* In the third section, we will problematize Khomeini's controversial legacy by examining Khomeinism after Khomeini. Ayatollah Khomeini's death did not put an end to Khomeinism; his contentious legacy is still alive and dominates current Iranian politics. The controversy over the presidential election in June 2009 captures the ambiguity and complexity of his legacy. The conclusion sheds some light on the conditions and possibility of post-Khomeinism.

I. AYATOLLAH KHOMEINI: FROM QUIETISM TO CONSTITUTIONALISM

Khomeini the quietist (1920s–1940s)

Ruhollah Khomeini, born into a clerical merchant family in Khomein in southwestern Iran, achieved prominence among the students of Ayatollah Abd al Karim Haeri (d. 1936) and received the degree of *itjihad* (independent judgment in legal matters) in 1936.[1] He was only thirty-three when he became known as the *marja-e taqlid,* meaning the source of emulation. Khomeini as a *marja-e taqlid* and a teacher did not restrict himself to the conventional teachings and habits of the *madraseh* (the seminary). By the 1940s Khomeini became a master synthesizer: in Qom's Feyziyeh Seminary he offered an unconventional curriculum, brought together the study of mysticism (*`irfan*), philosophy (*falsafeh*), ethics (*akhlāq*), and Islamic law (*sharī`ah*). Not only was he practicing how to combine *irfan* and politics, but he also was insisting on reconciling two opposing schools in clerical thought: *`irfan* and *sharī`ah*. Khomeini was "one of the few to have reached the stature of a leading jurisprudent, the highest level of theoretical mysticism and also to have become a highly-regarded teacher of Islamic philosophy. He was unique in being at the same time a leading practitioner of militant Islam."[2]

The young Khomeini's attitude to politics, however, was congruent with the long established apolitical tradition of the clerical institution. Political quietism and social conservatism best represent the dominant tradition of clerical Shiism. In this tradition the clergy remained apolitical and deferred to the monarchy. According to the traditional understanding of the doctrine of the Imamat, the leadership of the community rests solely with the imam. The last/twelfth imam gone into hiding/occultation (260/874) is the sole legitimate leader of the community, and it is believed he shall eventually return to establish the rule of Islam.[3] In the meantime, the community of believers ruled by illegitimate authority remains apolitical. The *`ulema'* (clerics) guide the community in religious matters and are responsible for the protection of the faith. Although a few clerics were politically active after the establishment of the Safavid dynasty, the clerical establishment remained largely apolitical, meaning it never proposed an alternative polity to the ruling authorities. Political quietism in the Shiite tradition, writes Hamid Enayat, resembles the pragmatic logic of "Sunni realism," meaning that the "supreme value in politics [is] . . . not justice but security—a state of mind which sets a high premium on the ability to rule and maintain 'law and order' rather than on piety."[4]

Nonetheless, because the authority of the Hidden imam is passed to the `ulema', the argument goes, they exclusively understand and interpret the *shari`ah* law. This suggests that "while power might lie with the temporal body, authority would naturally devolve onto the jurists." The Qajar dynasty (1794–1925) recognized this authority, but the Pahlavi monarchs (1925–1979) did not; this eventually caused tensions in state-clergy relations under the Pahlavi dynasty.[5]

After the death of Ayatollah Haeri in 1936, Ayatollah Mohamad Hossein Buroujerdi (d. 1961) became the supreme religious authority in Iran. Khomeini remained a quietist cleric so long as Ayatollah Buroujerdi, an important religious authority and a strong advocate of clerical quietism, was alive. The young Khomeini, although frustrated by Reza Shah's secular reforms, remained quietist, relying on the Shiite practice of *taqīyah,* or dissimulation, which permits people to deny their faith in order to continue its practice.[6] In 1941, the Allies replaced Reza Shah due to his pro-German stance with son, Mohamad Reza, as the new shah. The young shah welcomed religious activities in order to contain the supporters of the communist Tudeh Party connected the Soviet Union. The clerical establishment welcomed the new regime's policy, as it would strengthen its clerical institutions. The young Ayatollah was not an exception; he welcomed the change and remained quietist.

Khomeini the constitutionalist (1940s–1971)

Khomeini's transition from quietism to constitutionalism was prompted by the fear of secularism undermining the traditional role of the `ulema' in society. As a political activist Khomeini's first public statement came in a book published in 1945. The book titled

Kashf al-Asrar (The Discovery of Secrets) was essentially a detailed, systematic critique of an antireligious tract, but it also contained passages that were critical of the antireligious policy of the Pahlavi monarch. In this small polemical book Khomeini attacked secularism, Reza Shah's anticlerical policies, and a group of clergy who had offended the clerical establishment.[7] The book became the first statement of Khomeini's view on both constitutionalism and the Islamic state. "Government," Khomeini argued, "can only be legitimate when it accepts the rule of God, and the rule of God means the implementation of the *sharī'ah*."[8] But Khomeini did not challenge the institution of monarchy and remained a constitutionalist. He sought a supervisory (*nezarat*) role for the 'ulema'. This was in accord with Article 2 of the 1906 Constitution, as suggested by Shaykh Fazlollah Nouri, providing for a clerical committee to supervise laws passed by the *majles* (parliament). If on rare occasions the 'ulema' criticized the regime, writes Abrahamian, "it was because they opposed specific monarchs, not the 'whole foundation of monarchy.' "[9] Khomeini the constitutionalist was not an exception; he did not oppose the institution of monarchy.

In *Kashf al-Asrar* the form of government was not Khomeini's main concern as long as the *sharī'ah* law was enforced. Khomeini described the legal procedures and the constitutional arrangement in line of his constitutionalist approach to politics. He argued that

> if we say that the government (*hokumat*) and guardianship (*velayat*) is today the task of the *fuqaha* (religious jurists), we do not mean that the *faqih* (jurist) should be the Shah, the minister, the soldier or even the dustman. Rather, we mean that a *majles* that is . . . [run] according to European laws . . . is not appropriate for a state . . . whose laws are Holy. . . . But if this *majles* is made up of believing *mojtahids* who know the divine laws and . . . if

they elect a righteous sultan who will not deviate from the divine laws . . . or if the *majles* is under the supervision of the believing *fuqaha,* then this arrangement will not conflict with the divine law.[10]

Khomeini was clearly absent from politics in the years 1951–1953; he was unfriendly to the nationalist movement led by Mohammad Mosaddeq in the 1950s.[11] Khomeini was disappointed with the politics of quietism and was inspired by Islamist militants' idea of Islamic universalism but remained politically inactive and never publicly criticized Ayatollah Buroujerdi's policies.[12] It appears in retrospect that he understood that he had to establish "his credentials as a prominent religious leader before moving on to the political arena in order to both strengthen his standing within the religious establishment and widen his power base in general."[13]

Khomeini's real entry into politics came in 1962–1963 after the inauguration of the shah's reforms known as the "White Revolution." Ayatollah Buroujerdi's death in 1961 opened the space for Khomeini's involvement in politics and also left the religious institution with no single successor. Given the presence of older ayatollahs, Khomeini was a junior candidate for Buroujerdi's position. However, he seized the moment and published a collection of rulings on matters of religious practice (*resaley-e tozihol masael*), and with this book he made himself available to be recognized as the *marja-e taghlid.* The shah regime's difficulties with the White Revolution gave him the opportunity to emerge as a leading clerical opponent. Khomeini attacked the new electoral law enfranchising women as an un-Islamic law and the referendum endorsing the White Revolution as an *unconstitutional* procedure.[14] In response the shah sent paratroopers to attack Feyziyeh Madreseh, the religious seminary where Khomeini taught. The school was ransacked, Khomeini himself was arrested, and some students died. For Khomeini, this event showed the regime's hostility toward Islam and the clerical establishment. Khomeini was released from prison in 1964 and soon denounced the shah's tyrannical regime as being subordinate to US interests in Iran. When legal immunity was granted by the shah to American personnel for offences committed on Iranian territory, Khomeini furiously condemned this policy as humiliating to Muslims in their own country. In his words, "If someone runs over a dog belonging to an American, he will be prosecuted. . . . But if an American cook runs over the shah, the head of the state, no one will have the right to interfere with him. Why? Because they wanted a loan and America demanded this in return."[15] Khomeini was again arrested in 1964 and sent into exile in Turkey and then to Najaf, Iraq's most important Shiite shrine city. While in exile Khomeini "established himself as a major presence in Najaf."[16] Despite his physical absence from Iran, he maintained his influence among some Muslim political organizations inside Iran.

In *Kashf al-Asrar* Khomeini had argued in 1945 that the clergy should provide legal and moral guidance and not become politically involved. In return, the clergy expected respect for the *sharī'ah* and the clerical establishment. Khomeini's view as a constitutionalist remained unchanged until the 1970s despite the events of 1963.

II. THE MAKING OF KHOMEINISM: THE TRIUMPH OF A REVOLUTIONARY AYATOLLAH

Although prerevolutionary Iran never experienced a homogeneous Islamist political culture, Khomeinism dominated revolutionary Iran. Khomeinism was built upon a political and pragmatic reinterpretation of religious scripture that evolved into revolutionary populism.[17] Khomeinism is neither traditionalism nor fundamentalism; it symbolizes neither a premodern movement nor a postmodern phenomenon. It is not traditionalism, since Ayatollah Khomeini departed radically from the Shiite tradition of political quietism in the face of sociopolitical injustice. It is not fundamentalism, as the term "fundamentalism" derived from American Protestantism and implies the literal interpretation of scriptural texts.

Similarly, in spite of its critique of modernity, Khomeinism is not a postmodern phenomenon. Khomeinism explicitly associated itself with intellectual absolutism, insisting on the absolute representation of the Truth. Central to Khomeinism is its antihermeneutic claim, insisting that the *core* meaning of the Qur'an is absolutely clear and not open to interpretation. Postmodernity is largely antifoundational, while like other versions of Islamism, Khomeinism insists on some absolute a priori foundation as the basis of its ideology. Finally, it makes little sense to characterize Khomeinism as antimodern or even premodern, given its profound engagement with the modern world such as its ability to equip itself with modern technologies of organization, surveillance, warfare, and propaganda. Khomeinism refashioned and institutionalized a modern theocracy: the "whole constitutional structure of the Islamic Republic was modeled less on the early caliphate than on de Gaulle's Fifth Republic."[18] Ayatollah Khomeini's ideologized account of the tradition offered the country hope of relief from the ill effects of absolutism and imperialism and led to the formation of a nationwide populist revolutionary coalition. His political critique of the shah's absolutism and Western imperialism was more renowned than his theory of the *velayat-e faqih* (guardianship of jurist).

Khomeini the revolutionary (1971–1979)

In the early 1970s, "Khomeini was the first Shiite jurist to open the discussion (*fath-e bab*) of 'Islamic government' in a work of jurisprudence."[19] The theory of Islamic government was a departure point from constitutionalism. Khomeini began to change his position by suggesting that the whole institution of monarchy was illegitimate and that Muslims should be ruled by an Islamic government. He stated, "The Islamic government is constitutional in the sense that the rulers are bound by a collection of conditions defined by the Qur'an and the traditions of the Prophet. . . . In this system of government sovereignty originates in God, and law is the word of God."[20] He developed, through a series of lectures delivered in Najaf in the early 1970s, the novel idea that a just, knowledgeable, and faithful *faqih*, in the absence of the twelfth Shiite imam, was obliged to exercise both religious and political power. "The ruler," Khomeini argued "must have two characteristics: knowledge of the law and justice. He must have knowledge of the law because Islamic government is the rule of law and not the arbitrary rule of persons. In this sense only the *faqih* can be the righteous ruler."[21]

Khomeini's theory of the *velayat-e faqih* was a radical departure from the dominant traditional trends in Shiism.[22] The theory challenged the conventional Shiite doctrine of *Imamat,* which states that the legitimate leadership of the Muslim community belongs to the Prophet and his twelve successors or imams. Khomeini proposed the novel idea that "our duty to preserve Islam" by establishing an Islamic government "is one of the most important obligations incumbent upon us; it is more necessary even than prayer and fasting."[23] He suggested the task of creating an Islamic government that can be justified on the basis of the "secondary ordinances" (*ahkam-e sanaviye*), where the "primary ordinances" that is the *sharī'ah* laws are silent or not explicit.[24]

Ayatollah Khomeini established his doctrine of *velayat-e faqih* on two traditional and rational grounds.[25] The government is an essential component of Islam because the Prophet created an Islamic state. Moreover, the *sharī'ah* law cannot be fully implemented without an Islamic state; Islamic government is the only legitimate tool to put the Islamic rules into practice. Muslims cannot live under un-Islamic rule, and the implementation of *sharī'ah* law cannot be stopped during the Great Occultation: "Did God limit the validity of His laws to two hundred years? Was everything pertaining to Islam meant to be abandoned after the Lesser Occultation?"[26] The just *vali-ye faqih* is the only qualified ruler to undertake this task after the Prophet and the imams.

Khomeini initially stated, "Whatever is in [constitutional] accord with the law of Islam we shall accept and whatever is opposed to Islam, even if it is the constitution, we shall oppose."[27] He then increasingly came to believe that Islam was under greater threat from colonialism, "and thus shifted his emphasis from the constitution to Islam."[28] He argued that the Pahlavi regime was bent on destroying Islam because only Islam and the '*ulema*' can prevent the onslaught of colonialism.[29] Khomeini eventually rejected constitutionalism and monarchy: "Islam is fundamentally opposed to the whole notion of monarchy," he argued, because it is one of the most shameful "reactionary manifestations."[30]

Why and how did the constitutionalist Khomeini become a revolutionary? Why did it happen in the 1970s? Ayatollah Khomeini remained in close contact with Iran during his exile years and was deeply influenced by the waves of new ideas and radical trends in Iran. He, for example, read Al-e Ahmad's (1923–1969) pamphlet, *Gharbzadegi* (Westoxification), given his frequent use of the term in the late 1970s.[31] Moreover, Iranians outside the country also played a part in transforming Khomeini's views. In November 1973, Khomeini urged the Iranians to rise against the aggression of the Zionist regime while the shah was considered a friend of Israel. He attacked the shah for creating the Rastakhiz Party and opposed replacing Iran's Islamic calendar with that of the Achaemenid, known as the *Shahanshahi* calendar. He also condemned the shah's celebration of the 2,500-year anniversary of the Iranian monarchy, given the painful reality of Iranian society. By the 1970s, Khomeini was transformed into a populist and revolutionary Ayatollah with an ability to communicate with different groups of people.

The sociopolitical events of the late 1970s pushed Khomeini to become the leader of "the unthinkable revolution."[32] "Acting under another of its erroneous assumptions," the shah's regime requested that the Iraqi government expel Khomeini "in the hope of depriving him of his base of operations and robbing the Revolution of its leadership."[33] Khomeini went to France, which proved beneficial, as communication with Iran was easier from France because Khomeini's declarations were telephoned directly to Iran. His popular speech was articulated in the popular idioms and therefore united Iran's urban middle class and lower class under his charismatic leadership.

The shah was ultimately forced to leave Iran for the last time on January 16, 1979 and within two weeks Khomeini returned to Iran. On February 1 Khomeini received a tumultuous welcome in Tehran. Within ten days the old regime collapsed, and Khomeini established a new regime called the Islamic Republic of Iran. Ayatollah Khomeini spent the last two parts of his life under a polity he created. He successfully transformed the last monarchy into Iran's first republic. However, the republic he founded transformed Khomeini the revolutionary into Khomeini the *vali-ye faqih* (1979–1987) and eventually Khomeini the absolute *vali-ye faqih* (1987–1989).

Khomeini the vali-ye faqih *(1979–1987)*

In the absence of a common enemy, social and political differences in the aftermath of the revolution became more visible. There was division among the Islamists, nationalists of secular thinking, and various groups on the secular left. Each group held different opinions on the future of postrevolutionary politics. For Khomeini, the leader of the revolution, the future could only be an Islamic republic, but its nature remained undefined. Khomeini wanted to place the theory of *velayat-e faqih* as the leading idea of the revolution, merging clericalism and republicanism. Hence, both concepts were redefined. First, the Shiite "jurist law" was "transformed into the law of the state."[34] In his theory of *velayat-e faqih*, Khomeini redefined the role of clergy, suggesting that "in Islam there is no distinction between temporal and religious power. He rejected the prevalent notion that the jurists' task should be limited to understanding and interpreting the *sharī'ah*. They are not mere collectors of traditions; rather it is also part of their duty to implement the law."[35] In fact, the role of the imam, he suggested, "should be represented by a *faqih*, as the sole holder of legitimate authority."[36] In other words, Khomeini's definition of politics was an individual's conformity to the *sharī'ah*. For Khomeini, the structure of authority was divine and the state was instrumental in the implementation of the *sharī'ah*. Second, Khomeini also redefined the concept of republicanism in accordance with clerical rule. The people's participation in politics, or republicanism, resembled for Khomeini the traditional Islamic concept of *bay'a*, meaning the vote of allegiance to authority.[37]

Ayatollah "Khomeini was not setting up government in a vacuum but was taking over an existing one which had undergone considerable modernization in the course of the twentieth century."[38] To incorporate the theory of the *velayat-e faqih* into state institutions required time and experience. In appointing Mehdi Bazargan, a liberal Muslim, to head the interim government Khomeini was seeking time and experience for the clergy to eventually lead the new regime and consolidate Khomeinism.[39] In Paris Khomeini said "the `ulema' themselves will not hold power in the government" but instead "exercise supervision over those who govern and give them guidance."[40] But by the end of 1979, Iran had a quasitheocratic constitution, and by the summer of 1981 Khomeini's theory was in practice.[41] Ayatollah "Khomeini's personal role in the gradual transformation of the clergy into a 'clerical regency'—as Bazargan using the French term, called the new theocracy—was significant."[42] Khomeini as the *vali-ye faqih* wanted the clergy in the office of the president: the first clerical president and the Islamic Republic's third president was Ali Khamenei, then secretary general of the Islamic Republican Party and the future successor of Ayatollah Khomeini.

"Yet the results," as Brumberg put it, "were far from the theocracy that Ayatollah Khomeini had zealously proclaimed. Instead of producing a coherent constitutional map, the clerics blended several different ones, thus institutionalizing a new political order based on contending visions of authority," ranging from orthodox to pragmatist to democratic visions.[43] Khomeini's traditional and charismatic authorities were institutionalized in the constitution. The office of the *velayat-e faqih* and Khomeini as the *vali-ye faqih* brought together traditional, charismatic, and legal authorities in the making of the Islamic Republic. This was a "dissonant institutionalization,"[44] which caused many contradictions in the state of Khomeinism and much tension in the Khomeinist state.

The Iran-Iraq war provided Ayatollah Khomeini with a historic opportunity to consolidate his vision of the revolution. The unintended consequences of the eight-year war, the longest war in post-World War II,[45] were to change the state-society relationships and contribute to the reenchantment of the Iranian society. "If Iranians had entered the war as obedient subjects, they emerged from it with a keener sense of their own relationship to the state."[46] The legacy of the war was contradictory: it ironically strengthened both the state and the society, which both emerged with their self-confidence enhanced. To use Charles Tilly words, the war was instrumental in "state making," meaning "eliminating and neutralizing" the state's internal political rivals and enemies.[47] And yet the war changed relations between the state and society, as it simultaneously created a mass society with its demands unfulfilled. More importantly, the Khomeinist state was facing a growing tension between conservative elites or traditional right and revolutionary elites. By 1987, it became "too clear that the regime's emphasis on Islam, war, revolutionary discourse, and the persona of Khomeini were insufficient for governing Iran."[48] The crisis in the economy, the frustration and alienation in society, and the systematic deadlock and ideological factionalism in politics alarmed the regime, pushing the state to take some initiatives for change. "Perhaps more than anyone it was Khomeini who had woken up to this reality: the engine for change was Khomeini himself."[49] The change was aimed at the consolidation of the Islamic Republic. The institutionalization of the *velayat-e faqih* and rationalization of power, however, did not contribute to democratization but instead enhanced the power of the *vali-ye faqih* and made Khomeini more or less into an absolute (*motlaqeh*) *vali-ye faqih*.

Khomeini the absolute vali-ye faqih (1987–1989)

Three significant issues exemplified the transformation of Ayatollah Khomeini into the absolute *vali-ye faqih*. In all three issues, Khomeini was concerned about the future of the state he created.

THE ABSOLUTE RULE OF THE STATE OVER RELIGION

The elimination of so-called enemies of the *velayat-e faqih* brought to the fore divisions within the Khomeinist camp. These revolved "around the soul of the state," that is, "the characteristics of the government of *velayat-e faqih*" and "its Islamicity."[50] The first faction, the conservative or traditional right, backed by the *bazaari* merchants and the orthodox clergy, held a conservative position on the nature of the Islamic state and "wanted strict implementation of *sharī'ah* in the socio-cultural spheres."[51] The second faction, the revolutionary elites, by contrast "supported state-sponsored redistributive and egalitarian policies."[52] They also believed that primary Islamic ordinances (*ahkam-e awaliye*), derived from two Islamic sources of the Qur'an and the Tradition of the Prophet (the *Sunna*) were insufficient, and therefore Muslims living in modern times needed to issue secondary ordinances (*ahkam-e sanaviyeh*).[53] Ayatollah Khomeini trusted both factions. He appointed the six jurist members of the Guardian Council, the legislative body with veto power over the *majles'* bills, from the conservatives. At the same time he strongly supported the statist-revolutionary bills in the *majles* and the revolutionary plans provided by then Prime Minister Mir-Hossein Musavi (1980–1989). In the struggle between the two Khomeinist camps, "Khomeini shrewdly pursued his unique policy of 'dual containment.' "[54]

Khomeini's charisma was the backbone of his policy of "two-handed way," hiding the constitutional contradictions in the institutional setting of the Islamic Republic. By 1987, however, Khomeini's policy of "dual containment" was no longer effective, given the ever-increasing disagreements over economic, sociocultural, and military policies between the two factions. From December 1987 until his death in June 1989, Khomeini issued various decrees to clarify his sociopolitical positions and sided with the revolutionary camp.[55]

In December 1987, after continuous tensions between the conservative Guardian Council and the revolutionary *majles* over the tax bill and the labor law, Khomeini intervened and authorized the government to introduce bills essential to the interests of the state. In his speech he insisted, "The state can by using this power, replace those fundamental . . . Islamic systems, by any kind of social, economic, labor . . . commercial, urban affairs, agricultural, or other system, and can make the services . . . that are the monopoly of the state . . . into an instrument for the implementation of general and comprehensive politics."[56] When then President Ali Khamenei interpreted Khomeini's argument, suggesting that "the executive branch . . . should have a permanent presence in society . . . within the limits of Islamic laws and Islamic principles,"[57] Khomeini harshly responded by blaming Khamenei for misrepresenting his argument and his ruling. In January 1988 he made it clear that

> The state that is a part of the absolute vice-regency of the Prophet of God is one of the primary injunctions of Islam and has priority over all other secondary injunctions, even prayers, fasting and *haj*. . . . The government is empowered to unilaterally revoke any *sharia* agreement that it has conducted with people when those agreements are contrary to the interests of the country or of Islam.[58]

Khomeini as the absolute *vali-ye faqih* came to the view that all aspects of Islam were subordinate to the interests of the Islamic state. "From now on religion would serve the Islamic state rather than vice versa."[59] For Khomeini, as Brumberg put it, "the *faqih* was not merely the interpreter of the law, but in some sense the *vehicle* of law itself."[60] Khomeini, indeed, "implied that the vice regent of God had the authority to *create* both divine and secondary injunctions."[61] Even though "Khomeini in theory granted new and unparalleled powers to the *faqih*, he at the same time drastically undermined the religiousness of the regime and bolstered its populist-republican dimension."[62] Khomeini provided the state "with the authority not only to intervene in the economy but the right to use its discretion to suspend even the pillars of Islam."[63]

Ayatollah Khomeini's statement was bold but certainly not new. "Khomeini had long believed in the utilitarian tasks of government and had used the term *interests* in the context as far back as 1941."[64] This time, however, he clearly "broke from the historical position of the religious establishment in Iran with regard to state ordinances."[65] The statement was extremely significant, because "Khomeini emerged as a primary routinizer of his own charisma."[66] Khomeini as the absolute *vali-ye faqih* "by design or default" lay the foundation for greater tensions over his legacy and, indeed, over "the very nature and role of the state." The revolutionary Khomeinists sought to institutionalize "Khomeini's charisma in the *majlis* and government," while the conservative Khomeinists "tried to rescue the idea of charismatic rule by defending the investment of all authority in the *person* of the *faqih*."[67] Khomeini's exceptional statement in 1988, in sum, seemed to point toward an institutionalization of the absolute *velayat-e faqih*—a pragmatic rationalization, if not secularization, of the political order and the subjection of Islamic rulings to the interests of the Islamist rulers.

THE "POISONOUS CHALICE" OF THE PEACE

After accepting the ceasefire in the Iran-Iraq war, reported Khomeini's son, "he could no longer walk. . . . He never again spoke in public . . . and he fell ill and was taken to the hospital."[68] By 1988 Khomeini realized the war was no longer in the interests of the state and was undermining the very survival of the republic. Despite his fiery talks against imperialism and the infidel enemy, as the founding father of the republic Khomeini had no choice but, to use his own phrase, to drink from "the poisonous chalice" and save the state: "How unhappy I am because I have survived and have drunk the poisonous chalice of accepting the resolution. . . . At this juncture I regard it to be in the interest of the revolution and of the system."[69]

Ayatollah Khomeini accepted the ceasefire in the summer of 1988 and died in the summer of 1989. During this period Khomeini expressed his "absolute" authority in three specific events. First, following the end of the war, the People's Mojahedin Organization, the opposition group based in Iraq, launched a military attack against Iran. The regime response was harsh: the Mojahedin's forces were massacred on the battlefronts and several thousand jailed political opponents were executed in the prisons.[70] Second, Khomeini's *fatwa* against Salman Rushdie's novel *Satanic Verses* created much tension between Iran and the West. Third, after a decision by the Assembly of the Experts in 1985 it was expected that Khomeini's loyal student, Ayatollah Hossein-Ali Montazeri, would succeed him. Montazeri was the only high-ranking cleric who supported Khomeini's theory of *velayat-e faqih* and contributed in theory and practice to the institutionalization of the *velayat-e faqih*. However, Montazeri frequently criticized the violation of human rights by the regime. He challenged the regime's new reign of terror in the summer and autumn of 1988. Disappointed with Montazeri's reactions, Khomeini asked him to resign and ordered the Assembly of the Experts to meet and make a decision on the future leadership of the republic. The purge of the only Ayatollah loyal to the doctrine of the *velayat-e faqih* set the stage for the revision and the redefinition of Khomeini's doctrine of the *velayat-e faqih*.

THE SUCCESSION: THE RATIONALIZATION OF THE VELAYAT-E FAQIH?

There was one last work for Ayatollah Khomeini to fulfill before he died in June 1989: his succession. With Montazeri's dismissal, Khomeini needed to find a successor. The 1979 constitution was explicit in the theological qualifications of the *vali-ye faqih*, indicating in addition to all personal and political qualifications, only one among the grand ayatollahs as the prominent *marji`a*, or the source of imitation, could hold the office. The problem was that none among the grand ayatollahs was sympathetic to Khomeini's theory of *velayat-e faqih*. Moreover, the leading grand ayatollahs lacked the personal charisma or high political qualifications required for the office. However, there were a number of middle-ranking clerics who accepted Khomeini's theory and held the necessary political requirements. The pragmatic solution was to revise the constitution to save the Khomeinist state.

The 1989 constitution was a departure from the 1979 constitution. It expanded the power of the *faqih* by transferring the president's task of coordinating the three branches of government to the office of the *velayat-e faqih*. It made it explicit that the *vali-ye faqih* holds "absolute" power by adding the phrase *motlaqeh* to Articles 107–110, defining his absolute authority. The 1989 constitution, under Article 110, listed the expanded authority of the *vali-ye faqih*.[71] More importantly, Article 109 of the amended constitution separated the position of the *marji`a* from that of the *faqih*, setting the stage for the selection of a new *vali-ye faqih* who could be a middle-ranking cleric. As specified in Article 109, the *vali-ye faqih* no longer needed to hold the religious qualification of the *marj'a-e taqlid*, or source of religious emulation. Khomeini's theory of the *velayat-e faqih* "received a blow, as it effectively, in the long run, separated the position of the 'leader' from the institution of *marji'yat*, subordinating the latter to the state."[72]

Paradoxically, Khomeini's priority respecting the interests of the state led him to revive his own theory of the *velayat-e faqih* by reducing the theological qualifications needed and separating the position of the *marji'a* from that of the *faqih*. This surprisingly was the separation of religion from politics! The rationalization of the office of the *velayat-e faqih*, however, did not lead to the ascendancy of democratic authority in the republic. Rather, it was a boost toward greater institutionalization of political absolutism.

On 3 June 1989 Khomeini died. The elected Assembly of the Experts appointed Ali Khamenei as the new leader of the Islamic Republic. Khomeini died; Khomeinism, however, survived and became routinized. The routinization of charisma and the succession brought some significant changes to the fate and future of the Khomeinist state. First, the religious power shifted from the institution of the *velayat-e faqih* to the religious seminaries, and yet the political authority of the *vali-ye faqih* remained over and above the religious authority of the *marja-e taqlid*. Second, power was concentrated, not in the hands of a *vali-ye faqih* but in the office of the *velayat-e faqih*. Third, the routinization of charisma transferred power, not to the people but to the more authoritarian conservative faction of the state.

III. KHOMEINISM AFTER KHOMEINI: MULTIPLE FACES OF KHOMEINISM

Ayatollah Khomeini was "a unique product of unique historical circumstances" and thus "irreplaceable." It was Ayatollah "Khomeini who made the institution of the *velayat-e faqih* powerful, not the other way around."[73] Khomeini's charisma was not transferable to a successor. His successor, Ali Khamenei, who was designated by the ruling clergy, had neither religious credentials nor a charismatic personality, in Max Weber's terms, to be "awakened" or "tested." Thus, unlike Khomeini, who depended on his own charismatic authority, Khamenei was dependent on his conservative peers. Ali Khamenei's "lack of an independent base of support was the critical factor in his selection as the *faqih*; he did not seem threatening to the rival factions. Aware of his shortcomings, Khamenei in the early stage of his rule stayed above factions."[74] And yet, because he lacked the character required for mediating between the rival factions and balancing their power, he became closer to the conservatives with whom he shared attitudes and was indebted to their support.

The first republic (1979–1989) of the Khomeinist state was essentially a "one-man show" dictated by Ayatollah Khomeini.[75] Nonetheless, in the post-Khomeini era, with no charisma in politics, no war, and growing domestic opposition, disagreements over sociopolitical issues divided the Khomeinist forces. The post-Khomeini state went through four different political periods: the second republic (1989–1997), the third republic (1997–2005), the fourth republic (2005–2013), and the fifth republic (2013). Each republic presented a different face of Khomeinism.

The second republic (1989–1997), under President Hashemi Rafsanjani, routinized the revolutionary charisma and institutionalized the office of the *velayat-e faqih*. The neoliberal policy of reconstruction (*sazandegi*) weakened the social base of the regime, escalated elite factionalism, and forced the regime to open up public space and allow a limited degree of sociopolitical liberalization. The politics of *sazandegi*, neoliberal Khomeinism, prioritized economic development over political development; it resembled a conservative revolution or, to use Barrington Moore's analytical concept, a "revolution from above."[76] The policy was far from a success because Iran in the mid-1990s was experiencing a growing socioideological disenchantment. Civil society managed to challenge the repressive intentions of the state. For conservatives, the harsh truth to accept was a growing gap between their sociocultural values and those of the youth, the postrevolutionary generation. The state had failed to create the man/women or the society Ayatollah Khomeini had envisioned. The youth were socioculturally disenchanted, politically disappointed, and economically dissatisfied.

Religious and secular intelligentsia posed serious intellectual challenges to the ideological foundations of Khomeinism. Abdolkarim Soroush challenged authoritarian religious thinking: clerics, like other "professional groups," hold a corporate identity, "a collective identity and shared interest," and thus possess no divine authority.[77] The rule of the *vali-ye faqih*, Mojtahed Shabestari argued, is not divine and thus has to be subjected to democratic procedures. Ayatollah Montazeri came with a more accountable interpretation of the *velayat-e faqih*, suggesting that *velayat-e faqih* "does not mean that the leader is free to do whatever he wants without accountability."[78] The *vali-ye faqih* "we envisaged in the constitution has his duties and responsibilities clearly defined. His main responsibility is to *supervise*."[79] For Mohsen Kadivar, the "central question that the clergy faces today is whether it can preserve its independence . . . in the face of an Islamic state, since it does not want to fall victim to the fate of the Marxist parties of the former communist states."[80] He boldly argued that such a political version of the *velayat-e faqih* existed neither in the Qur'an, nor in the Prophet's, nor in the Shiite imam's traditions.[81]

By the late 1990s the intensity of Iran's factional politics was a fact, providing much opportunity for the unexpected victory of the reformist presidential candidate, Mohammad Khatami, on May 23, 1997. Khatami became the candidate for change and received the people's protest vote, making him a "Cinderella candidate"[82] and eventually an "accidental president"[83] of the Islamic Republic. The reformist republic stood on three intellectual pillars: Islamic constitutionalism, promoting civil society, and Islamic democracy. All three intellectual pillars were bound to the lasting legacy of Khomeinism, which created a limited and inchoate subjectivity never independent of the *vali-ye faqih*. The fall of the reformist republic (1997–2005) symbolized in part the crisis of *Khomeinism with a human face*.

The 2005 presidential election marked a new era in the Khomeinist state—an era of "neoconservative Khomeinism," which was consolidated in the June 2009 disputed presidential election. The president of Iran's fourth republic (2005–present), Mahmoud Ahmadinejad, was a product of the state-security apparatus, the office of the *velayat-e faqih*, and Iran's neoconservatives: a group of young members of Islamic Revolutionary Guards Corps cultivated in the postwar period. They attempted to revive the social base of the regime among the urban and rural poor, which has been eroded in the post-Khomeini era. The president of the fourth republic spoke about distributive social justice; promised to fight Iran's new class of mafia-like rentiers, the clerical noble-sons (*aghazadeh-ha*); and assured the poor they will bring the "oil money to their table." The irony is that neoconservative Khomeinists were blessed by the state's rents and shadow economy run by the revolutionary foundations controlled by the office of the *velayat-e faqih*.[84] Their populist slogans were instrumental in serving their pragmatist purpose, that is, to replace the old oligarchy with a new one and to establish a populist, centralized state backed by the lower classes and sponsored by petro dollars.

It is widely believed that with the rise of Iran's neoconservatives to power the Islamic Republic's social base might shift from the coalition of the *mullah*-merchant to that of the revolutionary security and military forces. For the first time, a Khomeinist (ex)military man and not a Khomeinist *mullah* is the president of the republic. The conservatives, in spite of their internal conflicts, gained complete control of the republic, and the absolute rule of the *vali-ye faqih* Khamenei seemed at hand. However, for the first time in the Islamic Republic, the public and the reformist elites have openly challenged the authority and legitimacy of the *vali-ye faqih* in the popular democratic Green Movement. In the presidential elections on 14 June 2013, Hassan Rouhani, a moderate and pragmatist conservative, was elected as the seventh president of the Islamic Republic of Iran. His four-year term, which started on 3 August 2013, brought to an end Iran's fourth republic (Ahmadinejad's presidency) and began Iran's fifth republic. (2013).

In addition to the nonideological, spontaneous, civic, and non-violent characteristics of Iran's Green Movement, the movement is distinctive for its pluralism; it includes reformist Khomeinists and secular and Muslim post-Khomeinists. Many of the reformist Khomeinists, who accompanied Khomeini on his return to Iran, are now in open revolt. The process of "de-Khomeinization," they believe, has damaged Khomeini's legacy; today Khomeini's Islamic Republic is neither Islamic nor a republic.[85] The reformist Khomeinists seek a peaceful transformation within the Khomeinist system, while the political spectrum of the Green Movement is both broader and more radical than the reformist discourse. In addition to the quest for free elections and civil rights, it seems Khomeini's legacy of the absolute *velayat-e faqih* is no longer acceptable to the public. Three decades after the practice of Khomeini's ideology, his legacy is contested: for the reformist Khomeinists, "de-Khomeinization" captures the core of the crisis. For others, the nation has gradually moved toward a new era: "post-Khomeinism."

CONCLUSION: TOWARD POST-KHOMEINISM?

In his book *Kitab al 'Asfar'* (Book of Journeys) the mystic-philosopher Molla Sadra discussed the "four journeys" of purification leading to a state of perfection. Khomeini was fascinated by this notion. He saw this (new) Platonic path of perfection as the path of the Prophet. In drawing upon Molla Sadra's "four journeys," Khomeini discussed this path of perfection in his lectures. The first journey is "from mankind to God" in which man leaves "the domain of human limitations" and purges his soul of all earthly desires. The second journey comes "with God in God"; this means man submerges himself in the oceans of secrets and mysteries to acquaint himself with the beauty of God. The third journey is from God to the people, when man returns to the people but is no longer separate from God, as he can now see His omnipotent essence. And the fourth journey is from people to people, in which man has acquired Godly attributes with which he can begin to guide and help others to reach God.[86] In this final stage the prophethood and the perfect man is realized; the perfect man is the imam and he is obliged to establish the *velayat* (guardianship) on earth, guiding the people and establishing an Islamic society. Ayatollah Khomeini's view of the absolute *velayat-e faqih* derives from his lifelong immersion in mysticism and (Platonic) philosophy, which rendered the absolute Truth, God's words, transparent to him. Such a mystic politician is an absolute *political* sovereign capable of overruling the *sharī'ah*. He does not implement or interpret the *sharī'ah*; he enjoys a full political agency/authority to act on behalf of the interest of the state. The interest and survival of the state/statesmen—*faqih*, not the *fiqh*—is the guiding principle of the Islamic state he envisioned. The events in post-presidential elections of June 2009 is a case in point where the doctrine of the absolute *velayat-e faqih* turns the Islamic Republic into a clerical leviathan accountable to itself, neither to God, nor people, nor human ethics.

Ayatollah Khomeini was a "master synthesizer." His life was full of contradiction. His thinking evolved over five distinct stages and his ideology was almost half a century in the making. Khomeini's transition from quietism to activism was prompted by the fear of secularism undermining the traditional role of the *ulama* in society. In the beginning, the form of state was not Khomeini's main concern as long as the *sharia* law was enforced. At the end, however, his theory of the absolute *velayat-e faqih* empowered the *vali-ye faqih* to unilaterally revoke *sharia* when it is contrary to the interests of the Islamic state.

Khomeini's most significant political legacy is the postrevolutionary Iranian regime, which can be divided into five Khomeinist republics, the nature of which has been "institutionally dissonant."[87] The state he created combined the theory of *velayat-e faqih* with republican institutions. The Khomeinist state is a mishmash of totalitarianism, authoritarianism, and (semi)democracy, while each republic presents a distinctive face of Khomeinism.[88] The first republic was essentially a "one-man show" dictated by Khomeini's populist and semitotalitarian politics. The absence of Khomeini's charisma in the second republic undermined the totalitarian character of the state, pushing the regime toward a limited degree of pluralism, while the crisis of legitimacy made the political system more authoritarian. The third republic aimed at refreshing the spirit of Iran's quest for democracy. However, the republic failed because it was bound by the institutional and intellectual legacy of Khomeini. The fall of the reformist republic was the failure of *Khomeinism with a human face*. The fourth republic was a product of the state-security apparatus, the office of the *velayat-e faqih*, and the extremist faction of Iran's conservatives, or *neoconservative Khomeinism*. The pragmatist president of the fifth republic challenged domestic and foreign policies of Ahmadinejd and has promised to pull Iran back from the brink of the negative economic growth, political repression, and international sanctions. It remains to be seen whether he is competent to accomplish this.

After three decades, Khomeini's legacy, the Islamic Republic of Iran, both is and is not what he envisioned. His legacy has been challenged at once by "de-Khomeinization" and "post-Khomeinism." For the reformist Khomeinists, "de-Khomeinization" was the official policy of the fourth republic.[89] Ayatollah Khomeini, it is argued, valued people's vote, recognized the *majlis* as the forefront of political affairs, encouraged open *itjihad* in religious thinking, and discouraged the involvement of the Revolutionary Guards in politics. While there is some truth to this argument, it can be argued that Ayatollah Khomeini himself started the process of "de-Khomeinization" after he transformed his doctrine of *velayat-e faqih* into the absolute *velayat-e faqih*. Ayatollah Khomeini was, in fact, the first and last *vali-ye faqih* he envisioned!

More importantly, the rise of the Green Movement suggests that Iran has gradually entered into a new era of "post-Khomeinism," thanks to the crisis of an *Islamic state* and the practice of Khomeini's doctrine of *velayat-e faqih*. If Ayatollah Khomeini's theory of *velayat-e faqih* was a radical departure from the traditional Shi'a political thought, his political legacy has actually contributed to another paradigm shift in the current debates over the possibility and conditions of "post-Islamism" in general and "post-Khomeinism" in particular. According to Asef Bayat, post-Islamism "represents both a *condition* and a *project*." It refers to a *condition* where Islamism, here Khomeinism, "becomes compelled, both by its own internal contradictions and by societal pressure, to reinvent itself." It is also a *project*, "a conscious attempt to conceptualize and strategize the rationale and modalities of transcending Islamism in social, political, and intellectual domains."[90] There is a continuity and change in Islamism and post-Islamism. Similar to Islamism, post-Islamism advocates the participation of religion in the public sphere. Contrary to Islamism, it rejects the concept of "Islamic state"; state is a secular entity no matter who the statesman is. Post-Islamism, post-Khomeinism in the Iranian context is a combination of "Islam *ism*" and "Islam *wasm*"!

NOTES

* Another version of this essay appeared in one section of the following journal article: Mojtaba Mahdavi, "One Bed and Two Dreams? Contentious Public Religion in the Discourses of Ayatollah Khomeini and Ali Shariati," *Studies in Religion* (2013; DOI: 10.1177/0008429813496102).

1. Hamed Algar, *Islam and Revolution: Writings and Declarations of Imam Khomeini* (Berkeley: Mizan Press, 1981), 14.

2. Baqer Moin, Khomeini: Life of the Ayatollah, London (New York: I.B. Tauris Publishers, 1999), 46–47.

3. The occultation of the last imam had two phases: the shorter phase and the complete occultation. During the first phase (874–941) four special deputies (*nuvvab-e khaas*) were in direct contact with the imam. After the death of the last deputy, the *ulama* have claimed to be the general deputies (*nuvvab-e aam*) of the imam.

4. Hamid Enayat, *Modern Islamic Political Thought* (Austin: University of Texas Press, 1982), 11.

5. Ali M. Ansari, *Modern Iran since 1921: The Pahlavis and After* (London: Pearson Education, 2003), 225.

6. Moein, *Khomeini: The Life of Ayatollah*, 56.

7. The book's real target was "the 'renegade' clergymen who in Khomeini's eyes had 'actively collaborated with him.' Indeed, it was a direct response to an attack on the clerical establishment in a pamphlet called Asrar-e Hezar Saleh (Secrets of a Thousand Years) written by Hakamizadeh, the editor of Homayon. Hakamizadeh and his colleagues including Ahmad Kasravi were strongly

disappointed with the religious establishment and its reactionary approach. See Baqer Moein, *Khomeini: The Life of Ayatollah*, 60–61.

8. Khomeini, *Kashf al-Asrar*, (Tehran: Nashr-e Safar, 1941), 291

9. Khomeini. *Kashf al-Asrar*, pp. 185–188, 226, quoted in Ervand Abrahamian, *Khomeinism: Essays on the Islamic Republic of Iran* (Berkeley and London: 1993), p. 20

10. Khomeini, *Kashf al-Asrar*, p. 185, quoted in Daniel Brumberg, *Reinventing Khomeini: The Struggle for Reform in Iran: The Struggle for Reform in Iran* (Chicago: The University of Chicago Press, 2001), p. 58.

11. The politics of quietism often benefited the shah. Ayatollah Buroujerdi, for example, congratulated the shah when he was brought back to power in 1953. Although, ayatollah Seyyed Abolqasem Kashani (1882–1962), Mojtaba Navab Safavi and his militant group, *Fadaiyan-e Islam*, believed in "political activism, Islamic universalism, anti-colonialism, and populism," they soon withdrew their support from Mossadeq. Khomeini "was a frequent visitor to Kashani's home." Moreover, when Navab Safavi was arrested Khomeini asked the authorities not to harm him. See Moein, *Khomeini: The Life of Ayatollah*, 66.

12. According to Khomeini after he succeeded to overthrow the shah, Mosaddeq's "main mistake was not to have got rid of the Shah when he was strong and the Shah was weak." Khomeini, *Sahifeh-ye Nur*, 3:36, quoted in Moein, *Khomeini: The Life of Ayatollah*, 66.

13. Moein, *Khomeini: The Life of Ayatollah*, 68

14. Abrahamian, *Khomeinism*, 10

15. Algar, *Islam and Revolution: Writings and Declarations of Imam Khomeini*, 181.

16. Ibid., 18.

17. Abrahamian, *Khomeinism*, 13–17.

18. Abrahamian, *Khomeinism*, 15.

19. Said Amir Arjomand, "Authority in Shiism and Constitutional Development in the Islamic Republic of Iran," in Rainer Brunner and Werner Ende, eds., *The Twelver Shia in the Modern Times: Religious Culture and Political History* (Brill: Tuta Pallace, 2001), 301.

20. Khomeini, "Islamic Government," in Hamed Algar, *Islam and Revolution*, 55.

21. Ibid.

22. Although Khomeini's interpretation of the theory of the *velayat-e faqih* was new, the concept was not new to the Shiite tradition. For an insightful discussion, see Farhang Rajaee, *Khomeini on Man, the State and International Politics* (Lanham: University Press of America, 1983).

23. Algar, *Islam and Revolution: Writings and Declarations of* Imam *Khomeini*, 75.

24. Ibid., 124.

25. Sami Zubaida, *Islam, the People and the State: Political Ideas and Movements in the Middle East* (London: I.B. Tauris, 2009), 16–17.

26. Algar, 42.

27. Huzeh-e Elmiyeh, *Zendeginameh-e Imam Khomeini* [A Biography of Imam Khomeini] (Tehran, n.d.), 95.

28. Hossein Bashiriyeh, *State and Revolution in Iran, 1962–1982* (Kent, UK: Croom Helm, 1984), 59–60.

29. Ayatollah Khomeini, *Khomeini va Jonbesh: Majmueh-ye Nameha va Sokhanraniha* [A Collection of Khomeini's Letters and Speeches] (Tehran: n.p. 1352), 58–60, 68–69.

30. Ruhollah Khomeini, "October 31, 1971, The Incompatibility of Monarchy with Islam," in Algar, 202.

31. Roy Mottahedeh, *The Mantle of the Prophet: Learning and Power in Modern Iran* (London; Chatto & Windus, 1986), 303. Moreover, waves of radical Islam reached Khomeini via young militant clerics influenced by Iran's People's Mojahedin Organization. Iranian student associations in Europe and North America, impressed by Shariati's ideas, pushed Khomeini toward radicalism.

32. Charles Kurzman, *The Unthinkable Revolution in Iran* (Cambridge: Harvard University Press, 2004).

33. In 1977, Khomeini's elder son, Mostafa, died suddenly in Najaf, likely assassinated by the shah's Security Police, SAVAK. Khomeini "bore this blow stoically," as he termed the tragedy "a divine blessing in disguise." The memorial ceremonies for Khomeini's son in Iran became a starting point for renewed uprising by the theological seminaries and members of the Iranian religious society. The shah's regime took revenge, publishing an insulting article in the daily *Ettela'at* by attacking Khomeini as an agent of foreign powers. In reaction, the people in Qom displayed anger and frustration. This was the first of a series of revolutionary demonstrations that spread across the country. Hamed Algar, *Islam and Revolution: Writings and Declarations of Imam Khomeini*, 19–20.

34. Said Amir Arjomand, "Authority in Shiism and Constitutional Development in the Islamic Republic of Iran," 302.

35. Ayatollah, Khomeini, *Velayat-e Faqih, Hokomat-e Islami* [The Rule of the Jurisprudent, Islamic Government] (Tehran: n.p. 1357), 28, 39–40, 77–79, quoted in Bashiriyeh, *State and Revolution in Iran*, 62–63.

36. Ibid.

37. According to one view, for Khomeini, the *vali-ye faqih* derives his *popularity* from people but his *legitimacy* is divine. Another interpretation suggests that both popularity and legitimacy of the *vali-ye faqih* derive from people, not God.

38. Arjomand, "Authority in Shiism and Constitutional Development in the Islamic Republic of Iran," 302.

39. Bazargan reluctantly accepted Khomeini's offer, hoping "he would be able to influence the new regime from within." See H. E. Chehabi, "The Provisional Government and the Transition from Monarchy to Islamic Republic in Iran," in Yossi Shain and Juan J. Linz, eds., *Between States: Interim Governments and Democratic Transitions* (New York: Cambridge University Press, 1995), 135.

40. Asghar Schirazi, *The Constitution of Iran: Politics and the State in the Islamic Republic*, John O'Kane, trans. (London: I.B. Tauris Publishers, 1997), 24.

41. After the fall of Bazargan's government in late 1979 and the dismissal of President Banisadr in 1981, the short "spring of freedom" was replaced by a long season of fear and frustration. The regime shut down all political parties and arrested, executed, or jailed the opposition. According to Abrahamian, the figures for the execution of the opposition were 600 by September, 1,700 by October, and 2,500 by December 1981; see Ervand Abrahamian, *Radical Islam: The Iranian Mojahedin* (London: I.B. Tauris Publishers, 1989), 220.

42. Quoted in Moin, *Khomeini: Life of the Ayatollah*, 247.

43. Brumberg, *Reinventing Khomeini: The Struggle for Reform in Iran*, 105.

44. Ibid., 100.

45. Dilip Hiro, *The Longest War: The Iran-Iraq Military Conflict* (New York: Rutledge Chapman and Hall, 1991).

46. Ansari, *Modern Iran since 1921: The Pahlavis and After*, 239.

47. Tilly, "War Making and State Making as Organized Crime," 181.

48. Mehdi Moslem, *Factional Politics in Post-Khomeini Iran* (Syracuse: Syracuse University Press, 2002), 72.

49. Ibid.

50. Ibid., 47.

51. The conservative Khomeinists have been supported by the Society of Combatant Clergy (*Jame'eh Rouhaniyat-e Mobarez*) and the Allied Islamic Society (*Jamiyat-e Mo'talefeh-ye Islami*).

52. The revolutionary Khomeinists have been supported by the Mojahedin of the Islamic Revolution Organization (*Sazman-e Mojahdin-e Enghelab-e Islami*) and the Society of Combatant Clerics (*Maj'ma-e Rouhaniyon-e Mobarez*). The central committee of the Islamic Republican Party, until its dissolution in 1986, was more inclined to the revolutionary Khomeinists and less to the conservatives.

53. Moslem, *Factional Politics in Post-Khomeini Iran*, 48–49.

54. Ibid., 65.

55. Khomeini also created a new institution; the Expediency Council (*Majma'e Tashkhis-e Maslehat-e Nezam*), an institutional mediator between the two Khomeinist camps in the *Majles* and the Guardian Council, paving the way for further institutionalization of the *velayat-e faqih*.

56. Khomeini, "Khomeini Ruling on State Powers Report," broadcast December 23, 1978, FBIS-NES-87, quoted in Brumberg, *Reinventing Khomeini*, 135.

57. "Khamene'i Delivers Friday Prayer Sermons," broadcast on Tehran Domestic-Service January 1, 1988, FBIS-NES-88-001, January 4, 1988, quoted in Brumberg, *Reinventing Khomeini*, 135.

58. *Ettela'at*, January 9, 1988, quoted in Moslem, *Factional Politics in Post-Khomeini Iran*, 74.

59. Moin, *Khomeini: Life of the Ayatollah*, 260.

60. Brumberg, *Reinventing Khomeini: The Struggle for Reform in Iran*, 135.

61. Ibid., 136.

62. Moslem, *Factional Politics in Post-Khomeini Iran*, 74.

63. Ibid.

64. Brumberg, *Reinventing Khomeini: The Struggle for Reform in Iran*, 136.

65. Moslem, *Factional Politics in Post-Khomeini Iran*, 74.

66. Brumberg, *Reinventing Khomeini: The Struggle for Reform in Iran*, 140.

67. Brumberg, *Reinventing Khomeini: The Struggle for Reform in Iran*, 136–137.

68. Ahmad Khomeini, *Yadegar-e Imam*, 6:468, quoted in Moin, *Khomeini: Life of the Ayatollah*, 270.

69. "Khomeini Message on *Hajj*, Resolution 598," broadcast July 20, 1988, FBIS-NES-88-140, July 21, 1988, quoted in Brumberg, *Reinventing Khomeini: The Struggle for Reform in Iran*, 142.

70. For an insightful account of this event, see Ervand Abrahamian, *Tortured Confessions: Prisons and Public Recantations in Modern Iran* (Berkeley: University of California Press, 1999).

71. The *vali-ye faqih* was given authority to delineate general policies and supervise the execution of decisions; to devise national referenda; to hold the supreme command of the armed forces; to declare war; to appoint, dismiss, and accept the resignation of the six jurists of the Guardian Council, the chief justice, the head of the national radio and television, the chief commanders of the Revolutionary Guard and of the armed forces. Moreover, Article 110 of the new constitution vested constitutional authority in the Expediency Council. In addition to its original task of acting as mediator between the *majlis* and the Guardian Council, the Expediency Council was elevated to a consultative body for the *vali-ye faqih*.

72. Moin, *Khomeini: Life of the Ayatollah*, 294.

73. Milani, *The Making of Iran's Islamic Revolution*, 225.

74. Milani, *The Making of Iran's Islamic Revolution*, 224.

75. Moslem, *Factional Politics in Post-Khomeini Iran*, 143.

76. See Barrington Moore, Jr., *Social Origins of Dictatorship and Democracy: Lord and Peasant in the Making of the Modern World* (London: Penguin Press, 1966).

77. See Soroush, "*Horriyyat va Rohaniyyat*" [Liberty and Clergy]," *Kiyan* 24, April–May 1995, 2–11, quoted in Brumberg, *Reinventing Khomeini*, 205.

78. "Montazeri on State's Road to Destruction," London *Keyhan*, October 10, 1994, EBIS-NES-94-231, October 10, 1994, quoted in Brumberg, *Reinventing Khomeini*, 215.

79. "Montazeri's Speech in Keyhan," December 4, 1997, available at http://eurasian-ews.com/iran/montadres.html, quoted in Brumberg, *Reinventing Khomeini*, 238.

80. Eric Rouleau, "La Republique Islamique d'Iran Confrontee a la Societe Civile," *Le Monde Diplomatique*, June 1995, available at http/www.mondediplomatique.fr/1995/06/rouleau/1542.html, quoted in Brumberg, *Reinventing Khomeini*, 238.

81. See Mohsen Kadivar, *Andisheh-ye Siyasi dar Islam* [Political Thought in Islam], vols. 1–2 (Tehran: Nay Publications, 1998).

82. Mohsen M. Milani, "Reform and Resistance in the Islamic Republic of Iran," in Esposito and Ramazani, eds., *Iran at the Crossroads*, 29.

83. Shaul Bakhash, "Iran's Remarkable Election," in Larry Diamond, Marc F. Plattner, and D. Brumberg, eds., *Islam and Democracy in the Middle East* (Baltimore: Johns Hopkins University Press, 2003), 119.

84. Ahmadinejad's colleagues such as Sadeq Mahsouli, minister of social welfare, and Mohammad Reza Rahimi, vice-president, among others, are members of the new oligarchy. The former is a billionaire real estate broker and the latter is another billionaire benefiting from exclusive political rents.

85. After the June 2009 events, Ayatollah Montazeri denounced *vali-ye faqih* Khamenei without mentioning his name. He explicitly argued, "This regime is neither Islamic nor a republic; it is a mere dictatorship. This is no longer the 'rule of the qualified faqih'; rather, it is the 'rule of the generals.' " Rasool Nafisi, "Where Is the Islamic Republic of Iran Heading?" *InsideIran*, September 23, 2009, available at http://www.insideiran.org/clerics/where-is-the-islamic-republic-of-iran-heading.

86. Moin, *Khomeini: Life of the Ayatollah*, 49–50.

87. Brumberg, *Reinventing Khomeini: The Struggle for Reform in Iran* (Chicago: University of Chicago Press, 2001), chapter 5.

88. See Chehabi, "The Political Regime of the Islamic Republic of Iran in Comparative Perspective," 48–70.

89. "Mir Hossein Mousavi's Interview with Kalameh," *Khordad*88, June 2, 2010, available at http://khordaad88.com/?p=1623#more-1623.

90. Asef Bayat, *Islam and Democracy: What Is the Real Question?* (Leiden: Amsterdam University Press, 2007), 18–19.

REFERENCES

Abrahamian, Ervand. *Radical Islam: The Iranian Mojahedin*. London: I.B. Tauris Publishers, 1989.

Abrahamian, Ervand. *Khomeinism: Essays on the Islamic Republic of Iran*. Berkeley: University of California Press, 1993.

Algar, Hamed. *Islam and Revolution: Writings and Declarations of Imam Khomeini*. Berkeley: Mizan Press, 1981.

Amir Arjomand, Said. "Authority in Shiism and Constitutional Development in the Islamic Republic of Iran." In R. Brunner and W. Ende, eds., *The Twelver Shia in the Modern Times: Religious Culture and Political History*. Brill: Tuta Pallace, 2001.

Ansari, Ali M. *Modern Iran since 1921: The Pahlavis and After*. London: Pearson Education, 2003.

Bakhash, Shaul. "Iran's Remarkable Election." In L. Diamond, M. F. Plattner, and D. Brumberg eds., *Islam and Democracy in the Middle East*. Baltimore: The Johns Hopkins University Press, 2003.

Bashiriyeh, Hossein. *The State and Revolution in Iran, 1962–1982*. Kent, UK: Croom Helm, 1984.

Bayat, Asef. *Islam and Democracy: What Is the Real Question?* Leiden: Amsterdam University Press, 2007.

Brumberg, Daniel. *Reinventing Khomeini: The Struggle for Reform in Iran*. Chicago: University of Chicago Press, 2001.

Chehabi, H. E. "The Provisional Government and the Transition from Monarchy to Islamic Republic in Iran." In Y. Shain and J. Linz, eds., *Between States: Interim Governments and Democratic Transitions*. New York: Cambridge University Press, 1995.

Chehabi, H. E. "The Political Regime of the Islamic Republic of Iran in Comparative Perspective." *Government and Opposition* 36, no.1 (2000): 48–70.

Enayat, Hamid. *Modern Islamic Political Thought*.Austin: University of Texas Press, 1982, 11.

Huzeh-e Elmiyeh. *Zendeginameh-e Imam Khomeini* [A Biography of Imam Khomeini]. Tehran: n.p., n.d, 95.

Kadivar, Mohsen. *Andisheh-ye Siyasi dar Islam* [Political Thought in Islam]. Vols. 1–2. Tehran: Nay Publications, 1998.

Khomeini, R. *Kashf al-Asrar*. Tehran: Nashr-e Safar, 1941.

Khomeini, R. *Khomeini va Jonbesh: Majmueh-ye Nameha va Sokhanraniha* [A Collection of Khomeini's Letters and Speeches]. Tehran: n.p. 1352/1974.

Milani, Mohsen M. *The Making of Iran's Islamic Revolution: From Monarchy to Islamic Republic*. Boulder: Westview Press, 1994.

Milani, Mohsen M. "Reform and Resistance in the Islamic Republic of Iran." In John L. Esposito and R. K. Ramazani, eds., *Iran at the Crossroads*. New York: Palgrave, 2001.

Moin, Bager. *Khomeini: Life of the Ayatollah*, London. New York: I.B. Tauris Publishers, 1999.

Montazeri, H. "Montazeri's Speech in Keyhan." December 4, 1997. Available at http://eurasianews.com/iran/montadres.html (July 12, 2006)

Mousavi, Mir Hossein. "Mousavi's interview with Kalameh," *Khordad*88, June 2, 2010. Available at http://khordaad88.com/?p=1623#more-1623 (January 21, 2013)

Moslem, Mehdi. *Factional Politics in Post-Khomeini Iran*. Syracuse: Syracuse University Press, 2002.

Mottahedeh, Roy. *The Mantle of the Prophet: Learning and Power in Modern Iran*. London: Chatto & Windus, 1986.

Schirazi, Ashar. *The Constitution of Iran: Politics and the State in the Islamic Republic.* John O'Kane, trans. London: I.B. Tauris Publishers, 1997.

Soroush, Abdolkarim. *"Horriyyat va Rohaniyyat"* [Liberty and Clergy]." *Kiyan* 24, April–May 1995, 2–11.

Zubaida, Sumi. *Islam, the People and the State: Political Ideas and Movements in the Middle East.* London: I.B. Tauris, 2009.

PART III

THE "INTELLECTUALS"
OF POLITICAL ISLAM

Chapter 6

Hassan Al-Turabi

PETER WOODWARD

INTRODUCTION

HASSAN AL-TURABI has been one of the most controversial figures in the Muslim world in the past half century. To his followers in Sudan he has been ideologically inspiring and a charismatic leader in national politics, while his political opponents have been known to regard him as fundamentally unprincipled. Outside Sudan younger educated Muslims have often found his writings imaginative and innovative, while to conservatives in the field of Islamic thought he has been seen to border on the heretical. Beyond the Muslim world he has been seen as an active supporter of terrorist movements, yet one who has also endeavored from time to time to engage with the non-Muslim world. If there is common ground in these differing judgments it is probably that he is clever, is pragmatic, and cultivates being enigmatic. Trying to assess Turabi as an ideologist only adds to this view. His writings are nowhere brought together into a coherent whole, rather both they and his speeches and interviews on various themes have emerged in a piecemeal manner down the years, often resulting in ambiguity as to where the consistent core of his thinking really lies. This ambiguity is heightened by what often appears to be a deliberate lack of precision in both his conceptual and practical positions. In applying his ideology through his political engagement, his record is similarly varied, leading his critics to see opportunism as often as principle in the positions he has adopted, with regard to both his ascent toward power and the way in which he exercised it following his coup in Sudan of 1989, the first time an Islamist regime had been established in the Arab and sunni world.

BACKGROUND

Turabi was born in 1932 and grew up in a small village in central Sudan, where his father was a *qadi*, administering the limited areas of Islamic law in what was in effect a British imperial administration (though legally the Anglo-Egyptian condominium in the Sudan), where civil law was essentially secular and largely founded on importing codes then applicable in India. ʿAbdalla al-Turabi ensured that his son Hassan had a rigorous education in all aspects of Islam alongside his secular studies in the state schools, and some see here a "traditional" background that was to survive Hassan al-Turabi's education in European-style institutions, which culminated in law degrees from the universities of Khartoum, London, and the Sorbonne.

However, if the British rulers were introducing secularizing trends, political mobilization in northern Sudan rested on building its major parties around sectarian Muslim identities that grew specifically from the nineteenth century, while having much older roots. Sufism had a long history in Sudan, including Turabi's illustrious forebear Hamad al-Turabi, which provided fertile soil for Mohammed Osman al-Mirghani, who arrived in Sudan in 1817, shortly before the invasion of Mohammed Ali's troops from Egypt that was to do much to define the country territorially over the next sixty years. Al-Mirghani established the *Khatmiyya tariqa*, which was to spread widely while accepting the new rulers. In the twentieth century *Khatmiyya* connections with Egypt were to survive, especially as political parties emerged after World War II with the Mirghani family becoming patrons of the National Unionist Party (NUP), which was also supported by Egypt, still hoping to achieve "The Unity of the Nile Valley." The NUP's great rival was the *Ummah* Party associated with the Mahdist movement. Mohammed Ahmed al-Mahdi had started the revolt that led to the overthrow of Turco-Egyptian rule (the *Turkiyya* as it was often known in Sudan) in 1885 and the establishment by his successor, the Khalifa Abdullahi, of an Islamic state that was to survive until the Anglo-Egyptian reconquest of 1898. In the following century al-Mahdi's heirs were to make a surprising comeback and after World War II created the *Ummah* Party. With their respective followings in the largely rural northern Sudan, the NUP and *Ummah* dominated both the nationalist era leading to independence in 1956 and the liberal democratic eras thereafter. Even during the long years of military rule from 1958–1964 and 1969–1985 the two parties remained active in various ways. While the sectarian-based parties dominated, the postcolonial state still showed the influence of imperialism's secularizing tendencies—as Turabi put it, "The disestablishment of the 'sharī'ah' and the imposition on Muslim societies of positive western laws"—especially in the attitudes of the Western-educated officials often known as the *effendiyya* (Turabi 1992, 6). Many of these retained their links to the major parties, often through family traditions, but others joined the small but significant Sudan Communist Party (SCP).

These developments provided the context within which Turabi was to evolve his own very distinctive Islamic ideology starting with his rejection of much of Sudan's experience. For him Sudan's history had been one in which Islam had been used in politics, rather than political life having been specifically based upon Islam. The Sufism that had been so dominant in Sudan was insufficiently political in essence; indeed its otherworldly spirituality in practice took Muslims away from the creation of an Islamic state and made them too accommodating of the secularizing processes that the imperial and postimperial state was imposing in the name of modernity. In addition the saintly leaders of the Sufi orders created and occupied a space between man and God, discouraging the individual's quest to actively pursue his or her direct experience of God and the living of a Godly life. Mahdism, which had a long tradition in Sudan preceding the late nineteenth-century movement (Hamad al-Turabi had twice proclaimed himself the Mahdi), was seen by Hassan al-Turabi as a form of revivalism. It rested on the vision of the decay of Islam and sought to return to a better age. It was thus backward looking, failing to engage with the issues of modernity, specifically Islamic modernity, which had come to lie at the core of Turabi's quest. He was also critical of the "official" clerical classes seeking to define Islam and widely influential in the Muslim world, where, far too often in his view, the state passed on its responsibilities with regard to the building of Islamic society. At the same time the clerics claimed a large measure of control through knowledge and interpretation of the Qur'an, rather than encouraging Islamic society as a whole in self-discovery of the true meaning of life, which involves adaptation in order to embrace and build Islamic modernity. All Muslims not only can but also should engage in the search for their own understanding of their religion and then implement it in their lives.

It is his stripping away of the above accretions of Islamic life that led to Turabi being regarded as a "fundamentalist," but he is not somebody who seeks a return to a golden age founded on strict enactment of Qur'anic verses and the *Sunnah* so much as looking forward and building afresh in the spirit of Islam applied to the modern age. Largely for that reason he has been seen as loosely connected to the ancient texts, which he rarely quotes, but rather as an interpreter who uses the style of the great texts on which Islam was founded to express what for him is the essence of the religion. The differentiation between original texts and interpretation today for him would lie in the totally changed circumstances of the contemporary world in which the building of Islamic modernity has to take place. Understandably his criticisms of so many of the existing manifestations of Islam have brought charges of apostasy from some, while also acting as an inspiration to others. Turabi believes that the search for modernity has even led some Muslims in the recent past away from the roots of their religion toward secularist ideologies such as nationalism and socialism in various forms, and these have had to be challenged by a new Islamic modernity, a line of thought that has given him another set of "modernist" critics.

IDEOLOGY

Turabi has in effect given himself a tabula rasa, and for his followers his inspiration has lain in having cleared away so many of the accretions of the past and then laid out a new feast. At its core is his conception of Islam, which lies in *ibtila'*, life's challenge to Muslims laid down by God. The modern world is a God-made world, one in which He has created a series of new challenges for Muslims, and it is through their responses to these that their faith is really put to the test. If they fail to rise to these challenges Islam will indeed degenerate in the face of globalizing secularism. But if they respond and rise to the challenge set by God they can shape a new world truly glorifying Him. In the state of the Muslim world today that means the need for *ibtila'* to be met by the recognition of the need for *tajdid*, renewal. But how is the meaning of *tajdid* to be appreciated having thrown off the accretions of centuries? It is here that *ijtihad*, the interpretation of Islamic law based on first principles, is so central and leads directly to the state, which Turabi believes has responsibility for that interpretation through the introduction and enforcement of the *Shari'ah*.

The state then is central to Turabi's understanding of the implementation of Islam, and the notion of an Islamic state is not the conjoining of two concepts but the pursuit and implementation of one, since Islam is inseparable from statehood, which lies at the center of the building of an Islamic society. In all this the Muslim world has fallen short, and Turabi is seen as a central figure in providing the theological basis for criticizing the existing states of the Muslim world whatever their particular character. The fault in this lies not only in Islam, as previously indicated, but also in Western imperialism, which has first divided the Muslim world, leaving a divided state structure that serves its interests rather than those of indigenous societies, and then co-opted Muslim rulers as local allies more on its terms than theirs, including false ideologies of modernity. The way ahead is toward a new *tawhid*, unification, of the *ummah*, the Muslim world, based upon an interpretation of first principles for the world of today and tomorrow, thus bringing together God, the ultimate sovereign, the rightly constituted Islamic state, and the society of believers.

It is Turabi's interpretation of these principles in public life that is seen as a major cause of the interest in him, especially his reputation for holding liberal and democratic views. Indeed it is the apparent marriage of Islam and democracy that has made him so attractive to the wider Muslim world in which this has become such an often raised subject. However for Turabi this is once more not a joining together of two concepts since it is God who is sovereign, and not the people as normally understood in Western views of democracy, and God's word has come down in the Qur'an and the *hadith*, so that there is an immediate circumscription of the nature of democracy. That is provided by the *Shari'ah*, which is God's law and as such not simply a manmade legal code, though as noted it is required that it be interpreted, codified, and implemented by the state.

> An Islamic form of government is essentially a form of representative democracy. But this statement requires the following qualification. First an Islamic republic is not strictly speaking a direct government of and by the people; it is a government of the *shari'ah*. But, in a substantial sense, it is a popular government since the *shari'ah* represents the conviction of the people, and therefore, their direct will. (Turabi 1983, 244)

With the *Shari'ah* in that framework he chooses not to use the word "democracy," a word usually associated with Western traditions, but rather to speak of *shura*, consultation, a long established concept in the Muslim world. *Shura* acknowledges that ultimate sovereignty rests with God while wishing the believers to participate in arriving at *ijma'*, consensus, with regard to the decisions pertaining to their society within the framework provided by the *Shari'ah*. This is popular government in the sense that it represents the theologically correct view of the people and thus amounts to a common or general will. *Shura* also implies an equality of all the citizens in the process of arriving at *ijma*. It also appears to imply that Turabi envisages a situation where *shura* is not associated with multiparty politics with all its competitive implications so much as an exchange of views among the believers as *ijma* is sought and, with

God's guidance, is eventually achieved. What has been fresh is the implied character of constitutionalism apparently associated with *Shari'ah* in Turabi's mind, which often appears to reflect practices associated with the West rather than those of the Muslim world: these include divisions of power, federalism, and an attractive range of freedoms, all of which were given considerable prominence in the campaign of the Muslim Brotherhood (which Turabi had led since 1964) under the banner of the National Islamic Front (NIF) in the multiparty elections of 1986. However, such constitutional aspects are only loosely presented rather than being spelled out clearly, for he sees himself expressing general principles while leaving it to others in formal government positions (which he chose not to hold after the coup of 1989) to handle the details: power without responsibility in the eyes of his critics.

Turabi's approach to democracy, which appeared to be that of liberalism in an Islamic context, led to criticisms of him for a series of steps that seemed opportunistic, though it is possible to argue that there is an underlying consistency. The first occasion was his agreement to national reconciliation with President Nimeiri in 1978. Turabi had been imprisoned by the military ruler who had seized power in 1969 and the Muslim Brotherhood had proved bitter opponents of the regime: yet from Turabi's perspective Nimeiri's turn to reconciliation opened a door of opportunity. He became attorney general, while the movement was to undertake a period of entryism into many areas of the state, the full extent of which was not to become apparent for several years. In 1983 Nimeiri introduced *Shari'ah,* and though it was not specifically the work of the Muslim Brotherhood it was regarded by the movement as a step in the right direction. Following Nimeiri's downfall in 1985, the Brotherhood returned to the liberal democratic path, fighting the 1986 elections as the NIF and obtaining 18 percent of the vote.

It was in and out of subsequent coalition governments until itself staging a coup in 1989, an obviously undemocratic move. However it can be argued that Nimeiri's *Shari'ah* was under threat. Civil war in southern Sudan, which had reopened in 1983 after ten years of peace, was intensifying and after much maneuvering it appeared that peace might be negotiated, though only at the price of suspending *Shari'ah*, a measure demanded by the predominantly non-Muslim south. That would be a major setback for Turabi and his followers and it was judged better to seize power than to risk a setback on the path to the Islamic state they sought.

Once in power Turabi's approach could also be seen in his effort to push his Islamic democracy agenda. Following the introduction of revised *Shari'ah* he became the leading promoter of moves toward a non-multi-party national assembly. Later, having become leader of the assembly, he sought in 1999 to challenge President Omar al-Beshir and his military-security colleagues in the name of progressing from military to "democratic" government. However, Beshir responded by suspending the Assembly and ousting Turabi. The latter then formed his own party, the Popular Congress Party (PCP), and with the promise of liberal democratic elections in 2009 (which was contained in the Comprehensive Peace Agreement of 2005 between the rulers of north and south Sudan), Turabi returned to the campaigning mode he had used in the 1986 elections. To his critics this long record put opportunism above principle, while to his defenders he had responded to the changing context while consistently pursuing his path toward his vision of an Islamic democracy, showing the flexibility he had always argued Muslims are required to do.

That Turabi's approach to democracy is ultimately theological based on *Shari'ah* is also reflected in his apparent liberalism. He is noted for the way in which he has called for greater openness within

Muslim societies, which some have seen as a call for "civil society": but this is less civil society as understood in Western liberal societies—groups operating independently of the state—than organizations committed to expressing aspects of Muslim society within the framework provided by the *Shari'ah*. It thus involves encouraging the development of a truer Muslim society, which at one time Turabi appeared to think should precede the establishment of an Islamic state. "An Islamic state evolves from an Islamic society" was his view before his 1989 coup (Turabi 1983, 241). Indeed from national reconciliation in 1977 the Muslim Brotherhood had been building up its own activities in civil society. Part of this was with regard to Islamic charitable activities. The growing charities were intended to challenge the influence of Western nongovernmental organizations (NGOs) and assist in the growth of the Islamic movement as a whole. In addition the universities and the small business sector were targeted by the movement as it expanded its membership. In this it was helped by fund raising among the many Sudanese working in the Gulf and Saudi Arabia and by the Islamic banking movement, which grew rapidly in Sudan and elsewhere with capital from the oil-rich states.

However, just as context produced his change with regard to democracy in 1989, so the relationship between civil society and the state had to be turned upside down. The work of the 1980s was incomplete, and the state was now required to embark upon a program of intensified reshaping of society. Non-Islamic NGOs, especially Sudanese "secular" NGOs, were faced by harassment and worse, which resulted in a number of leading Sudanese being persecuted or leaving the country. Meanwhile the state embarked on "the civilizational project" as it was known. It involved a whole range of activities intended to create the true Muslim society but had limited success. De Waal has written of the project's limitations with regard to certain rural areas, while Simone, a researcher brought in by the regime itself, was to describe its lack of progress even in the capital (de Waal 2004, 89–99; Simone 1994). Turabi's critics complained that the attempt to create Islamic society from above contributed to the most repressive actions by the state in Sudan since it became independent in 1956 and reports by many bodies, including the United Nations, have supported this view.

This process of building Islamic society was closely linked to human rights; another area where the potential for paradox in Turabi's thought is often discussed. He has been a defender of human rights, especially in areas such as freedom of thought and freedom of religion, but again in an Islamic context. Contemporary human rights are too often associated with the Enlightenment and depicted therefore as manmade, whereas in Turabi's view man himself is the work of God and under his supreme law, *Shari'ah*. Indeed he has even argued that modern human rights theory is in reality itself derived historically from earlier Islamic thought. Apart from criticism of his argument stretching legal and political history, the reality of human rights following his 1989 coup included practices that even Turabi himself was forced to concede were un-Islamic.

One subject in which Turabi's apparent liberal interpretation of human rights is frequently brought up is that of women, a subject on which he first came to prominence in 1973. In his view women have been held back in Muslim societies, but less by anything specifically included in Islam than by the theological and social developments since that time. Thus in all areas of life, including education in particular, women are to have equal rights with men and are to be regarded as active members of the community rather than confined in domestic incarceration. As well as the practice of patriarchy in some Muslim societies, the principle of avoiding situations that permit un-Islamic relations between the sexes has been exaggerated:

instead greater active incorporation of women in all areas of life is to be encouraged. However, women too are part of the Muslim society that is governed by *Shari'ah*, and there are thus standards to which they have to conform while offering personal freedoms from sometimes stifling customary constraints found in parts of the Muslim world. As a result the Muslim Brotherhood fostered women's activities under its aegis, and they became in time a growing and prominent part of the movement. Nevertheless there were women who were less amenable to the "Islamic call" as represented by the Brotherhood and more influenced by the "modern forces," as more secularist movements were often known, and they too had to be challenged. The result was that after 1989 many "uncooperative" women lost their jobs, while in areas such as dress and informal economic activities others were harshly treated for much of the following decade.

Another noted area of Turabi's apparently liberal approach lies in his views on art, which appear to bring out his breadth and his opposition to materialism. While the Muslim world has long appreciated poetry and calligraphy, its approach to the visual arts was too restrictive in his view. The reason, he has argued, has lain in undue influence on avoiding the creation of religious idols or art forms that could be construed as undermining Islam's moral code. However this has been taken to extremes by some clerics in particular and instead Turabi believes that the arts, and the media generally, have a greater part to play in society though once again within a clear Islamic context in which a fusion is reestablished. But instead of a liberation of the arts in Sudan after 1989 many of the practices of the generally easygoing northern Sudanese society, such as music and traditional dancing, were cracked down on for a decade before there was a general easing of the restrictions. How far this easing with regard to civil society as a whole reflected a view amongst the

Islamists that their transformation had been achieved and how far it grew from the split in which Turabi was involved and subsequent pragmatism by the military rulers remains a matter of debate.

Turabi's attitude to non-Muslims within an Islamic state is also open to interpretation. On the one hand he put the need for Islamists to construct a specifically Islamic state at the center of his thought, but on the other he sought to present his thought as open with regard to other faiths. The issue arose especially in respect to *jihad*. Turabi has been keen to emphasize that *jihad* is a comprehensive term denoting effort for the Islamic cause and did not simply imply the exercise of armed force. It was a particularly sensitive issue in a context in which successive Sudan governments had been waging a war since 1983 in the predominantly non-Muslim south, where there was a significant Christian community. Whatever was expressed ideologically, in practice the government forces were encouraged to believe that they were engaged in *jihad* in the south and in other areas such as the Nuba Mountains, while soldiers killed in action were heralded in the media as martyrs. It appeared increasingly that few non-Muslims believed that there was the absence of discrimination against them that Turabi claimed should exist; though after his ousting in 1999 he did return to this point, including saying that the conflict was not after all a *jihad*.

Turabi's emphasis on the centrality of the Islamic state in protecting truly Muslim societies gave rise to consideration of his ideas on international politics. Here it becomes apparent that the distinction is fundamentally between those states that are Islamic and should bind together as such and the rest of the world. But first, beyond the Islamic state properly constituted, one must return to his vision of the Muslim world as a whole being in need of *tajdid*, renewal, following centuries of degeneration and division. Again there is a need to return to first principles, and they are far from the Westphalian model so dominant in the contemporary international system. Indeed he believes that there has been a "failure of the territorial national state model," which imperialism had endeavored to impose and construct upon the Muslim world (Turabi 1992, 7). In talking of the Muslim world Turabi is aware that there are complex multiple identities and that these all have their part to play in the reality of the modern world. People have understandable reasons for identifying themselves from family through a series of other layers, including what may be the imposed contemporary state system to *Dar al-Islam*, the Muslim commonwealth, where "Final loyalty must be rendered."

> The Islamic community of believers is unitary and integrated, but it is a structured association with complex bonds and balances that gives coherence and equilibrium, assuring therein the embodiment of the Islamic values of freedom, unity and justice among men. (Turabi 1992, 2)

The end of the Cold War, he argued, gave particular opportunity for the renewal of the *ummah* to take place. One factor was the growth of modern Islamic movements across the Muslim world giving rise to a new awareness of what should and could be achieved. This had been aided by the growth of new forms of mass communication that had penetrated Muslim societies as much as any others around the world. The collapse of the "socialist" world constructed by the Soviet Union removed what had been an alluring and sometimes supportive power for some in the Muslim world. Other major events included the Iranian Revolution in 1979, which had shown that power could be taken from the West's collaborators; and in particular the Gulf War in which predominantly Western troops had deployed on a vast scale in the center of the Muslim world. This had encouraged a new mood that "threatens to wipe out liberal nationalist and socialist tendencies and [will] proceed to take its international course" (Turabi 1992, 7).

How was this to be achieved? True there had been an international organization in existence since the 1960s, the Organization of the Islamic Conference (OIC), but this had been inadequate in Turabi's view. It was supported by states that had had close relations with the Western world and thus it was, "politically impotent and totally unrepresentative of the true spirit of community that animates the Muslim people" (Turabi 1992, 8). Following the coup of 1989 Turabi himself set up and led a new organization, based in Khartoum, called the Popular Arabic and Islamic Conference (PAIC). It invited a heterogeneous range of representatives from groups including Hizbollah, Islamic Jihad, Hamas, and the Palestine Liberation Organization as well as various veterans from the *mujahadin* campaign in Afghanistan against the USSR, including Osama Bin Laden, who lived in Sudan from 1991 until 1996. All were dubbed "brothers in Islam" and seen as part of Turabi's vision of a united *jihad* by the Muslim world in all its diverse parts, even including sunni and shi`a, which contributed to his somewhat ambiguous view of Iran. While the PAIC made a significant contribution, the Muslim world as a whole was looking for a new beacon to set an example of a true Islamic state, with the clear implication that this was what Turabi was inspiring and guiding into being in Sudan itself.

The final vision was of the reestablishment of the Muslim caliphate, but not the same as that which had ended following the collapse of the Ottoman Empire after World War I. The caliphate would in future be less a central political authority than a symbolic leadership of Muslim communities. These would exist under *sharī`ah* as decentralized and democratic but recognizing their ultimate unity as fellow Muslims. "There is no standardization of language or cultural forms as long as an essential minimum of Arabic is assured everywhere and that social life-styles observe the common standards of the *Shari'ah*" (Turabi 1992, 3). As for the non-Muslim world, one finds once more a degree of ambiguity. Clearly Muslim minorities living in predominantly non-Muslim societies were to be supported in whatever ways were necessary and encouraged to keep and develop their faith. Non-Muslims in Muslim countries were to be accorded their rights since freedom of religion was recognized in Turabi's writings, though that did not detract from Muslims engaging in proselytism. A similar attitude was shown toward non-Muslim countries. Turabi both believed in struggling for the Islamic cause and at the same time encouraged interfaith dialogue, especially with leaders of Christian denominations.

The element of struggle for Islam also gave rise to questions about his understanding of *jihad*. While, as mentioned, he saw *jihad* as an effort for Islam broadly understood, he did not rule out violence on behalf of the cause. This became particularly clear in 1995, when Egyptian Islamists received assistance from Sudan in seeking to assassinate President Hosni Mubarak in Addis Ababa. Turabi described the would-be assassins as "messengers of the Islamic faith" (Collins 2008, 216). However he did also say that justifiable acts of violence in the name of promoting Islam should seek to avoid killing civilians as far as possible.

CONCLUSION

If Turabi had confined himself to being a theorist his thought would have attracted interest and perhaps served as an inspiration for some. But he has been an ideologist in the fullest sense of the word, turning his ideas into programs of action in Sudan and beyond, which have themselves excited widespread discussion and often critical judgment. He himself has blamed many of the shortcomings in practice on those carrying them out rather than the underlying ideas and intentions themselves and, after his removal from power in 1999, on the military in particular; yet it can be argued that they are based in his thought itself. Many of his fellow believers, while accepting the ultimate sovereignty of God, are of the view that there have been inherent dangers in the vagueness and lack of textual reference in Turabi's writings. Since the state, and the *Shari'ah* for which it is responsible, is so central it requires tighter definition and clearer constitutional arrangements with adequate legal and political accountability. This in turn will help to clarify the relationship between society and the state that appeared in effect to be reversed in Turabi's thinking by his coup of 1989. This, and much else that has flowed directly or indirectly from his thoughts and actions, leads his Muslim critics to argue that the source of authority is less God as revealed in the texts than Turabi himself as he interprets God's purpose.

REFERENCES

Al-Turabi, Hassan. 1983. The Islamic State. In *Voices of Resurgent Islam*, ed. John L. Esposito. Oxford University Press, 241–251.

Al-Turabi, Hassan. 1992. "Islam as a Pan-National Movement and Nation States: An Islamic Doctrine on Human Association." Nationhood Lecture presented at the Royal Society of Arts, April 27, London.

Burr, J. M., and Robert O. Collins. 2003. *Revolutionary Sudan: Hassan al-Turabi and the Islamist State,* 1989–2000. Leiden: Brill.

Collins, Robert O. 2008. *A History of Modern Sudan.* Cambridge: Cambridge University Press.

De Waal, Alex, ed. 2004. *Islamism and Its Enemies in the Horn of Africa.* London: Hurst.

El-Affendi, Abdelwahab. 1991. *Turabi's Revolution: Islam and Power in Sudan.* London: Grey Seal.

Gallab, Abdullahi A. 2008. *The First Islamist Republic: Development and Disintegration of Islamism in the Sudan*. Burlington: Ashgate.

Hamdi, Mohamed Elhachmi. 1998. *The Making of an Islamic Political Leader: Conversations with Hassan al-Turabi*. Boulder: Westview.

Ibrahim, Abdullahi Ali. 2008. *Manichaean Delirium: Decolonizing the Judiciary and Islamic Renewal in the Sudan, 1898–1985*. Leiden: Brill.

Simone, T. Abdou Maliqalim. 1994. *In Whose Image?: Political Islam and Urban Practices in Sudan*. Chicago: Chicago University Press.

Chapter 7

Rashid Al-Ghannushi

AZZAM TAMIMI

Rashid GHANNUSHI was born on June 22, 1941 in southeastern Tunisia. The youngest of ten brothers and sisters, he grew up in a traditional and observing Muslim community. Within his large extended family, he was particularly impressed by his maternal uncle, Al-Bashir, a staunch supporter of Arabism and a great admirer of its leader President Nassir of Egypt and a member of the Bourguiba-led national liberation movement against the French occupation authorities.

Developing an interest in modern Western literature, in his teens Ghannushi read Arabic translations of Tolstoy's *War and Peace*, Gorky's (1868–1936) *Mother*, and Dostoyevsky's *Crime and Punishment*. He also read some of the works of Irish writer Bernard Shaw (1856–1950), French author Victor Hugo (1802–1885), and American novelist Ernest Millar (1899–1961). The Arab novelists he read included Najib Mahfuz, Yusuf al-Siba`i, Muhammad Abd Al-Halim Abdullah, and Colin Suhail.

When aged eighteen, Ghannushi left the village in 1959 for the capital in pursuit of education at the ancient Arabic-medium A-Zaytouna Institute. The three years he spent in the city exposed him to the identity crisis the conflict between modernity and tradition had created in his country.

In his final high school year, Ghannushi studied philosophy and became passionately fond of arguing about theoretical issues. Yet, the years he spent studying at this historic Islamic institution did not quench his thirst for knowledge nor answer his many questions. Worse still, the Institute's curriculum failed to secure him with confidence about his Islamic faith. Outside the classroom the public sphere was dominated by a Western lifestyle and little within it related to Islam. The students' community of this supposedly religious institution had every reason to be alienated from religion.

Influenced by his maternal uncle, Ghannushi grew up as a Nassirist, a supporter and believer in the pan-Arabism of President Nassir who ruled Egypt between 1952 and 1970. His love and admiration for the Arab *Mashriq* and his displeasure with the situation in Tunisia prompted him to seek refuge in Egypt in pursuit of further education. In 1964, he enrolled with the Faculty of Agriculture at Cairo University. But no less than three months later he was forced to quit because the regimes in Cairo and Tunis decided to reconcile their differences. The presence of anti-Bourguiba students in Egypt was no longer welcome.

Ghannushi thought of escaping to Albania but was advised by a fellow student to go instead to Syria. Once there, he enrolled for a BA in philosophy at Damascus University, where he studied from 1964 to 1968.

While still a student, Ghannushi took time off in 1965 to embark on a seven-month tour of Europe. He traveled by road from Syria to Turkey then on to Bulgaria, Yugoslavia, Germany, France, Belgium, and the Netherlands, earning his living by taking up whatever menial job was available to him.

Intellectually, Ghannushi remained loyal to Nassirism up to the second year of his stay in Damascus. During that period, he underwent a transition from a romantic Arabist to a committed ideologue of Arab nationalism as propagated by Sati` al-Husrai (1879–1968), whose writings were the Arabists' main source of inspiration. Yet, he soon started having misgivings. The foundations of the nationalist ideology crumbled more and more as he progressed in the study of philosophy and as he took a more active part in the intellectual debates of the students' community in Damascus. Soon, his Arab nationalism readings were substituted by Islamic ones. During the last two years of his study in Damascus, he read Muhammad Iqbal, Abu al-`Ala al-Mawdudi, Sayyid Qutb, Muhammad Qutb, Hassan al-Banna, Mustafa al-Siba`i, Malik Bennabi, and Abu al-Hassan al-Nadwi in addition to more traditional writing in various Islamic disciplines.

Searching for a camp that could accommodate both his Arabism and Islamic faith, Ghannushi joined a group of Syrian nationalist students who, after spending hundreds of hours debating the Arab situation and the means of bringing about an Arab renaissance, started having their doubts about the nationalist discourse. In their company, he moved from one Islamic study circle to another, acquainting himself with Islam and Islamic movements. He met with members the *Ikhwan* (the Muslim Brotherhood), with a group of followers of Shaykh Nassir al-Din al-Albani and with some elements of Hizb al-Tahrir al-Islami (the Islamic Liberation Party). In addition, he made the acquaintance of a number of scholars who were active in Damascus at the time, such as Shaykh Habannaka, Shaykh Adib al-Salih, Shaykh Sa`id Ramadan al-Buti, Shaykh Wahba al-Zuhayli, and Jawdat Sa`id, whom he thought was a very distinguished and impressive personality.

The divorce with nationalism led Ghannushi to the rediscovery of Islam. The night of June 15, 1966 was a turning point and a landmark in his life; that was the night he embraced what he called the true Islam, Islam as revealed and not as shaped or distorted by history and tradition. That night he felt he was reborn with the determination to review and reflect on all that which he had previously conceived.

Following his graduation from Damascus University in the summer of 1968, Ghannushi left Syria for France to pursue his postgraduate studies in philosophy at the Sorbonne. He had not been back to Tunisia since he left it in 1964. France seemed the right place to go. For, should he hope to be recognized in Tunisia upon his return home, he needed to have acquired an academic qualification from France.

Most of the Tunisian students in Paris at the time were communists or Arab nationalists. As a committed Islamist by then, it would have been unthinkable, let alone comfortable, for him to associate with any of these. Soon a small nucleus of Islamist Tunisian students took shape. In addition to Ghannushi, the group included Ahmida Enneifer and Ahmed Manai. In the meantime, Ghannushi frequented a circle at the local mosque belonging to Tablighi Jama`at, a branch of the Indian-based apolitical movement founded in 1926 by the Sufi scholar Mawlana Muhammad Ilyas (1885–1944). The rule within the *Tabligh* group was such that new recruits were expected to make a four-month pilgrimage to Pakistan, and in the case of a "cultured" recruit like Ghannushi it would have been seven months, where he would have undergone initiation and would have been fully indoctrinated. He would have gone there had it not been for an unexpected turn of events.

Upon the completion of his first year of study in Paris, Ghannushi was summoned home to see his mother, whom he was told was rather sick. He traveled home by land via Spain in the company of his elder brother, who was dispatched on a rescue mission to fetch young Ghannushi and deliver him from the "claws" of extreme religiosity.

On the way back home, Ghannushi had an opportunity to stop by at the grand mosque in Cordoba that had been turned into a museum. There, he wrested a guard who endeavored to prevent him from praying at the mosque. Then, transiting in Algiers, he met Algerian Islamic thinker Malik Bennabi for the first time.

Instead of returning to Paris to resume his studies, Ghannushi decided to stay at home. The country was in better shape than he expected. It was not family pressure that succeeded in holding him back but what he believed were promising signs of Islamic revival. A study circle he accidentally came across in one of the mosques convinced him that his country needed him.

Working as a high school philosophy teacher, he joined others in founding *al-Jama'a al-Islamiya* (the Islamic Group). The group used as a platform the government-sponsored Qur'anic Preservation Society (QPS). For a number of years henceforth, he and other founding members of *al-Jama'a*, Shaykh Abdelfattah Moro, al-Fadhil Al-Baladi, Salih bin Abdullah, and Ahmida Enneifer, traveled regularly to Algeria to attend Malik Bennabi's annual Islamic Thought Seminar. This was the period, from 1970 to 1972, that saw Ghannushi's gradual conversion from Qutb's school of thought to that of Bennabi, whose critique of Qutb was the first in a series of experiences that shook his confidence in the thought of al-Mashriq (Arab East).

Ghannushi first drew Tunisian public attention when an article by him entitled "Baramij al-Falsafah wa Jil al-Daya'" (The Philosophy Curriculum and the Generation of Loss) was published in a leading Tunisian daily newspaper. Sharply criticizing the education system in Tunisia, the article rejected the notion that Western ideas were absolutes accepting them only as possible, albeit partial, explanations of human conduct and of human history. At the same time, he started reading the Qur'an with a new insight. He discovered that, in the Qur'anic discourse, the economy was an essential dimension. He began to realize that a comprehensive reading of Islam would lead one to conclude that economic, political, sexual, and social factors had already been sufficiently emphasized in the Qur'an, and therefore denying the effect such factors have on people's lives, as he used to do, was a mistake.

Upon his return to Tunisia from France, Ghannushi conceived a thought acquired through reading the writings of *Ikhwan* leaders and ideologues including Hassan al-Banna, Sayyid Qutb, Abdel-Qadir ʿAwdah, Muhammad al-Ghazali, and Yusuf al-Qaradawi as well as the writings of Mawdudi. Yet, until the Tunisian government outlawed *al-Jamaʿa al-Islamiya* in 1973, the group emulated the method of the *Tabligh Jamaat*. The banning of the group prompted him to question the utility of the open activity of the *Tabligh*, which might have worked more successfully in an open environment such as that of India or Pakistan or of Western Europe, where basic freedoms are guaranteed. From then on, *al-Jamaʿa* was compelled to adopt an *Ikhwan* style of dual, clandestine/public, activism.

Working locally, it did not take Ghannushi long to reconnect with what he discovered to be a Tunisian Islamic legacy treasured by the country's most prestigious institute, al-Zaytouna, whose scholars played a significant role in the modernization endeavor that preceded the colonial era. Ghannushi deemed it essential for him and his group to be perceived as the rightful inheritors of the nineteenth-century Tunisian reform effort of Khayr al-Din al-Tunsi (1810–1899), prime minister and author of a book entitled *Aqwam al-Masalik fi Ma'rifat Ahwal al-Mamalik* (The Surest Path to Learning the Conditions of States).

As part of his mission to reconnect with the Tunisian Islamic legacy, Ghannushi returned to al-Zaytouna in search of his roots, studying the writings of Tunisian Islamic thinkers, which together with those of Bennabi constituted what he called the *Magharibi* Islamic heritage.

By the mid-seventies, Ghannushi's Islamic movement acquired a Tunisian characteristic that, according to him, was the product of the interaction of three main components: (1) *al-tadayun al-taqlidi al-Tunisi* (the traditional Tunisian religiosity), which is composed of three elements: the *Maliki* school of jurisprudence, the *ash'ariyah* doctrine of theology, and Sufism; (2) the *salafi* religiosity, of the type he embraced initially following the example of the *Mashariqi* Islamic thought; and (3) *al-tadayun al-'aqlani* (rational religiosity).

In the second half of the seventies, Ghannushi and his group started interacting and communicating with other political and intellectual groups within Tunisia, including the nationalists and the leftists. This coincided with arrival in Tunisia of some of the writings of former members of the *Ikhwan* in Egypt such as Fathi Osman. These writings, which were critical of the *Ikhwan*, prompted a revival of what Ghannushi called *al-turath al-islami al-'aqlani* (the Islamic heritage of rationality) as expressed by the *Mu'tazilah* school of thought.

The strategy of *'aqlana* soon led to a split. Some of Ghannushi's colleagues wanted to pursue it further while others were apprehensive that it might eventually lead to undermining the sacredness of revelation itself by emphasizing reason at the expense of the text. The rationalists, known later as *al-yasar al-islami* (the Islamic left), wanted also to restore recognition and respect for Western culture.

The rationalists' critique of the *Ikhwan* targeted in particular the thought of Sayyid Qutb, whose theory of *jahiliyah* (barbarity) called for *mufasalah* (alienation and departure) from blasphemous society by the community of believers, which he considered to be the *ummah*.

Ghannushi did not entirely disagree with the rationalists' critique of Qutb. Nor did he disagree with them on the need to restore respect for the reformist school of the nineteenth and early twentieth centuries. However, he did not condone their skeptical attitude toward the sacred text, nor did he accept the extension of their critique to the entire *Ikhwan-Salafi* school. Above all, he disliked their suggestion that the *al-burguibiyah* (Bourguibism, referring to the reforms introduced by President Bourguiba) was an extension of the Tunisian reformist school of Khayr al-Din and al-Tahir al-Haddad.

From the mid-seventies to the early eighties Ghannushi's thought and the development of his movement's political standing were influenced by a series of major developments. Locally, there was the liberal democratic current that emerged in Tunisia in the second half of the seventies followed by the 1978 violent confrontation between the trade unions and the government. Regionally, there was the Iranian Revolution and the sociopolitical thought of the Islamic movement in Sudan under the leadership of Hassan al-Turabi.

The communication with the Tunisian democrats coincided with demands for *muhasaba* (accountability) and *ma'sasah* (institutionalization) by some members of *al-Jama'a al-Islamiya*. These demands prompted the convening of a general conference in 1979, the year of the Khomeini-led Iranian Revolution, henceforth referred to as *al-mu'tamar at-ta'sisi* (the Founding Conference). In addition to adopting a constitution, the conference elected for the first time the top leadership of the movement, which consisted of a *shura* council, an executive bureau, and a president. Ghannushi was the first president.

As democracy was rapidly becoming a primary issue for political opposition trends within Tunisia, including his own, Ghannushi felt the need to revive the democratic thought of nineteenth-century Islamic reformers that had been obscured by the proliferation across the Arab region of the antidemocracy thought, primarily as expressed in the writings of Sayyid Qutb.

The Khomeini-led Islamic Revolution had a considerable impact on Ghannushi and his Tunisian Islamic movement. One important intellectual contribution of the Iranian Revolution was its presentation of the conflict between the poor and the rich as a conflict between the oppressor and the oppressed. The Iranian Revolution seemed to shake what had remained of the foundations of *Mashariqi* thought. Ghannushi was particularly impressed with what he believed was Khomeini's success in uniting behind him all political trends within Iran by mobilizing the oppressed in the name of Islam. Ghannushi's enthusiasm for the Iranian Revolution led him to regard Khomeini a *mujaddid* (a renewer). He believed that three such persons existed in the twentieth century: al-Banna in Egypt, Mawdudi in India, and Khomeini in Iran.

A visit to Sudan in 1979 acquainted Ghannushi with a different model of Islamic activism. The most striking aspect of this model was the liberal attitude toward women. In the Sudanese model women participated fully in the political and social programs of the Islamic movement. In contrast, the Tunisian Islamists had been influenced by *Mashariqi* thought, which was highly critical of the status of women in the West and warned against the dangers posed to family life by liberal attitudes.

Back in Tunisia in 1980, Ghannushi delivered a speech in which he strongly criticized his movement's previous position on women and called for a review in favor of affirming the principle of equality between the sexes. He called for the immediate lifting of any restrictions by members of his group on the education of women and stressed the need for training and developing Islamic women leaders. His remarks reflected a radical change of position, especially as he stressed that the innocent mixing of men and women was not prohibited and that polygamy was not an Islamic duty.

Until about 1984, Ghannushi strongly opposed the Tunisian Personal Status Code and denounced the law prohibiting polygamy. Yet, in 1988, encouraged by Ben Ali's announcement upon assuming power that he would democratize the regime, Ghannushi announced that his movement accepted the Personal Status Code.

Earlier in 1981, Bourguiba Prime Minister Mohamed Mzali announced that his government would allow the formation of political parties in prelude to calling for parliamentary elections. In response, Ghannushi, who a year earlier took the precautionary measure of dissolving al-Jama`a, announced the formation of the of the Mouvement de la Tendence Islamique (MTI). The MTI manifesto expressed the movement's commitment to democratic process, including pluralism and the sharing and alternation of power, and stated that the democratic process should exclude no one, not even communists, and affirmed that the electoral process was the source of legitimacy.

On July 17, 1981, the leaders of MTI and five hundred of its members were arrested. Imprisoned from 1981 to 1984, Ghannushi later said he felt his incarceration was a break he used for contemplation and reflection. In prison, he memorized the Holy Qur'an and studied a number of classical works in different Islamic sciences. He read Ibn Taymiyah, Abu Hamid al-Ghazali, Ibn Rushd, Ibn Hazm, al-Zamakhshari, al-Qarafi, Ibn `Ashur, and a number of more contemporary authors including the Iraqi Shiite philosopher Baqir As-Sadr.

In 1983 he started working on the draft of a treatise, which he entitled *al-Mujtama' al-Tunisi: Tahlil Hadari* (Tunisian Society: A Civilizational Analysis), with the purpose of reflecting on the path of the movement and the situation of society so as to reinforce positive elements and avoid negative ones, to clarify the image of the aspired civilizational alternative and to determine the short-term objectives and the means of accomplishing them. In addition, he undertook a number of projects, one of which was to study a translation of a book on women by Roger Garaudy, which inspired him—together with his recent experience in Sudan—to write a treatise on women rights and on the status of women inside the Islamic movement. One other important project he undertook while in custody was the translation of a booklet authored by Malik Bennabi entitled *al-Islam wa al-Dimuqratiyah* (Islam and Democracy), which inspired him to begin working on his most important book, *al-Hurriyat al-'Amma fi al-Dawla al-Islamiya* (Public Liberties in the Islamic State).

While in prison, he wrote a piece about the centrality of the Palestinian issue and another one about the relations with Iran in which he criticized the Iranians for the first time since their revolution. This was in response to what was communicated to him of an attack launched in an Iranian Revolutionary Guards' bulletin against a number of Islamic movements in the Arab world, including the Muslim Brotherhood of Egypt and the MTI of Tunisia, accusing them of being counterrevolutionaries and lackeys of the West.

Following his release from prison, and in response to what he perceived as a concentrated endeavor to undermine the guarantees that Islam provided to safeguard public and individual liberties and to protect the rights of political and religious minorities and the rights of women, Ghannushi set out to defend Islam and refute all those allegations made against its social and political systems. As he embarked on this mission he discovered that so much distortion had also been made about the nature of the Western civilization itself and most importantly about the concept of democracy. He felt obliged to remove himself from the tide of everyday life and devote it to the task of finishing what he had started in prison, working on his public liberties book. But no sooner had he finished working on the manuscript than he was once again arrested and held in detention.

In August 1987, Ghannushi and eighty-nine other MTI leading members were brought to trial before the State Security Court, accused of inciting violence and seeking to change the nature of the state. Ghannushi's death sentence was commuted to life imprisonment with labor but Bourguiba ordered a retrial insisting on a death sentence. However, on November 7, 1987, Bourguiba was toppled in a bloodless coup and the new president, Zine El Abidine Ben Ali, ordered the release of Ghannushi and his comrades.

The initial period of President Ben Ali's era saw a commitment to the creation of a multiparty system. In an attempt to gain recognition under a new law, Ghannushi, in December 1988, changed the name of his organization from of the MTI to Harakat al-Nahdah (The Renaissance Movement, written in English as Ennahda), dropping the reference to Islam from its title.

Still not officially licensed despite having lodged an application, Ennahda members ran as independents competing for 129 of the 141 available parliamentary seats in the elections of April 1989. Ennahda-backed independents emerged as the largest opposition force, winning 14.5 percent of the national vote and as much as 30 percent in some urban centers, including Tunis, the capital. On June 6, 1989 Ennahda's application for the status of a political party was rejected, leaving its supporters liable to prosecution on grounds of membership in an illegal organization, an offence punishable by up to five years' imprisonment. Despite Ennahda's impressive showing at the polls, none of its candidates were returned to parliament. In fact, all seats in parliament were awarded to candidates from the ruling Rassemblement Constitutionel Démocratique (RCD) party.

The elections, which were supposed to mark the beginning of a new era of national reconciliation, triggered a government campaign aimed at the complete uprooting of the Tunisian Islamic movement.

In May 1989 Ghannushi fled the country ending up in London, where he has remained ever since. Ghannushi seemed to take the entire organization into exile with him. His departure was to be followed by a series of measures by the regime of President Ben Ali aimed at discrediting and crushing Ennahda once and for all. In January 1991, Ghannushi's deputy Abd al-Fattah Mourou fell victim to a government-sponsored defamation campaign that brought an end to his career. In February of that same year, an arson attack on the ruling party's offices in the Bab Souika district, allegedly carried out by members of the movement, was seized upon by the government as proof of the violent and antidemocratic nature of Ennahda.

Having felt responsible for what had happened to the movement, Ghannushi preferred to leave the task of pursuing the political struggle to somebody else while dedicating his life in exile to further scholarship and to the completion of unfinished writings. But Ennahda members insisted there was a much greater benefit for the movement in his dedicating a greater part of his time and effort to the leadership of the movement. His exiled comrades believed that in view of the tough circumstances experienced by their movement and their country, Ghannushi was obliged to remain in the field where he was most needed.

It was in his exile in London that Ghannushi finally had the opportunity to return to his book and finish it. Published by the renowned Centre of Arab Unity Studies in Beirut in 1993, *al-Hurriyat al-ʿAmma fi al—Dawla al-Islamiya* (Public Liberties in the Islamic

State) is an important reference in contemporary Islamic political thought, especially on the discussions within the house of Islamism on issues such as civil liberties, democracy, and the aspired to system of good governance.

In his book, Ghannushi defines the ideal system of governance as one that recognizes and protects the dignity of man and provides guarantees for stemming despotism and creating the right climate for the blossoming of man's potential. It is the system in which the political, economic, and cultural gaps between the "ruled" and the "ruler" diminish until they disappear altogether.

While admiring the achievements of liberal democracy, Ghannushi is sharply critical of its philosophies underpinning a worldview that according to him drives a wedge between the soul and the body and is therefore incapable of balancing man's different needs. He believes that an Islamic model of democracy may arise out of a marriage between liberal democratic tools and procedures on the one hand and the Islamic code of ethics and values on the other, thus averting some of the negative features of liberal democracy and its many broken promises. He laments, however, that the emergence of this model in the Muslim world is hindered by a number of obstacles. Ghannushi's ideas about the obstacles impeding democratization in the Arab world, and particularly in the North African region, are subsequent to the publication of his public liberties book and may be the outcome of contemplating the failure of the democratic processes in both Algeria and Tunisia.

The late nineties saw Ghannushi write, in Arabic, about some of these obstacles for the first time. Undoubtedly, his first ten years of exile in London gave much food for thought, having had the opportunity to discuss these ideas with a good number of other Arab exiles as well as with Western thinkers whom he met individually or at workshops and conferences.

He came to the conclusion that the enforced secularization of Arab societies, which began during colonial days, as well as the erosion of traditional institutions, which equaled modern-day civil society institutions, are the main obstacles hindering democratization. Furthermore, foreign powers, which constitute the New World Order, and local elites that share interests with these powers would not want to see genuine democratization in this part of the world simply because they believe it would harm their mutual interests.

While Ghannushi is critical of secularism as a whole, he does distinguish between Western secularism and the secularism that evolved, and is being advocated, in the Arab and Muslim countries. While the evolution of secularism in the West was associated with the need by reformists, especially during the Renaissance, to free their societies from the constraints imposed on them by the Church, secularism in the Arab and Muslim societies was imported by the colonial authorities and imposed by autocracies that took shape in the postcolonial era. Rather than bring about democratization, the Arab version of secularism of which Ghannushi is critical has given rise to some of the most despotic and corrupt regimes in modern history.

Ghannushi's more recent book *Muqarabat fi al-'Almaniyya wa al-Mujtama' al-Madani* (Approaches to Secularism and Civil Society) has documented his ideas on secularism and civil society. These ideas were developed through a series of encounters and exchanges with academics and thinkers he met during his stay in London including John Keane, John Esposito, Ernest Gillner, John Voll, Luis Cantori, Abd al-Wahhab al-Messiri, Fahmi Huwaidi, Muhammad Salim al-'Awwa, and Tariq al-Bishri.

Ghannushi has argued strongly against the monopoly of the concept of civil society by Arab secularists who deny such a status to Islamic institutions in Arab societies. As far as he is concerned all nongovernmental organizations (NGOs) qualify for the category of civil society whether they are secular or religious. Ghannushi is unprecedented within Islamic intellectual circles in his theory that civil society is an Islamic concept and that religion consolidates civil society whereas secularism, especially the model imported to the Muslim world under the guise of modernization, weakens it.

Among contemporary Islamic thinkers and activists, Rashid Ghannushi is distinguished by his daring and innovative endeavors to introduce new dimensions in contemporary Islamic thought. The impact of his ideological and intellectual standing has extended well beyond the frontiers of Tunisia. His contribution to modern Islamic thought lies in his comprehension of both traditional Islamic litera-ture and modern Western theories and in his strong belief in the compatibility of Islam with Western thought in matters concerning the system of government, human rights, and civil liberties.

Unlike other Islamic thinkers who espouse the democratic cause, Ghannushi is both a thinker and a leader of an Islamic move-ment. Perhaps this is one reason he has acquired acceptability within many Islamic circles at the global level. However, this may in some other respect be a source of vulnerability. His position as leader of the main opposition party in his country requires him to take certain political factors into consideration, and this in turn is bound to give an impression of an inconsistency in his discourse. As a political leader he has been, on more than an occasion, compelled to make compromises, the most notable of which was his decision to remove the reference to Islam from the name of his movement in order to qualify for registering as a legal political party and reversing the movement's position vis-à-vis the Tunisian Personal Status Code to which he was previously vehemently opposed.

Undoubtedly, Ghannushi's dual role as a political activist and a political thinker imposes a limitation on his mission as thinker engaged in the project of Islamic revival. On certain occasions Ghannushi speaks more as a politician while on others speaks more as a thinker employing a discourse that corresponds to the level and nature of his audience. Sometimes it is too sophisticated for an average Muslim to relate to. Sometimes it is more of political analysis than of philosophical argumentation. On occasions it may even be too populist.

Being a political leader can be a liability in addition to being a heavy burden. The events that led to his exile and the banning of his movement have cost Ghannushi some popularity among his own followers. Yet, he never hesitated to take the blame for his movement's failures, an attitude that is rare among Arab opposition leaders. He regretted trusting President Ben Ali, who upon coming to power promised to start a new democratic era of freedom and power sharing that turned to be a despotic era of oppression and persecution. While some disgruntled and former members of the movement charge that Ghannushi was not qualified as political leader, he continued to be democratically elected as leader of Ennahda.

As a thinker and political leader, Ghannushi's primary concern has been to see the restoration of just and good governance to his own country Tunisia as well as Muslim lands. He has advocated democracy as the best means of achieving this objective, arguing within Islamic circles that the difficulty to extrude, completely, democratic procedures and mechanisms from their liberal philosophical packaging should not be an excuse for Muslims to deprive themselves of the opportunity to get rid of the authoritarian regimes that burdened them and hampered their progress for many decades.

In pursuit of political reform Ghannushi has followed the footsteps of nineteenth- and twentieth-century reformists such as Rifa'a al-Tahtawi (1801–1873), Khayr al-Din al-Tunsi (1810–1899), Jamal al-Din al-Afghani (1838–1897), Muhammad ʿAbduh (1849–1905), Abd al-Rahman al-Kawakibi (1849–1903), Muhammad Rashid Rida (1865–1935), al-Tahir al-Haddad (1899–1935), Muhammad Iqbal (1877–1938), and Malik Bennabi (1905–1973), building on their achievements and learning from their experiences. Like most of these reformers, he has tried to assimilate specific Western concepts and ideas, incorporating them into the Islamic discourse on reform and revival. His objective, like theirs, has been the accomplishment of an Islamic renaissance that is founded in Islamic values and capable of benefiting, at the same time, from the positive aspects of Western modernity.

While a firm believer that Divine Revelation for Muslims is the ultimate frame of reference, Ghannushi sees in Western modernity positive aspects that are not only of great benefit but may also be indispensable for a modern Islamic revival.

Ghannushi remains a very important and influential Islamic thinker whose contribution to Islamic political thought will undoubtedly be remembered by future generations and reflected upon by posterity just as he himself used to reflect upon the contributions of great men such as al-Tunisi, Afghani, Iqbal, and Bennabi.

GHANNUSHI'S PUBLISHED BOOKS IN CHRONOLOGICAL ORDER

Tariquna Ila al-Hadara, al-Maʿrifa Publications, Tunis, 1975.

Al-Haraka al-Islamiya wa al-Tahdith, Dar al-Jeel, Beirut, 1980.

Maqalat [Articles], a collection of Ghannushi's articles, Dar al-Karawan, Paris, 1984.

Huquq al-Muwatanah, Huquq Ghayr al-Muslim fi al-Mujtamaʿ al-Islami, The International Institute of Islamic Thought, Virginia, 1993. (First published in Tunisia in 1989.)

Al-Qadar ʿInda Ibn Taymiyah, Halq al-Wadi, Tunis, 1989.

The Right to Nationality Status of Non-Muslim Citizens in a Muslim Nation. Translated by M. A. al-Iryan, Islamic Foundation of America, 1990.

Min al-Fikr al-Islami fiTunis [From the Islamic Thought], Dar- al-Qalam, Kuwait, 1992 (two volumes).

Al-Mar'ah al-Muslimah fi Tunis Bayna Tawjihat al-Qur'an wa Waqi' al-Mujtama' al-Tunisi, Dar al-Qalam, Kuwait, 1993.

Al-Hurriyat al-'Amma fi al-Dawla Al-Islamiyya [Public Liberties in the Islamic State], Markaz Dirasat al-Wihda al-'Arabiyah, Beirut, 1993.

Al-Mabadi al-Asasiya li al-Dimuqratiya wa-Usul al-Hukm al-Islami [The Basic Principles of Democracy and the Fundamentals of Islamic Governance], Al-Furqan Publications, Casablanca, 1994.

Muqarabat fi al-'Ilmaniyyah' wa al-Mujtama' al-Madani [Approaches to Secularism and Civil Society], Maghreb Center for Researches & Translation, London, 1999.

Al-Harakah al-Islamiyyah wa Mas'alat al-Taghyir [The Islamic Movement and the Question of Change], Maghreb Center for Researches & Translation, London, 2000.

OTHER ENGLISH BIBLIOGRAPHY

F. Burgat and W. Dowell, *The Islamic Movement in North Africa*, Austin, TX: University of Texas Press, 1993.

J. Davis, *Between Jihad and Salaam: Profiles in Islam*, New York: St. Martin's Press, 1997.

M. Dunn, "The Al-Nahda Movement in Tunisia: From Renaissance to Revolution," in *Islamism and Secularism in North Africa*, ed. John Rudy, London: Macmillan, 1994.

A. El-Affendi, "The Long March Forward," in *The Inquiry*, October 1987.

K. Elgindy, "The Rhetoric of Rachid Ghannouchi," *Arab Studies Journal*, Spring 1995.

M. Hamdi, *An Analysis of the History and Discourse of the Tunisian Islamic Movement al-Nahda—A Case Study of the Politicization of Islam*, Ph.D. dissertation, School of Oriental and African Studies, University of London, July 1996.

E. Hermassi, "The Islamicist Movement and November 7" in *Tunisia: The Political Economy of Reform*, ed. I. William Zartman, Lynne Rienner, London, 1991.

N. Hicks, *Promise Unfulfilled: Human Rights in Tunisia Since 1987*, The Lawyers Committee for Human Rights, New York, October 1993.

L. Jones, "Portrait of Rachid al-Ghannouchi" *Middle East Report*, July–August 1988.

D. Magnuson, "Islamic Reform in Contemporary Tunisia: Unity and Diversity" in *Tunisia: the Political Economy of Reform*, ed. I. William Zartman, Lynne Rienner, London, 1991.

A. Zghal, "The New Strategy of the Movement of the Islamic Way: Manipulation or Expression of Political Culture?" in *Tunisa: the Political Economy of Reform*, ed. I. William Zartman, London: Lynne Rienner, 1991.

Chapter 8

Yusuf Al-Qaradawi

BETTINA GRÄF

EGYPTIAN SCHOLAR AND ACTIVIST

THE Egyptian-born Yusuf al-Qaradawi is one of the most popular and at the same time highly controversial religious scholars in today's Sunni Islam. He was born in 1926 in the village of Saft al-Turab in the Nile Delta into a rural family of modest means.[1] His father died when he was two years old. He was then raised in his mother's family, who were fruit merchants. He received his primary education in a Qur'anic school (*kuttab*) and memorized the Qur'an at the age of ten. In 1939 he entered an Azhari school in Tanta, a commercial and industrial center in the Egyptian province Gharbiyya, and subsequently went to study at Azhar University in Cairo in 1949. Al-Qaradawi first enrolled in the Faculty of Theology (*usul al-din*) and later transferred to the Arab Language Faculty. He graduated in 1953 as the top student in his class.

Al-Qaradawi got involved in politics at an early age. He was in his teens when he became an admirer of Hassan al-Banna, the founder of the Egyptian Muslim Brothers, after listening to his speeches during the 1940s. In 1942–1943 al-Qaradawi became a member of the Brothers himself. Founded in 1928, the Muslim Brothers advocated an Islamic set of rules in all spheres of life and fought against the appropriation of Egypt by the British colonialists. In the years preceding the Egyptian revolution of 1952 al-Qaradawi took part in student strikes and demonstrations against the British protectoral power. He traveled to Upper Egypt, Syria, Jordan, and Palestine on behalf of the Brothers. In addition he became committed to the modernization of al-Azhar, advocating, among other things, the introduction of English into the curriculum and the admission of female students. During those days, he received the unfailing support of his mentor, the Muslim Brother and Azhar scholar Muhammad al-Ghazali (1909–1996).[2]

Al-Qaradawi was arrested after Hassan al-Banna's assassination in 1949. In 1954, under the Nasser administration, he was twice interned in the military prison of Cairo, along with thousands of fellow Muslim Brothers; and the Brothers were again banned, this time for good, although they continued to exist. Following his release from prison in 1956, al-Qaradawi resumed his studies but not his involvement with the Muslim Brothers. He was officially banned from preaching and teaching in public. Part-time employment at the Ministry of Awqaf and giving private lessons enabled him to make his living.

Before entering al-Azhar in 1957 to undertake further studies, he spent one year at the Department of Arabic Language and Literature at the Arab League's Institute of Higher Studies. For a short period in 1957 he was even allowed to preach at the Zamalek mosque. He passed the qualifying examination at al-Azahr's Faculty of *Usul al-Din* and decided to specialize in Qur'an exegesis and *Hadith*. A year later he started working in the Department of Culture at al-Azhar University. Departmental director Muhammad al-Bahy and the grand imam (Shaykh al-Azhar), reformist scholar Mahmud Shaltut, both encouraged al-Qaradawi to compose his first and most influential book to date, *The Lawful and the Prohibited in Islam*, which was published in 1960. Shortly afterward, in 1961, al-Qaradawi applied for a position at one of al-Azhar's institutes abroad. He left Egypt and went to Qatar, where he was sent to direct a newly established institute of religious studies in Doha. He taught the son of the emir in Ramadan, Shaykh Khalifa b. Hamad Al Thani, who would later become the emir of Qatar (1972–1995). When the Egyptian authorities refused to extend al-Qaradawi's stay in Qatar, the emir offered him a permanent position and a Qatari passport.[3]

Qatar has been an important location for al-Qaradawi in many respects. First, this is where he lived for nearly two-thirds of his life and where his children were born and went to school (although they later left Qatar and went to study in Europe and the United States).[4] Second, upon arriving in Doha he immediately began to preach and give religious instruction during Ramadan. He was also instrumental in shaping the religious education system in Doha, which used to be part of the same Wahhabi and Hanbali branch of Islam as neighboring Saudi Arabia. Third, with the help of his Qatari passport he was able to cross national borders without difficulties.[5] Fourth, he had the means and resources to invite fellow colleagues to Qatar and often played a key role in organizing meetings for scholars and activists, including Muslim Brothers from Egypt and beyond.[6] In comparison to Egypt, Qatar was a safe haven where one could meet and work without interference.

However, al-Qaradawi has never lost contact with Egypt. Ever since Anwar al-Sadat succeeded Nasser as president of the country in 1970, al-Qaradawi has been travelling to his home country regularly. In 1973 the Azhar University awarded him his doctoral degree for his thesis on almsgiving in Islam (*zakat*). In the same year he became director of the Department of Islamic Studies at the newly founded College of Education at Qatar University. This was transformed into the Shari'ah Faculty in 1977–1978, and he served as dean there for many years. He founded the Centre for Sunna and Sira Studies in 1980 as part of Qatar University. Most of his employees there later went to work for the newly established Internet portal IslamOnline.net.

Since the 1970s he has traveled widely throughout the Arab world, as well as to Europe, the United States, Canada, Australia, and Asia, including Japan. He has been invited to conferences to deliver lectures and give interviews. Since the first Islamic banks and investment companies were established in the early 1970s, he has served as consultant or as a member of the board of advisers.[7] He is an associate of major Islamic institutions such as the Board of Trustees of the International Islamic University in Islamabad (created in 1980), the Union des Organisations Islamiques de France (UOIF, founded in 1983), and the Oxford Centre for Islamic Studies (founded in 1985). He is also a member of the Islamic Fiqh Academy of the Muslim World League (founded in Mecca in 1962) and the Organization of the Islamic Conference (since 2011 the Organization of Islamic Cooperation, founded in Rabat in 1969).

After al-Qaradawi retired, he spent the academic year 1990/1991 in Algeria as chairman of the Higher Institutes of Islamic Studies. He never returned to al-Azhar nor did he go back to the Muslim Brothers although he was asked to become their supreme leader (*al-murshid al-'amm*) twice, the last time in 2002 after the death of Mustafa Mashhur. However, at the age of eighty-four he returned to lead the prayer at Tahrir Square in Cairo in February 2011 one week after Hosni Mubarak was swept away by the Egyptian revolution.

BOOKS AND SUBJECTS

To date Yusuf al-Qaradawi has written over 100 books—mostly paperback—and many journal articles. He addresses at least three different groups: scholars of Islamic jurisprudence, activists seeking the reform of contemporary society, and a wider public that goes beyond the circles of intellectuals and activists. He is involved in debates about Islamic jurisprudence (*fiqh*) and its conflicted relationship with social reality (*fiqh al-waqi'*), Islamic reformist thinking since the nineteenth century, and the so-called Islamic Awakening (*al-sahwa al-islamiyya*), which has evolved since the 1970s.[8] His main concerns are the economy in Islam, the role of women in society, education and the bringing up of children, art and entertainment, colonialism, the issue of Palestine, secularism, and minorities. This last addresses both the life of non-Muslims in Muslim societies and that of Muslims in non-Muslim societies (*fiqh al-aqalliyyat*).[9] In his published work he has dealt with notions of *tajdid* (renewal), *al-hall al-islami* (the Islamic solution), and *taysir* (ease), as well as the newly coined concepts of *wasatiyya* (moderation or the middle way) and *shumuliyya* (comprehensiveness).[10]

Besides *The Lawful and the Prohibited in Islam* (1960),[11] al-Qaradawi's best-known books include *The Islamic Awakening between Rejection and Extremism* (1982),[12] *Creative Legal Reasoning in the Present between Discipline and Detachment* (1994),[13] *Secular Extremism in Confrontation with Islam. The Examples of Turkey and Tunisia* (2001),[14] *Study in Maqasid al-Shari'a. Between Universal Intentions and Specific Texts* (2006).[15] Only *The Lawful and the Prohibited in Islam* and *The Islamic Awakening between Rejection and Extremism* are translated into English.[16] His dissertation *Fiqh al-Zakat* on alms in contemporary Islam, which does not address as wide a readership as his other books, was published in two volumes in 1971. Al-Qaradawi also writes poetry. But although he was raised in an environment where Sufi practices were usual, he was never attracted by Sufism or Sufis.[17]

His books are mostly composed as parts of various series, such as the Series toward an *Intellectual Unity for the Activists of Islam*,[18] which is a commentary on Hassan al-Banna's "Twenty Principles,"[19] or the one on *Ease in Islamic Jurisprudence for the Contemporary Muslim in the Light of Qur'an and Sunna*,[20] which brings together al-Qaradawi's books on contemporary Islamic religious practice. Another popular publication is the Series for the *Guidance of the Awakening*[21].

Al-Qaradawi's writings have developed over time and he has revised his opinion on certain topics, for example on the participation of women in social and political life,[22] on democracy and political pluralism,[23] and on the concept of *wasatiyya*.[24] These changes are best illustrated in his fatwa collections, which are his only hardcover publications.[25] They have been published so far in four volumes by the publishing house Dar al-Qalam in Kuwait (1979, 1993, 2003, and 2009) with many reprints, including those by other publishers.

Al-Qaradawi's self-definition as a scholar and activist as well as details of his life and thoughts can be found in his memoirs, *Son of the Village and the Kuttab: Characteristics of the Trajectory*, four volumes of which have been published so far.[26]

CALL FOR THE COLLECTIVE AWAKENING OF ARAB–ISLAMIC IDENTITY

Yusuf al-Qaradawi is considered to be intellectually independent of the major Islamic institutions, which in the last century mainly served national interests, as is the case with al-Azhar in Egypt.[27] His work takes up the ideas of the early twentieth-century Islamic reformers. In contrast to those scholars, however, al-Qaradawi does not base his thoughts on the adaptation of Islam to modern requirements. His goal is to develop Islamic answers to the questions of the era. What lies behind this is the notion of an Islamization of modernity and the attempt to give the modern age an Islamic face. Since the 1970s he has applied himself to the so-called Islamic Awakening project (*al-sahwa al-islamiyya*). As a consequence of a new religiosity among the population after Nasser's socialist experiment failed, including the—in the eyes of many—disastrous defeat in the Six Day War in 1967 (*naksa*), Islamic scholars and intellectuals began to push for Islamic renewal in both Egypt and other societies. Al-Qaradawi is regarded to this day as one of the leading minds of a transnational network of Islamic intellectuals pursuing similar goals in their respective nation-states. What they have in common beyond an interest in national affairs is a moral allegiance to the Islamic community (*umma*).[28] Just like al-Qaradawi, most of these intellectuals are close to the Muslim Brothers but without necessarily being organized into Islamic factions. These scholars and intellectuals communicate beyond national borders, for example, via journals, such as *al-Muslim al-Muʿasir, al-Umma, al-Ijtihad,* or *al-Manar al-Jadid.*

INSTITUTIONAL NETWORKING

Another way for those scholars and activists to communicate is via the International Union for Muslim Scholars (IUMS), founded in Dublin in 2004 with Yusuf al-Qaradawi as chairman. The intellectual Muhammad Salim al-ʿAwwa, the attorney for the Egyptian Wasat Party, became the secretary-general, with the former Mauritanian justice minister ʿAbdallah Bayn Bihi, the Shiite cleric

Ayatollah Muhammad ʿAli al-Taskhiri, and the Ibadite Shaykh Ahmad al-Khalili as his deputies. The union established its own website in Arabic, which puts out news as well as publishing studies and pronouncements.[29] IUMS describes itself as a nongovernmental body, whose objective is to establish a global Islamic authority (*al-marjiʿiyya al-islamiyya al-ʿalamiyya*). The main characteristics of IUMS are that it is Islamic (i.e., it represents all Islamic schools and groupings), global, people oriented, independent (i.e., it is not connected to governments or political parties), scientific (referring to ʿ*ilm*, i.e., a union of ʿ*ulama*'), missionary, and moderate. The union's basic principle is to apply a middle way for the Islamic community of the middle (*al-minhaj al-wasat li al-umma al-wasat*). The main points in the IUMS's founding declaration, which specifies the work of the union, are first the opposition to undemocratic ruling principles in Islamic countries and second the enforcement of equal legal and legislative rights for men and women.

In 1997, drawing on the American model, Yusuf al-Qaradawi, together with other scholars and intellectuals, founded the European Council for Fatwa and Research (ECFR, www.e-cfr.org), a body he also chairs, although he does not speak any European languages.[30] The questions of European Muslims, sent in by electronic or conventional mail, confront the scholars with the realities of life in Europe. The answers are for the most part pragmatic, mainly due to the fact that European legislation does not allow the fatwa council unlimited leeway. The ECFR scholars argue, for example, that Muslim girls in France should go to school without having to wear a headscarf, as the main concern there is their education. In spite of that, the headscarf ban imposed by the French government has been fiercely criticized.

The *fatawa* issued by the ECFR support the idea of making Muslims in Europe proper citizens. Participation in non-Muslim cultural practices may be allowed, but cultural assimilation is by and large rejected. The scholars' reasoning is based upon what is called the law for minorities (*fiqh al-aqalliyyat*).[31] According to al-Qaradawi there are several principles of legal decision making in the European context, the two most important being the understanding of the reality of daily life (*fiqh al-waqi'*) and the task of making life easy for Muslims and not difficult and full of interdictions (*fiqh al-taysir*). The favored method is called collective reasoning (*ijtihad jama'i*), because no single person may judge the complex social and political changes at work.

Two other recently established institutions connected to this transnational network of Muslim scholars and intellectuals around al-Qaradawi are the Wasatiyya Center in Kuwait, founded in 2006, and the recently founded Al-Qaradawi Center for Islamic Moderation and Renewal in Doha, which is part of the Qatar Foundation.[32]

ELECTRONIC NETWORKING

Yusuf al-Qaradawi is involved in print as well as electronic media production in the name of Islam, even though he lacks the technical skills to produce it himself. He has had a weekly program on Qatar TV since the launch of terrestrial television in Qatar in 1970, in which he answers letters sent in by viewers from the Gulf.[33] Since its inception, Qatar TV has consistently televised his Friday prayer at 'Umar b. al-Khattab Mosque in Doha. Since 1993 it has also broadcast via satellite and reaches a larger audience beyond the Gulf countries. A worldwide audience of millions has seen him on television since 1996 in the program *Shari'a and Life*–shown weekly on satellite channel Al Jazeera since 1996–during which he explains his interpretation of Islamic normativity in layman's terms.[34] In 1997 he was one of the first scholars to launch his own website in the Arabic language, Qaradawi.net. The Internet portal IslamOnline.net, which was founded in Doha and used to be the largest of its kind until it was split up in 2010, was also established with al-Qaradawi's support.[35] It has been online since 1999 in Arabic and English. The body behind the website is the Al-Balagh Cultural Society, which was established in 1997 on the initiative of the Qatari Maryam Hassan al-Hajari, a Information Technology (IT) student from the University of Qatar, and the Qatari Hamid al-Ansari, a religious scholar from the Shari`ah Faculty of the University of Qatar. In the beginning the project was supported and financed by the University of Qatar; later it was supported by donations and the merchandising of its own products. Its headquarters and IT development unit used to be based in Doha, while most of the content has been produced in its Cairo offices.[36] On its homepage al-Qaradawi wrote in missionary style: "It is our duty to acquaint all people in this world with our religion until they understand it, become interested in it, seek it and convert to it."

His extensive exposure in various types of media, which also includes numerous videos on YouTube, has assisted the fast and wide dissemination of his texts and *fatawa*. And it is in no small part due to this that he is the subject of controversial discussion. Web logs, or blogs, which first appeared around 2003, give an impression of how al-Qaradawi's arguments are received around the world. Here one can find both vehement adversaries and fervent supporters.[37]

RECEPTION

A lot of Muslim intellectuals hold him in high esteem for his ideas on the reform of Islamic jurisprudence. A voluminous Festschrift was given to him on the occasion of his seventieth birthday in

1996.[38] The authors are admirers of al-Qaradawi and most of them are themselves scholars, intellectuals, and activists, like the Egyptian jurist Tariq al-Bishri, the Tunisian philosopher Rashid al-Ghannushi, the Egyptian political scientist Hiba Ra'uf 'Izzat, and the Morrocan jurist Ahmad al-Raysuni. From this book one gets a picture of al-Qaradawi drawn by more than sixty friends and followers on various topics, ranging from portraits of al-Qaradawi as scholar (*'alim*), legal interpreter (*mujtahid*), jurist (*faqih*), or preacher (*da'i*) to texts on his jurisprudential methodologies, his commitment to Islamic banking, Islamic internationalism, or on the issue of Palestine.[39] This admiration is echoed by intellectuals in Europe and America. Tariq Ramadan, for example, quotes Yusuf al-Qaradawi extensively.[40]

In the political field, the scholar occupies, to some degree, the role of a diplomat or ambassador in the dialogue between European politicians and so-called moderate Islamists. Both Ken Livingstone, London's former mayor, and French foreign minister Michel Barnier expressed their thanks in letters to al-Qaradawi as a result of his explicit condemnation of hostage takings and attacks by radicals in 2005.[41] Recently, Efraim Halevy, former head of Mossad, the Israeli secret service, even asked Prime Minister Benjamin Netanyahu to negotiate with al-Qaradawi.[42]

The general public, including many Muslims in Europe, revere him as a scholar who does not shy away from contemporary questions. Due to his unmistakable opposition to neoliberal politics he has also become a conciliatory figure for many nonactivist Muslims. But he has many opponents too. These include, on the one hand, people with a left-wing and/or secular orientation who are concerned about the authority of the clerics and Islam in general becoming too pronounced.[43] On the other hand, al-Qaradawi is criticized by Salafi-oriented authors, in whose eyes he is too permissive.[44] From time to time his fatwas also cause tensions with the religious establishments in Egypt or Saudi Arabia, as was the case when he declared his approval of Palestinian suicide attacks[45] or recently when he called for the killing of Mu'ammar al-Ghaddafi in February 2011 via Al Jazeera.

Among academic researchers he is viewed as a reformer of Islamic jurisprudence and one of the leading figures in the Islamic movement.[46] He is also referred to as being at the forefront of a group of "superstar" religious scholars and a spokesperson of contemporary global Islamic discourse.[47] Some label him as an advocate of liberal Islam[48] but this notion is refuted by others: he may be regarded as moderate in comparison to radicals but this is by no means tantamount to his being a liberal.[49]

RENEWAL OF ISLAMIC JURISPRUDENCE (*TAJDID AL-FIQH*)

Al-Qaradawi defines the renewal of *fiqh* as one of the cornerstones of his method.[50] The emphasis on renewal was also a prominent part of wider intellectual debates about the relationship between tradition (*taqlid*), authenticity (*asala*), and contemporary Islam (*al-islam al-mu'asir*) in the last quarter of the twentieth century. These debates are closely related to the discussions about reform (*islah*) that took place at the end of the nineteenth century and the beginning of the twentieth century in the Arab regions and in Asia.

Supported by the readings of legal expert 'Abd al-Razzaq al-Sanhuri (1895–1971), al-Qaradawi distinguishes his approach from the notions of positive law upheld by Western societies, be they socialist or liberal capitalist. He is interested in the subject because of his conviction that a modern interpretation of *shari'a* is not possible without a profound knowledge of its foundational texts and traditions of interpretation.[51] Proper renewal (*al-tajdid al-haqq*) means a development from within (*tanmiyat al-fiqh al-islami min dakhilihi*).[52] However, it is, according to him, a basic principle that there should be no renewal of those parts of *fiqh* that are regarded as fixed (*thawabit*). This includes all rules that are clearly written in the *Qur'an*, for example, the five pillars of Islam or the laws governing inheritance and marriage. It includes further matters that *shari'a* provides clear rulings on, such as the prohibition of alcohol, pork, and usury.

All other parts of *shari'a*, which are considered flexible (*al-muruna*), that is, which do not explicitly contain positive rulings or interdictions, can and should be interpreted with regard to the relevant contemporary questions. Based on this he suggests a program of renewal for *fiqh* in seven steps. He calls for:

1. the systematization of the principles of Islamic jurisprudence (tanzir al-fiqh al-islami).

2. the undertaking of comparative studies (al-dirasat al-muqarana).

3. the creative interpretation of the sources (ijtihad). Here he suggests a reassessment of the different classical methods of consensus (ijma'), analogical reasoning (qiyas), courteous action (istihsan), and consideration of the public good (istislah).[53] Furthermore ijtihad should be accomplished collectively (ijtihad jama'i).[54]

4. the codification of fiqh (taqnin al-fiqh).

5. the compilation of an updated encyclopedia of fiqh (al-mawsu'a al-fiqhiyya al-'asriyya).

6. the production of scientific editions of legal literature (ikhraj 'ilmi l-kutub al-fiqh).

7. the publication of the old handwritten manuscripts (nashr al-makhtutat al-fiqhiyya).

Al-Qaradawi lays strong emphasis on the significance of the classical legal texts. This is due to the fact that legal and religious scholars have been under attack from intellectuals and activists since the 1950s.[55] He is convinced that in order to reform society a reinvigoration of their position and their methods is needed.[56]

MODERATION

Yusuf al-Qaradawi describes his doctrine as the school of the middle way (*wasatiyya*).[57] Based on the phrase *"ummatan wasatan"* from the Qur'an 2/143 ("a justly balanced community" or "a community of the middle" according to different translators), al-Qaradawi argues in favor of an even-handed approach in the implementation of Islamic jurisprudence by legal scholars. The term *wasatiyya* is given various similar descriptions in al-Qaradawi's texts: it is not merely a characteristic of *fiqh* but the nature of Islam, the soul of Islam, one of the general qualities of Islam, the strongest course within the Islamic awakening movement, al-Qaradawi's method and the outstanding characteristic of the Islamic community. First, on the functional level, *wasatiyya* represents a dissociation from both too rigid (i.e., literal) and too free (i.e., oriented to the public interest) interpretations of *fiqh*.[58] Second, in the political field, it stands for the introduction of Islam as a social system that presents an alternative to liberal capitalist and socialist systems. Third, within the realm of Egyptian politics (and Arab politics as a whole), it implies a dissociation from both secular and militant Islamic tendencies and seems to offer a way out of political crisis. Fourth, in the religious sphere, it serves to give Islam a special status when compared to other religions (especially Judaism and

Christianity). And fifth, it functions as a counterbalance to terms like radical Islam.

USE OF VIOLENCE AS POLITICAL MEANS

Al-Qaradawi rejects violence as a means of changing society, except when it comes to defending the "most sacred things of Islam." In his opinion, one of these things is Palestine. In the context of the second Intifada in 2001 he expressly endorsed suicide attacks carried out by Palestinians.[59] However, he does not term these as such, since suicide is forbidden in the Qur'an, but refers to them rather as acts of martyrdom. In his view, Palestinians had no other option than to use their bodies as deadly weapons in order to preserve unhindered access to their sacred sites and to demand a just division of the country.[60] Moreover, even though women and children were among the victims of suicide bombings in Israel, he defended these acts, arguing that Israeli society is a society of soldiers. Since everyone could potentially be drafted for military service, there are no civilians in Israel according to al-Qaradawi. This proclamation led the US authorities to revoke al-Qaradawi's entry visa to the United States and deny him entry into the country pending further notice.

Other suicide attacks with an Islamic identification have been condemned by al-Qaradawi, including the attacks of 9/11 and the ones in Madrid in 2004, as well as the suicide missions in Iraq, London, Mumbai, Sharm el-Sheikh, and Turkey in the following years. Following the London bombings he reaffirmed that civilians (a term which, in his words, along with women, children, and the elderly, also covers journalists and aid organization workers) should under no circumstances be involved in armed conflicts.[61]

GENDER RELATIONS

In his writings, al-Qaradawi advocates living according to Islam with the aim of introducing a contemporary Islam into everyday life. Since the 1990s al-Qaradawi has been speaking out in favor of legal equivalence for men and women, based on the Qur'an 9:71.[62] Here, the appeal is directed at both sexes, in the belief that men and women are allies, consult with and protect one another, observe the prayers, give *zakat*, and obey God. Accordingly, he concludes, every verse in the Qur'an applies equally to both women and men, except in passages where one of the two genders is specifically addressed. Measured against the standards of liberal democracies, this interpretation can scarcely be considered emancipated, especially in light of the fact that on important issues, such as inheritance laws, men and women are clearly treated unequally.

However, as a legal reformer, al-Qaradawi sees it as his duty to interpret the existing texts of the Qur'an and Sunna, rather than to invent completely new rules. As long as he is acting within the framework of Islamic jurisprudence, he consciously binds himself to certain principles, as in the case of gender equality. Yet, what he offers is the development of a flexible Islamic doctrine that is oriented to the lives of Muslims. This means that scholars, and he insists that it should be scholars, along with knowing the Qur'an and its legal interpretations, must also study modern life, for example by seeking a dialogue with the general public instead of treating its members as ignorant and infidels, as radical interpreters do.[63] As he wrote in the periodical *al-Manar al-Jadid* in 1998, "The doctrine must be adapted when the time, the place and the circumstances of the people change."[64]

DEMOCRACY AND PLURALISM

In the late 1980s, Yusuf al-Qaradawi as well as other activists and intellectuals started to concern themselves with terms such as democracy, the constitution, and party pluralism.[65] Rather than strictly rejecting these terms, they are taken up, adapted, and equated with legal structures and forms of government existing in the Islamic tradition, thus constructing an Islamic form of democracy.[66] Al-Qaradawi sees, for example, the parliament as the legitimate arena for legislation and as an effective means of controlling rulers, an opinion that puts him in opposition to Qutb or Mawdudi who were against a legislative assembly.[67] Islamic scholars nevertheless occupy a central position in al-Qaradawi's envisioned system, as they control those in power, while also offering their advice to the population.

This issue is of vital importance to him, yet it also reveals the challenges to his democratic models, for if the guardians of religious books can decide on what is allowed or prohibited in a society, the freedoms of thought, opinion, and religion are possibly at risk, even when he is proposing a position in the middle (*wasati*).[68]

His commitment to democracy may therefore turn out to be less robust than his rhetoric sometimes suggests. A telling example of this is his view on pluralism (*ikhtilaf*). He distinguishes between two types of disagreement, the one offering alternatives and the other constituting opposition or contradiction. This latter form is forbidden, which means that, in al-Qaradawi's view, disagreement is only possible between otherwise like-minded people and is not meant as a contest between people with different worldviews as in the idealized liberal understanding of democracy.

CONCLUSION

In many respects, Yusuf al-Qaradawi is a key figure in helping us to understand contemporary Islamic discourse. Born in the mid-1920s, he acts as a link between the early publicists and reformers of Islamic thinking at the beginning of the twentieth century and today's Sunni Islamic intellectuals and activists.

At the beginning of his career al-Qaradawi was, like many of his contemporaries, involved in the anticolonial struggle against the British in the Arab regions. Since the official end of colonialism he has grappled with other adversaries: Salafism and secularism. Subscribing to the notion of *wasatiyya* he has occupied a position between these two poles; he neither advocates literal interpretations of the holy sources as Salafis do nor does he authorize the neglect of religion (*din*) in the course of modernization. The Gulf region and Europe play an important role in this regard, because each represents for al-Qaradawi one side of the two extremes that he struggles with. Another struggle al-Qaradawi undertakes is against the instrumentalization of Islam by different nation-states and he also writes in condemnation of the religious extremism in Egypt and elsewhere.

Al-Qaradawi thinks of the renewal of Islamic jurisprudence (*tajdid al-fiqh*) as the best means available to confront all these different challenges. Several principles of legal decision making are relevant in this context, the two most important being the understanding of the local reality of daily life (*fiqh al-waqi'*) and the task of making life easy for Muslims and not difficult and full of interdictions (*yusr la 'usr*). In addition, he pleads for close cooperation between the different denominations of Islam.

Al-Qaradawi sees himself as independent from the institutions of any nation-state and from political parties although one can doubt his independency from the state of Qatar due to his manifold entanglements with its ruling family. Nevertheless he does not use only the exclusive forms of scholarly communication, such as giving sermons in the mosque, issuing fatwas face-to-face and teaching, but also various kinds of mass media for the dissemination of his message and for networking. Al-Qaradawi is one of the scholars who publicly brought Islamic legal discourse into focus. He is always openly involved in discussions and uses global electronic mediascapes, although he and his assistants sometimes underestimate their peculiar dynamics, as for example during the second Intifada when he legitimized Palestinian suicide attacks in various media.

Al-Qaradawi is a co-founder of different independent organizations that are distinct because of their translocal and global orientation. He seems to have understood at an early stage that belonging to Islam under modern conditions can only be defined by faith and not by territory. His mission therefore is to strengthen the de-territorialized global Islamic community. Meanwhile he has become his own best role model for the kind of position scholars should hold in today's society: as teacher, preacher, counselor, monitor, and admonisher.

NOTES

1. For an excellent account of al-Qaradawi's life (based on his memoirs *Ibn al-qarya wa-l-kuttab*, 2002, 2004, 2006), see Gudrun Krämer 2006, 184–200. Further information can be found in Wenzel-Teuber 2005, 35–47 and Gräf and Skovgaard-Petersen 2009, 1–12.
2. Muhammad al-Ghazali was expelled from the Muslim Brothers in 1953; see Krämer 2006, 196 and al-Qaradawi 2000.
3. al-Qaradawi, 2004, 172f.
4. In 1958 al-Qaradawi was married; he has seven children by his first wife.
5. al-Qaradawi, 2004, 271.

6. al-Ansari, 2001, 401–438.

7. Cf. Krämer 2006, 191 and Tammam 2009, 67. See also Mariani 2003.

8. Cf. Salvatore 1997 and Zaman 2004 and 2006.

9. Cf. Caeiro 2010.

10. For commentary on the term *taysir* see Krämer 2006 and Gräf 2010; for *tajdid* and *wasatiyya* Baker 2003; for *shumuliyya* al-Qaradawi 1991 and al-Khateeb 2009b.

11. *al-Halal wa-l-haram fi l-islam*, 1960.

12. *al-Sahwa al-islamiyya bayna l-jumud wa-l-tatarruf*, 1982.

13. *al-Ijtihad al-muʿasir bayna l-indibat wa-l-infirat*, 1994.

14. *al-Tatarruf al-ʿilmani fi mawajahat al-islam. numudhaj Turkiya wa-Tunis*, 2001. See also Masud 2005 and Larrson 2010.

15. *Dirasa fi fiqh maqasid al-shariʿa. bayna l-maqasid al-kulliyya wa-l-nusus al-juz'iyya*, 2006.

16. *The Lawful and the Prohibited in Islam* has been translated into many languages.

17. Though he was inspired by Muhammad al-Ghazali's book *Ihya' ʿulum al-din*, cf. Krämer 2006, 185.

18. *Silsilat nahwa wahda fikriyya li-ʿamaliyyin li-l-islam*.

19. Cf. Zaman 2004, 134. Euben and Zaman calls it an "extraordinary series of books.…In its focus not on the Islamic foundational texts but rather on the work of an Islamist founding father, there are no parallels to this work in Islamist literature." Euben and Zaman 2009, 224 Fn 1.

20. *Silsilat taysir al-fiqh li-l-muslim al-muʿasir fi daw' al-qur'an wa-l-sunna*.

21. *Silsilat rasa'il tarshid al-sahwa;* see also Gräf 2010.

22. See Stowasser 2001 and 2009.

23. Cf. Euben and Zaman 2009.

24. Cf. Gräf 2009.

25. *Min hady al-islam. fatawa muʿasira* (From Guidance for Islam. Contemporary Fatwas), 1979, 1993, 2003, and 2009.

26. *Ibn al-qarya wa-l-kuttab. malamih sira wa-masira*, 2002, 2004, 2006, and 2012.

27. Cf. Salvatore 1997 and Skovgaard-Petersen 2009.

28. Cf. Nafi 2004, al-Khateeb 2009a, and Euben and Zaman, who state that allegiance to the Islamic community has since 1924 been defined not by territory but by faith; Euben and Zaman 2009, 54.

29. http://www.iumsonline.net/ar, cf. Gräf 2005.

30. Cf. Caeiro 2010.

31. See al-Qaradawi 2001; for an analysis and translation into German, see Schlabach 2009.

32. Qatar Foundation is a large organization that was founded in 1995 in Doha as an NGO by the wife of the Emir of Qatar. It has established branch campuses of eight international universities at its Education City. Qatar Foundation's general tendency for international exercise of influence became visible to a wider public when it announced the shirt sponsorship deal over five years with FC Barcelona

in 2010, http://news.bbc.co.uk/sport2/hi/football/europe/9276343.stm, accessed May 13, 2013.

33. Cf. al-Qaradawi 2006, 240.

34. Cf. Galal 2009.

35. Cf. Gräf 2010.

36. Today the Cairo part has its own site called OnIslam.net; cf. Abdel-Fadil 2010.

37. See, for example, http://en.wordpress.com/tag/yusuf-al-qaradawi.

38. It was published as a book in 2003 by the publishing house *Dar al-Salam* in Cairo: *Yusuf al-Qaradawi. kalimat fi takrimihi wa-buhuth fi fikrihi wa-fiqhihi muhdat ilayhi bi-munasabat bulughihi as-sab'in.*

39. See also Talima 2001.

40. Cf. Ramadan 2004. See also Larsson 2010.

41. Cf. Greater London Authority 2005.

42. According to news printed in *al-Yawm al-Sabi'* newspaper after al-Qaradawi preached at Tahrir Square on February 24, 2011, available at: http://www.youm7.com/News.asp?NewsID=357624. See also the commentary by editor-in-chief of *Asharq Alawsat* Tariq Alhomayed, published on February 26, 2011: http://www.asharq-e.com/news.asp?section=2&id=24305.

43. In 2005 'Abd al-Razzaq 'Id published a critical monograph on al-Qaradawi, in which he tried to make sense of his arguments from his own secular perspective. In doing so, he aligned himself with the French intellectual and specialist in Islamic studies Muhammad Arkoun; cf. Gräf 2009; see also Helfont 2009.

44. As early as 1976 Salih al-Fawzan, a well-known author from Saudi Arabia, wrote a commentary on al-Qaradawi's first and most famous publication from 1960. Al-Fawzan does not agree with al-Qaradawi's details and comments and offers his own more severe interpretations. Two other, more recent publications by authors who can be described as Salafi are in line with this argumentation, Sulayman Ibn Salih al-Harashi 1999 and Ibrahim 'Abduh al-Shafrawi 2001.

45. Euben and Zaman talks about al-Qaradawi's "significant ambiguities." Euben and Zaman 2009, 227. Cf. also Hamzah 2005 and Gräf 2010.

46. Cf. Salvatore 1997 and Nafi 2004.

47. Cf. Mandaville 2007 and Zayid 2007.

48. Kurzmann 1998.

49. Krämer 2006. Zaman speaks of a general hostility of *'ulama'* to liberal conceptions of civil society; cf. Zaman 2004, 131, see also Hallaq 2012.

50. Al-Qaradawi 1986. Cf. Baker 2003, Wenzel-Teuber 2005, and Gräf 2010.

51. Cf. Zaman 2004.

52. Cf. Gräf 2010, based on al-Qaradawi 1973 and 1986.

53. Cf. Zaman's discussion of the controversial notion of the common good (*maslaha*) in al-Qaradawi's writings; Zaman 2004, 134f.

54. Cf. also Nafi 2004.

55. Cf. Krämer 1999, 274 and Zaman 2004, 129.

56. See also Zaman 2002.

57. Cf. Gräf 2009.

58. Cf. also Zaman 2004, 136 and 145.

59. Euben and Zaman 2009, 227.

60. In al-Qaradawi's words the new weapons of "those deemed weak," a Qur'anic expression; cf. Euben and Zaman 2009, 227.

61. Al-Qaradawi, Bombing Innocents: IAMS's Statement: http://web.archive.org/web/20050729032302/http://www.islamonline.net/English/In_Depth/ViolenceCausesAlternatives/Articles/topic08/2005/07/01.shtml, accessed January 4, 2012.

62. Cf. Stowasser 2001, 2009 and Roald 2001.

63. Al-Qaradawi's severe criticism of Sayyid Qutb's latest texts can be placed in this context, cf. al-Qaradawi 1994.

64. Al-Qaradawi 1998, 6.

65. Al-Qaradawi has never outlined a state theory but sees his "al-Islam wa-l-dimuqratiyya," in *Min hady al-islam. fatawa mu'asira* [From Guidance for Islam. Contemporary Fatwas], vol. 2, 1993, 636–651, *Min fiqh al-dawla fi l-islam* [The Understanding of State in Islam] 1997, and *al-Din wa-l-dawla* [Religion and State] 2006; see Zaman 2004 and Euben and Zaman 2009.

66. Cf. Krämer 1999 and Euben and Zaman 2009.

67. Cf. Euben and Zaman 2009, 226f.

68. See Krämer's article on al-Qaradawi and apostasy, 2006.

REFERENCES

Abdel-Fadil, Mona. 2011. "The Islam-Online Crisis: A Battle of Wasatiyya vs. Salafi Ideologies?" *Online Journal of the Virtual Middle East*, available at: http://www.cyberorient.net/article.do?articleId=6239. Accessed May 13, 2013.

al-Ansari, Muhammad b. 'Abdallah. 2001. *Fadilat al-shaykh 'Abdallah al-Ansari. Waqi'a wa-l-ta'rikh*. Doha.

Baker, Raymond William. 2003. *Islam without Fear: Egypt and the New Islamists*, Cambridge MA: Harvard University Press.

Caeiro, Alexandre. 2010. "The Power of European Fatwas: The Minority Fiqh Project and the Making of an Islamic Counterpublic" *International Journal of Middle East Studies* 42, no. 3: 435–449.

Euben, Roxanne L., and Zaman, Muhammad Q., eds. 2009. *Princeton Readings in Islamist Thought: Texts and Contexts from al-Banna to Bin Laden*. Princeton: Princeton University Press.

al-Fawzan, Salih Ibn-Fawzan Ibn-ʿAbdallah. 1976. *al-Iʿlam bi-naqd kitab al-halal wa-l-haram*, Jamiʿat al-Imam Muhammad Ibn-Saʿud al-Islamiyya. Riad: al-Matabiʿ al-Ahliyya li-l-Uffsit.

Galal, Ehab. 2009. "Yusuf al-Qaradawi and the New Islamic TV." In Gräf, Bettina and Jakob Skovgaard-Petersen, eds., *The Global Mufti. The Phenomenon of Yusuf al-Qaradawi*, London: Hurst, 149–180.

Gräf, Bettina. 2005. "In Search of a Global Islamic Authority." *ISIM Review* 15: 47.

Gräf, Bettina, and Jacob Skovgaard-Petersen, eds. 2009. *The Global Mufti. The Phenomenon of Yusuf al-Qaradawi*. London: Hurst.

Gräf, Bettina. 2010. *Medien-Fatwas@Yusuf al-Qaradawi: Die Popularisierung des islamischen Rechts*. Berlin: Klaus Schwarz Verlag.

Greater London Authority (ed.). 2005. *Why the Mayor of London Will Maintain Dialogues with All of London's Faiths and Communities. A Reply to the Dossier against the Mayor's Meeting with Dr Yusuf al-Qaradawi*. London.

Hallaq, Wael B. 2012. *The Impossible State: Islam, Politics, and Modernity's Moral Predicament*, New York: Columbia University Press.

Hamzah, Dyala. 2005. "Is There an Arab Public Sphere? The Palestine Intifada, a Saudi Fatwa and the Egyptian Press." In Salvatore, Armando, and Mark Le Vine, eds., *Religion, Social Practice, and Contested Hegemonies. Reconstructing the Public Sphere in Muslim Majority Socities*, 181–206. New York: Palgrave.

al-Harashi, Sulayman Ibn-Salih. 1999. *al-Qaradawi fi l-mizan*. Riad: Dar al-Jawab.

Helfont, Samuel. 2009. *Yusuf al-Qaradawi: Islam and Modernity*. Tel Aviv: Moshe Dayan Center, Tel Aviv University.

ʿId, ʿAbd al-Razzaq. 2005. *Sadanat hayakil al-wahm, naqd al-ʿaql al-fiqhi: Yusuf al-Qaradawi bayna l-tasamuh wa-l-irhab*. Beirut: Dar al-Taliʿa.

al-Khateeb, Motaz. 2009a. *Yusuf al-Qaradawi faqih al-sahwa al-islamiyya: sira fikriyya tahliliyya*. Beirut: Markaz al-Hidara li-Tanmiyyat al-Fikr al-Islami.

al-Khateeb, Motaz. 2009b. "Yusuf al-Qaradawi as an Authoritative Reference." In Gräf, Bettina, and Jakob Skovgaard-Petersen, eds., *The Global Mufti. The Phenomenon of Yusuf al-Qaradawi*, 85–108. London: Hurst.

Krämer, Gudrun. 1999. *Gottes Staat als Republik. Reflexionen zeitgenössischer Muslime zu Islam, Menschenrechten und Demokratie*. Baden-Baden: Nomos.

Krämer, Gudrun. 2006. "Drawing Boundaries. Yusuf al-Qaradawi on Apostasy." In Sabine Schmidtke, ed., *Speaking for Islam. Religious Authorities in Muslim Societies*, 181–217. Leiden: Brill.

Kurzman, Charles. 1998. *Liberal Islam. A Sourcebook*, 196–204. New York: Oxford University Press.

Larrson, Gören. 2010. "Yusuf al-Qaradawi and Tariq Ramadan on Secularisation: Differences and Similarities." In Marranci, Gabriele, ed., *Muslim Societies and the Challenge of Secularization. An Interdisciplinary Approach*, 47–64. Heidelberg: Springer.

Mandaville, Peter. 2007. *Global Political Islam*. New York: Routledge.

Mariani, Ermete. 2003. "Youssef al-Qaradawi: pouvoir médiatique, économique et symbolique." In Mermier, Franck. éd., *Mondialisation et nouveaux médias dans l'espace arabe*, 35–45. Lyon: Maisonneuve et Larose.

Masud, Khalid M. 2005. "The Construction and Deconstruction of Secularism as an Ideology in Contemporary Muslim Thought." *Asian Journal of Social Science* 33, no. 3: 363–383.

Nafi, Basheer M. 2004. "Fatwa and War: On the Allegiance of the American Muslim Soldiers in the Aftermath of September 11." *Islamic Law and Society* 11, no. 1: 78–116.

al-Qaradawi, Yusuf. 1971. *Fiqh al-zakat. dirasa muqarana li-ahkamiha wa-falsafatiha fi dhaw' al-qur'an wa-s-sunna*. Beirut: Mu'assasat al-Risala.

al-Qaradawi, Yusuf. 1973. *Shariʿat al-islam saliha li-l-tatbiq fi kull al-zaman wa-l-makan*. Cairo: Dar al-Sahwa.

al-Qaradawi, Yusuf. 1986. *al-Fiqh al-islami bayna l-asala wa-l-tajdid*. Cairo: Maktaba Wahba.

al-Qaradawi, Yusuf. 1991. *Shumul al-islam*. Cairo: Maktaba Wahba.

al-Qaradawi, Yusuf. 1994. *al-Ijtihad al-muʿasir bayna l-indibat wa-l-infirat*. Beirut: Amman.

al-Qaradawi, Yusuf. 1998. "Fiqh al-waqiʿ wa-taghayyur al-fatwa." *al-Manar al-Jadid* 3: 6–15.

al-Qaradawi, Yusuf. 2000. *Shaykh Muhammad al-Ghazali kama ʿaraftuhu. rihlat nisf al-qarn*. Cairo: Dar al-Shuruq.

al-Qaradawi, Yusuf. 2001. *Fi fiqh al-aqalliyyat al-muslima. hayat al-muslimin wasat al-mujtamaʿat al-ukhra*. Cairo: Dar al-Shuruq.

al-Qaradawi, Yusuf. 2002, 2004, 2006. *Ibn al-qarya wa-l-kuttab. malamih sira wa-masira*. Cairo: Dar al-Shuruq.

Ramadan, Tariq. 2004. *Western Muslims and the Future of Islam*. Oxford: Oxford University Press.

Roald, Anne-Sofie. 2001. *Women in Islam. The Western Experience*. London: Routledge.

Salvatore, Armando. 1997. *Islam and the Political Discourse of Modernity*. Berkshire: Ithaca Press.

Schlabach, Jörg. 2009. *Scharia im Westen: Muslime unter nicht-islamischer Herrschaft und die Entwicklung eines muslimischen Minderheitenrechts für Europa*. Berlin: Lit-Verlag.

Skovgaard-Petersen, Jakob. 2009. "Yusuf al-Qaradawi and al-Azhar." In Gräf, Bettina, and Jakob Skovgaard-Petersen, eds., *The Global Mufti. The Phenomenon of Yusuf al-Qaradawi*, 27–54. London: Hurst.

Stowasser, Barbara Freyer. 2001. "'Old Shaykhs, Young Women', and the Internet: The Rewriting of Women's Political Rights in Islam." *The Muslim World* 91: 99–119.

Stowasser, Barbara Freyer. 2009. "Qaradawi On Women." In Gräf, Bettina, and Jakob Skovgaard-Petersen, eds., *The Global Mufti. The Phenomenon of Yusuf al-Qaradawi*, 181–212. London: Hurst.

Talima, 'Isam. 2001. *Yusuf al-Qaradawi: faqih al-du'at wa-da'iyat al-fuqaha'*. Damascus: Dar al-Qalam.

Tammam, Husam. 2009. "Yusuf al-Qaradawi and the Muslim Brothers. The Nature of a Special Relationship." In Gräf, Bettina, and Jakob Skovgaard-Petersen, eds., *Global Mufti. The Phenomenon of Yusuf al-Qaradawi*, 55–84. London: Hurst.

Wenzel-Teuber, Wendelin. 2005. *Islamische Ethik und moderne Gesellschaft im Islamismus von Yusuf al-Qaradawi*. Hamburg: Verlag Dr. Kovac.

2003. *Yusuf al-Qaradawi. kalimat fi takrimihi wa-buhuth fi fikrihi wa-fiqhihi muhdat ilayhi bi-munasabat bulughihi as-sab'in*. Cairo: Dar al-Salam.

Zayid, Ahmad. 2007. *Suwar min al-khitab al-dini al-mu'asir*. Cairo: Maktabat al-Usra.

Zaman, Muhammad Q. 2002. *The Ulama in Contemporary Islam. Custodians of Change*. Princeton: Princeton University Press.

Zaman, Muhammad Q. 2004. "The Ulama of Contemporary Islam and their Conception of the Common Good." In Salvatore, Armando, and Dale Eickelman, eds., *Public Islam and the Common Good*, 129–156. Leiden: Brill.

Zaman, Muhammad Q. 2006. "Consensus and Religious Authority in Modern Islam: The Discourse of the 'Ulama." In Krämer, Gudrun, and Sabine Schmidtke, eds., *Speaking for Islam: Religious Authorities in Muslim Societies*, 153–180. Leiden: Brill.

Chapter 9

Mohammad Khatami

MAHMOUD SADRI AND AHMAD SADRI

BIOGRAPHICAL SKETCH

SEYED MOHAMMAD KHATAMI was born October 14, 1943 to a notable clerical family in the central town of Ardakan in Yazd province and grew up with two brothers and four sisters. The designation "Seyed" signifies that his family is descended from the Prophet of Islam, which, in the Shi`a tradition, confers the black color to his turban. Mohammad Khatami's father, Rouhollah Khatami was an erudite and trusted local cleric who founded a seminary in Ardakan and served as the "imam of Friday prayer," the highest clerical position in town, immediately after the Islamic revolution of 1979. Mohammad completed his primary and secondary education in local schools while completing the introductory courses in religious studies in his father's seminary in town. In 1961 he entered the Qum seminary and in two stints over the course of a decade reached the highest level of studies, *Dars e Kharej* (postgraduate seminars for elite students preparing to become Muslim jurists), at which time he was both an advanced seminarian and a lecturer. In 1970 he entered the University of Isfahan and graduated with a BA in philosophy and later obtained an MA in education from the University of Tehran. While in Isfahan, Mr. Khatami met and collaborated on scholarly and political projects and in the context of the Islamic Student Association with Ahmad Khomeini and Mohammad Montazeri, sons of two of Iran's foremost clerical dissidents: Ayatollah Khomeini and Ayatollah Montazeri. These connections helped place Khatami in the leadership ranks during the first years of the Islamic revolution. Mr. Khatami was later affiliated with "Tarbiat Modarres" University as a lecturer. His chosen field of study at this time was political philosophy. In these years he published a book on the Islamic political philosopher, Al Farabi. In 1974, Mohammad Khatami married Zohreh Sadeghi, a niece of the legendary leader of the Lebanese Shi`a community, Imam Mousa Sadr. They have two daughters and a son together.[1]

THE REVOLUTIONARY YEARS

Given his intellectual and spiritual upbringing and his training both in the seminary and in modern educational institutions, one would have expected Khatami to emerge as a reform-minded cleric and a professor of humanities had the revolution not happened. Even with all his preoccupations, Khatami has managed to teach a number of courses in Iranian universities and to publish twenty-one books, by the last count, during the past three decades. This oeuvre includes, of course, several compendiums of his speeches and articles but there are volumes, also, on political philosophy, democracy and dictatorship, dialogue of civilizations, and civil society. Four of his books are available in English.[2]

One year before the revolution, Khatami briefly replaced Mr. Beheshti, an astute cleric at the helm of Iran's impending revolution, as the director of Islamic Center in Hamburg, allowing Beheshti to return to Iran and pursue his revolutionary agenda as a trusted lieutenant of Ayatollah Khomeini. Upon his return to Iran, Mr. Khatami won a seat in Iran's first postrevolutionary parliament as a representative of his region, Ardakan and Meybod, from 1980 to 1982. During this period, Khatami was also appointed as the head of Iran's semiofficial popular daily, *Keyhan*, by Ayatollah Khomeini.

Mr. Khatami's first prominent governmental position came in 1982, when he was appointed the minister of culture and Islamic guidance by Prime Minister Mirhossein Mousavi. At the same time, he was given major responsibilities in Iran's war effort against Iraq, as the head of the joint command of the armed forces and the director of Iran's War Propaganda Headquarters. Khatami's reputation and immaculate record of service within the ranks of Iran's revolutionary elites led to a second ministerial appointment in the government of President Ali Akbar Hashemi Rafsanjani in 1989. This was the post that Khatami resigned in 1992 to protest his frustrated attempts to grant the printed media greater freedoms. Khatami did not leave stealthily. In addition to a detailed and strongly worded letter of resignation in which he assailed the organized opposition of the "regressive and reactionary" elements against his reforms, he orchestrated a highly visible and well attended public appreciation/farewell event in Tehran's opera house ("Talar e Vahdat"), in which representatives of politicians, artists, university professors, clergy, students, and politicians praised him for his intellectual integrity and liberal temperament.[3] The next five years mark a hiatus in Khatami's career during which he held the posts of advisor to President Rafsanjani and director of the National Library. He was also a member of Iran's High Council of Cultural Revolution, which was charged with revising the curriculum of Iran's institutions of high learning. At this time it appeared that Khatami's political career was winding down. His new position at the margins of the Tehran's political scene was a virtual retirement job.

KHATAMI'S RISE AS THE POLITICAL FACE OF THE REFORM MOVEMENT

In retrospect, Khatami's resignation from his ministerial position over his liberal convictions helped him emerge as the presidential candidate for the nascent reform movement that took Iran's 1997 presidential elections by storm. To the surprise of everyone, including the reformist leaders, Khatami handily won the election by a landslide of a little under 70 percent majority, trouncing, most notably, the establishment's favorite candidate, Ali Akbar Nategh Nouri, to become the Islamic Republic's fifth president. He acknowledged the collective effervescence that brought him to power in his inaugural speech on August 4, 1997 by describing it as an "epic of historical proportions." The presence of women, intellectuals, and the youth who had been absent on the scene ever since the heady days of the 1979 revolution helped immortalize not only Khatami's triumph but also the birth of the "reform movement" that came to be known as "the May 23 Movement" (*Jonbesh e Dovvom e Khordad*) the day of Khatami's 1997 electoral victory. It is noteworthy that Khatami at the moment of his victory was only the political face of the Iranian reform, an intellectual and political movement that had been in gestation for a decade.[4] The intellectual pedigree of reform dates back to the disappointing end of the Iran-Iraq war (1988) when a battle-hardened and formerly idealistic segment of the Iranian revolutionary cadre elite cut itself off its ideological and Islamist moorings and came together in a government sponsored think tank[5] and an independent monthly journal (*Kian*) to form the nucleolus of the religious and political aggiornamento of the Islamic Republic. Others, such as a majority of the formerly radical "students supporting the Line of Imam" (Daneshjouan e Khatt e Emam was the organization behind the taking of the American hostages that led to an international crisis lasting from late 1979 to early 1981), who had become disenchanted with the country's autocratic leadership, also joined this nucleus. Mr. Khatami's connection to this core group was tenuous and tangential.

At this time, Khatami was a mildly liberal and thoughtful politician with excellent connections and a respectable revolutionary dossier at the margins of both the intellectual and political scenes in Tehran. The reason he found himself in a position to run as the candidate of reform was his clerical garb, his personal connections, and his revolutionary credentials. And the reason such qualities mattered had more to do with the political system of the Islamic Republic than either the predilections of Khatami or the preferences of the reformists. The byzantine political system of the Islamic Republic makes election to high office dependent on the approval of the Guardian Council,[6] a right-wing body that is invested with the right to vet candidates[7] for elective office under articles amended to the Iranian constitution in 1995. The reform movement and indeed any party hoping to slate a candidate for presidency cannot afford to ignore the wishes of the Guardian Council—which has not been shy about imposing its partisan wishes by disqualifying up to 99 percent of the candidates, even when they appear to have current elected offices, established Islamic profiles, and revolutionary credentials.[8]

It is in this context that Mohammad Khatami, his scholarly nature, and nonconfrontational style notwithstanding, became indispensable for the reform movement. While Khatami was a reluctant candidate in his first term, it would not be an exaggeration to state that he was forced by the above circumstances to run for his first term of presidency as well as for his second term (2001) and his brief candidacy for a third term in the presidential elections (2009). The reformers begged, cajoled, and pressed Khatami to run not because he was the best-qualified or the most willing candidate but because they feared that anyone else would have been unceremoniously disqualified. Those who have, during the course of the past decade, underlined the shortcomings of Khatami as a political leader (including the authors of this essay) do so with the knowledge that the prime mover of Khatami's political career was not his personal ambitions or political goals but the flawed democracy of the Islamic Republic that prevents natural representatives of political parties from running for elected office.[9]

By the end of Khatami's first presidential term it was evident that he was neither able to fight the intransigence of entrenched right-wing theocrats[10] nor willing to deliver on the promise of democratization of Iran that was the ultimate objective of the reform platform. But the reformers like Saeed Hajjarian who had no other horse in the presidential race, found themselves begging Khatami to run again.[11]

At this time Khatami's sins were mostly those of omission. Most gave him the benefit of the doubt. His inaction was generously construed as wanting to pick his fights. After all he had shown some courage in confronting the state-sponsored serial murderers of dissidents at the outset of his presidency. Khatami's persistence led to the arrest of four highly placed officials in the Ministry of Information caught for the murder of fifteen Iranian intellectuals, artists, and political figures and the plot to murder many more. The reformist constituency remained hopeful that maybe, just maybe, he would use his second term to good use. Based on his popularity, necessities of the political structure, and wishful thinking, Khatami won his second term by a clear majority.

But he did so without giving a single campaign promise. He had not pledged to act more in keeping with the wishes of the reform movement or to stand up to the right wing. The Guardian Council had already disqualified and eliminated Khatami's reformist challengers, offering him the leadership of the reformist constituency on a silver platter. In other words the right-wing Guardian Council usurped the functions of "primaries" in the Iranian elections.

That is not to say that Khatami was even eager to run. He appeared to have burnt out. He had fought, in his first run, a defensive and losing battle against the sustained sabotage of the right wing that by Khatami's own count had fomented a crisis for every nine days of his presidency. He was visibly reluctant to go through another grueling term. But the bizarre political system (through the agency of right-wing opponents and reformist friends) "forced him" to accept the candidacy for the highest elected office of the land. It is little wonder then that in the wake of his easy victory in 2001 Khatami's sins of omission turned into sins of commission. He had not asked for the office and he had no appetite to fight the legal and extralegal conspiracies of the right wing at the risk of triggering more crises and bloodshed.

President Khatami had won his second presidential term amid widespread dissatisfaction and disaffection with his administration's inability to achieve a modicum of success in realizing the reform movement's objectives: liberalizing the civic sphere, greater transparency, and a tangible responsibility for the unelected block of the Iranian regime. To add to the domestic opposition to Khatami's ideals and policies, the price of oil plummeted during this period causing economic hardships beyond his control. The discontent of the 2001 election was marked by lower voter participation and, more indirectly, by an abundance of popular jokes (that reportedly Mr. Khatami himself enjoyed) about his "do-nothing" and "perpetually smiling" profile.

Signs of exhaustion were written all over Khatami's second-term leadership. Shortly after being elected he dismissed the plight of the unjustly imprisoned journalists, quipping, "How do we know they have not violated the law?" Then he proceeded to choose a more right-wing cabinet than he had in his first term in office—despite the fact that in 2001 he had a sympathetic parliament (the sixth parliament dominated by reformists) on his side and was no longer beholden to right-wing power brokers such as Rafsanjani.

This preemptive surrender angered many of his supporters. Shortly after this period Khatami was bitterly criticized by reform-minded intellectuals (including Abdolkarim Soroush, Said Hajjarian, and Mohsen Kadivar) for lacking the courage of his convictions, for his crippling legalism and conservatism, and for missing "golden opportunities" to advance the cause of reform as a president. Some among the reform-minded critics of Khatami (e.g., Mohsen Kadivar and Abbas Abdi) had from the very beginning prophesied that Mr. Khatami, despite all his irrefutable virtues, would not be suitable for presidency. They now had proof.[12] At this point some reformers even started to talk about slating the former "reconstruction president," Ali Akbar Hashemi Rafsanjani as the reform candidate. But he had been savaged by some of the reform publications (for malfeasance and political oppression) at the outset of the reform reign and it would have taken the reformers a paradigm shift to contemplate such a change in course. In short, reformers had little choice but to support Khatami for a second term despite the evidence of his first term and hope against hope that he would somehow change into a real, hardball politician.

Abdolkarim Soroush, the quintessential reform ideologue and theoretician, argued that Khatami's convictions themselves suffered from lack of inner coherence and clarity. He claimed, in the manner of a true intellectual, that it was the inner inconsistencies of Khatami's ideas that led to his notorious indecisiveness.[13] He had failed to stop the brutal, vigilante takeover of the dormitories of the University of Tehran (summer of 1999) and the judiciary's subsequent mass closure of ninety reformist newspapers. Later in his second term (2003) Khatami first started a bold gambit in the form of "twin bills" to expand presidential powers and to enact media freedom, but he was forced to withdraw these proposals under mounting pressure from the right wing. On occasions like this Khatami was reduced to dithering silence as he watched the right wing pick off (assassinate, imprison, defame, and fire) his close associates and allies (student activists, journalists, and parliamentarians) and stymie or roll back reform legislation.

By the end of his second term the disappointment of Khatami's followers was palpable. It was true that he had accepted the job somewhat reluctantly and that the right-wing pressure was enormous. But based on his popular mandate he could have engaged in symbolic action. His critics asked, When his right-wing rivals shut down the reformist press and brutalized the protesting students could he have not gone on a political fast? When the hanging judges of the right-wing judiciary imprisoned his lieutenants and other reformists, could he have not gone to visit them in prison? Was there no alternative between supine passivity and enticement of violence? Had Khatami ignored the beckoning of Fortuna for the path of safety, mediocrity, and appeasement? Had he wasted a unique historical opportunity to transform Iran's decrepit political system? These questions may never be fully answered even in carefully drawn historical counterfactuals. Social scientists who were observing the Iranian scene at the time of transition from Khatami to Ahmadinejad went from depicting the closing of an Iranian equivalent of the French Revolution's "Thermidor" period to adumbrating an Iranian version of the Chinese Revolution's experience of "return of the radicals."[14]

Nevertheless, today, despite the great disappointments of Khatami's two terms of presidency, he remains enormously popular (both at home and abroad) for his decency, civility, and liberality. Actually, it could be said that his international reception dwarfs his domestic popularity. Mohsen Kadivar relates that as a domestic critic of Mr. Khatami he was pleasantly surprised by the level of support Khatami enjoyed abroad and among the educated classes.[15] In 2001 the United Nations designated the year as the "Year of the Dialogue among Civilizations" to support Khatami's doctrine to counter Samuel Huntington's theory of "Clash among Civilizations." He remains popular for his proposal on the international scene, and several other initiatives have followed in the footsteps of his original proposition.

KHATAMI IN THE POST-KHATAMI ERA

In 2005 Khatami was constitutionally barred from running for a third term and since the vetting agencies of the regime had disqualified three of the most capable reform candidates, including Khatami's younger brother, an MD and the secretary general of Iran's "participation front" from running, the compromise reform candidate, Dr. Mostafa Mo`in, a lackluster former minister of higher education was defeated by the establishment's candidate, Mr. Ahmadinejad. The fact that reformers had achieved little under Khatami was a factor in the defeat of the reform platform at this time. Also the political backlash of the United States' twin invasions of Afghanistan (for which the Khatami government had acted as a virtual ally but received no rewards but a place on the Axis of Evil from the Bush administration) and Iraq explains the appeal of Ahmadinejad's hardline foreign policy. Khatami's soft approach had won him acceptability, but it had not brought home the "beef" on issues ranging from obtaining a civilian fleet for Iranian airlines to the peaceful use of nuclear energy, and Ahmadinejad knew how to exploit these sensitive nationalist issues.

During the first Ahmadinejad term Khatami returned to his cultural and intellectual activities. However, institutions that pursued his agenda such as "Center for the Dialogue of Civilizations" and "The Rain Foundation" faced dwindling state support and mounting harassments. The election of 2009 marked another watershed in Khatami's role in Iranian politics. He was persuaded by an enormous public campaign waged by artists and intellectuals to stand for a third term of presidency against Ahmadinejad (February 2009). Khatami initially accepted the nomination under pressure but withdrew later in favor of his colleague Mirhossein Mousavi. Such a development does not surprise those who have followed his career.

The charges of fraud in the election of June 2009 that brought Ahmadinejad to power and the ensuing tragic and bloody suppression of the protest rallies led to the birth of the "Green Movement." Within a month after the disputed election and the widespread incarceration and torture of the reformist politicians and intellectuals, Khatami publically denounced the show trials and extraction of forced confessions. He publicly called for a referendum on the legitimacy of the Ahmadinejad's government. Among the arrested were Mr. Khatami's brother, Mohammad Reza Khatami, the embattled leader of "Islamic Iran's Participation Front," his chief of staff, several deputy ministers of his administration, and other close and prominent colleagues and collaborators such as Mostafa Tajzadeh, Mohsen Aminzadeh, and Said Hajjarian. Khatami continued to appear in prestigious international forums as the World Economic Forum in Davos, Switzerland even after these events. In 2006 alone he had fifteen international addresses. Eventually the government revoked his passport and prevented him from flying to Japan on a lecture tour. Later, they blocked his website as well. This, too, is bound to boost his profile as a beloved and popular, though embattled and besieged, dissident in Iran. These days, as Mr. Ahmadinejad's two-term presidency is coming to a disgraceful end with international isolation, economic sanctions, threats of invasion, a precipitous decline in the value of Iranian currency (to one-third of what it was before he took over), and his fall from grace even among the right-wing circles, people cannot help waxing nostalgic about the halcyon days when their Smiling Seyed managed the affairs of Iran in a turbulent world.[16]

In his "Politics as a Vocation" The German sociologist Max Weber describes a good politician as one who is idealistic without being dogmatic, uses power to achieve political goals rather than basking in the glory of the office, and ultimately lives "for" rather than "off" politics.[17] On this scale Khatami can be counted as an excellent politician. But one must also factor in the time, the place, and the political matrix. In normal times Khatami might never have chosen "politics as his vocation." When Khatami did find himself at the helm of Iranian presidency he discharged his duties honorably. What he failed at was not the job he was elected for but a higher mission: to lead the reform movement's thrust to democratize the Islamic Republic. He could have helped the revolution molt out of its hardened exoskeleton and take wing in a new century. Khatami could have been a contender, possibly the greatest leader Iran has had since the days of Cyrus. But, like President Carter before him, Mohammad Khatami has become Iran's best ex-president.

KHATAMI'S DISTINCTIVE DISCOURSE

Lest our account of the intricate contingencies surrounding President Khatami's political life leave the reader with the impression that he is simply a creature of the ebbs and flows of Iran's postrevolutionary realpolitik, we must emphasize that Khatami's discourse on cultural openness, human rights, political participation, and civic liberties has left an indelible mark, not only on Iranian political culture but on the entire Islamic world. This effect is not due to the originality of Khatami's ideas. On the contrary, he treads on the path paved by Iranian and Islamic reformers of the nineteenth and twentieth centuries, who were, in their turn, indebted to the eighteenth- and nineteenth-century European liberal tradition.[18] Rather, what is remarkable in Khatami's discourse is that it is the first time in Islamic history that a committed Muslim, indeed, a clergyman, and a political leader, the fifth president of the Islamic Republic of Iran, proposes these decidedly modern and liberal ideas—and means them. These are ideas that we in the Islamic world have come to expect from idealist academics and exiled intellectuals.

Khatami's pragmatic political agenda is present, in embryonic form, in his letter of resignation from the ministry of culture in 1992. It is endowed, with not only ideals and ideas concerning meaning of Islam and nature of man but with an acute awareness of the nature of entrenched opposition to it and the political groundwork needed to overcome it. Khatami elaborates on this thesis in the ensuing decades. The same ideas are in full bloom and expressed triumphantly in his first-term inaugural speech on August 4, 1997 at the Islamic Consultative Assembly (Majles)

The legitimacy of the government stems from the people's vote. And a powerful government, elected by the people, is representative, participatory, and accountable. The Islamic government is the servant of the people and not their master, and it is accountable to the nation under all circumstances. The people must believe that they have the right to determine their own destiny and that the power of the state is bound by limits and constraints set by law. State authority cannot be attained through coercion and dictatorship.[19]

Again, what is stunning about these proclamations is not the content but the position of the speaker and the forum in which it is delivered. Khatami's sustained belief in the compatibility of Islam, democracy, and modernity and his natural tendency toward civility and respect has thus engendered nothing short of a cognitive shift in the Iranian political discourse. Even those Iranian politicians who disagree with him find themselves borrowing his rhetoric of human rights and liberties. The only exception to this rule is the kind that proves the rule. His greatest detractors are the rank and file extremists and xenophobic fundamentalists who find the very ideas of democratic right to self-determination, natural liberties, and freedom of conscience as noxious and deleterious to Islam.[20] Thus, Khatami has acquired the right kind of friends and enemies to ensure him a place in the history and political philosophy of modern Iran and Islam.

NOTES

1. Seyed Mohammad Khatami, Iran Chamber Society. Accessed October 10, 2010. http://www.iranchamber.com/history/mkhatami/mohammad_khatami.php. Profile: Mohammad Khatami, BBC, 2001, 2003, Accessed October 5, 2010. http://news.bbc.co.uk/2/hi/middle_east/1373476.stm.http://news.bbc.co .uk/2/hi/middle_east/3027382.stm. Encyclopedia Britannica, "Mohammad

Khatami," Accessed October 10, 2010. http://www.britannica.com/EBchecked/topic/316504/Mohammad-Khatami. Wikipedia, "Ahmad Khatami," Accessed October10,2010. http://en.wikipedia.org/wiki/Mohammad_Khatami. Robert Worth, *New York Times*, July 20, 2009. http://topics.nytimes.com/top/reference/timestopics/people/k/mohammad_khatami/index.html. Mohammad Khatami, Mehran Kamrava, "Mohammad Khatami," in *Iran Today, An Encyclopedia of Life in the Islamic Republic*, vol. I: A–K.

2. خاتمی، محمد مهسید سندگینا حیاتنامه, Accessed October 01, 2010. http://www.hayat-name.blogfa.com/post-103.aspx. Mohammad Khatami's official website, Accessed September 8, 2010. http://www.khatami.ir.

3. Mohsen Kadivar, نشزنی، دغدغههایحکومتدینی, 1380 On Khatami's letter of resignation, see Wikisourse.org. Accessed November 4, 2010. http://fa.wikisource.org/wiki/%D9%86%D8%A7%D9%85%D9%87_%D8%A7%D8%B3%D8%AA%D8%B9%D9%81%D8%A7%DB%8C_%D9%85%D8%AD%D9%85%D8%AF_%D8%AE%D8%A7%D8%AA%D9%85%DB%8C_%D8%A7%D8%B2_%D9%88%D8%B2%D8%A7%D8%B1%D8%AA_%D8%A7%D8%B1%D8%B4%D8%A7%D8%AF.

4. Mahmoud Sadri and Ahmad Sadri, "Three Faces of Violence: Cognitive, Expressive, and Traditionalist Discourses of Discontent in Contemporary Iran," in *Iran Faces the New Century* (Routledge, 2007), London. For the reference to Khatami's 1997 inaugural speech, see Mohammad Khatami, *Islam, Liberty and Development* (Binhamton University, 1998), 136.

5. Center for Strategic Studies under the Institution of Presidency, Tehran.

6. "Guardian Council of the Constitution" is a sort of supreme court composed of six Shiite jurists directly appointed by the supreme leader and six legal experts appointed by the head of the judiciary. The head of judiciary is himself appointed by the supreme leader. So, the supreme leader appoints half of the members of this body by direct writ and the other half are appointed by his appointee.

7. "Nezarat-e Esteswabi."

8. The most notorious of vetting of this body to date is the disqualification of the senior revolutionary cleric, the former, two-term president and the head of the "Expediency Council" Akbar Hashemi Rafsanjani in the presidential elections of 2013.

9. Ahmad Sadri, *Khatami's Swan Song*. http://www.drsoroush.com/English/Interviews/E-INT-HomaTV.html.

10. Under the leadership of Ayatollah Ali Khamenie, the Supreme Leader of the Islamic Republic of Iran.

11. Zhila BaniYaghub, *Hajjarian's Criticisms of Khatami*. http://www.zhila.org/spip.php?article147.

12. Mohsen Kadivar, *Interview with Mahmoud Sadri*, October 3, 2010, unpublished manuscript.

13. Abdolkarim Soroush. تذبذبعمليخاتميريشهدرتذبذبفكزيايشاندارد. http://www.drsoroush.com/Persian/News_Archive/F-NWS-13830903-Gooyanews.htm. نامهعبدالكزيمسزوشبهمحمدخاتمی. http://autnews3.blogspot.com/2008/04/blog-post_5875.html. Abdolkarim Soroush, *Interview with Daryoush Sajjadi.* http://www.drsoroush.com/English/Interviews/E-INT-HomaTV.html.

14. Mathew C. Wells, Thermidor in the Islamic Republic of Iran, *British Journal of Middle Eastern Studies*, 26, no. 1 (May 1999): 27–39; Jack A. Goldstone, The Return of the Radicals, in *Iran, Project Syndicate, A World of Ideas.* http://www.project-syndicate.org/commentary/goldstone1/English.Dateaccessed, September 28, 2007.

15. Mohsen Kadivar, *Interview with Mahmoud Sadri*, October 3, 2010, unpublished manuscript.

16. It was this enduring popularity that led to the campaign to slate Mr. Khatami as the reformist candidate in the presidential elections of June 2013. Entirely in character, he resisted the pressure and backed Akbar Hashemi Rafsanjani for the position.

17. Max Weber, "Politics as a Vocation" in *From Max Weber*, ed. Hans H. Gerth and C. Wright Mills (Oxford University Press, 1946), 77–128.

18. MahmoudSadri, "Liberalism, Islamic," in *Iran Today: An Encyclopedia of Life in the Islamic Republic*, ed., Kamrava and Dorraj, Westport, Connecticut 300–307.

19. MohammadKhatami, "Covenant with the Nation," Presidential inaugural speech at the Islamic Consultative Assembly (Majles), in *Islam, Liberty and Development* (IGCS, Binghamton University, 1998), Binghamton, N.Y 150–151.

20. For a recent example, see Tebyan.com. Accessed, November 7, 2010 http://www.tebyan.net/Weblog/SAEIDAN/post.aspx?PostID=102923.

Chapter 10

Abdolkarim Soroush

BEHROOZ GHAMARI-TABRIZI

INTRODUCTION

IF Ali Shari`ati was the intellectual par excellence of the Islamic revolution, Abdolkarim Soroush represents one of the most significant postrevolutionary intellectual attempts to end that revolutionary fervor. A prolific writer, Soroush has made important contributions to the advancement of Islamic theology and political philosophy. There are three distinct periods in the development of his thought: (1) critique of Marxism and its influence on Islamist political ideology, (2) epistemological critique of Islamist truth claims, and (3) hermeneutical approach to the Divine text and Prophetic tradition. Whereas during the first period he contributed to the consolidation of postrevolutionary state power, he emerged as one of the most vociferous critics of Islamism, particularly after the death of Ayatollah Khomeini in 1989, during the second and third periods.

CRITIQUE OF MARXISM AND ITS INFLUENCE ON ISLAMIST POLITICAL IDEOLOGY

Abdolkarim Soroush was born in Tehran in 1945 into a lower-middle-class Muslim family. He was named Hossein,[1] for his birth fell on

ʿĀshura, the day commemorating the martyrdom of Hossein, the third Shiʿte imam. After earning a degree in pharmacology from Tehran University, he went to London in 1972 to pursue his studies in chemistry. Although he finished a Master's degree in chemistry, soon thereafter, he concentrated his academic work on the philosophy of science. As a devout Muslim, he remained aloof to the political activism of Iranian students in Europe, which was primarily informed by Marxist ideologies. At the time, Marxian political and philosophical ideas had even penetrated militant Muslim groups, the most influential of which was the Organization of People's Mujahedin (OPM). Despite his reservations about political militancy, he participated in Muslim Youth Association meetings in the United Kingdom.

During his association with the Muslim student movement in the United Kingdom, Soroush emerged as a popular speaker and later as a prolific writer. Like other Muslim intellectuals of his period, such as Morteza Motahhari and Ali Shariʿati, he considered Marxism to be the main intellectual threat that had estranged Iranian intellectuals from their own religion and culture. Unlike Shariʿati, who articulated an Islamic liberation theology, an Islam of *telos*, Soroush engaged Marxism outside its emancipatory politics. He focused on the logical inconsistencies of its philosophy and what he perceived as the totalitarian implications of the materialist conception of history. Shariʿati's indisputable success in attracting the younger generation of Iranian intellectuals to his Islamist ideology afforded Soroush an eager audience who at the time remained oblivious to the fundamental distinctions between competing hermeneutics of Islam.

The result of Soroush's early preoccupation with the critique of Marxism was a series of books in each of which he chastised the "illusive ideology of liberation" from a neopositivist standpoint sheathed in Mulla Sadra's philosophical realism.[2] In the introduction of his treatise on Mulla Sadra's thesis of "(Trans) Substantial

Motion" (*harkat-e johari*), he lamented that contemporary generations of Muslims were gradually losing the courage to think independently, to be innovative and original. He declared that they had grown "inept" and "hopeless"; they had become "timid and reluctant to consider positions on which foreigners have not inscribed their stamp of approval. Intellectual independence, the courage to think creatively, and *ijtihad* are the most urgent responsibilities that face Muslims today" (Soroush 1982, 9). The time had come, he declared in the same introduction, "to emit the fragrance of our culture and offer it to those seekers who trust the aroma of a scent and are not bewitched by the promotional squawking of the scent seller" (Soroush 1982, 10).

The publication of his treatise on Mulla Sadra marked a defining moment in Soroush's intellectual and political life. First, by introducing Mulla Sadra to a new generation, he dismissed the orientalist fallacy of the continuous decline of post-Peripatetic Islamic philosophy. He showed that more than three hundred years after the Golden Age of the Islamic Renaissance, in the early seventeenth century, Mulla Sadra brought together the rationalist philosophy of Ibn Sina (*Mashā'*), the Illuminationism (*Ishrāq*) of Shahab al-Din Suhrawardi, and the Gnostic teachings of Ibn ʿArabi to create a metaphilosophy (*al-hikma al-mutaʿāliya*) through which he offered new resolutions to the centuries-old predicament of existence, reality, essence, and their relation to God.

Moreover, Soroush addressed these questions within the frame of Shiʿite theology, with significant stress laid on its principle of imamate and the imperative of *ijtihad*. Soroush concluded his short but meticulously argued treatise by proposing that:

For the first time, the doctrine of substantial motion introduced two fundamental elements to Islamic thought: first, the historicity

of existence; second the concomitant internal tumult and restless-
ness and external calm and tranquility of the phenomenon....
Rather than being a thing, the world is an unremitting process of
becoming.... The inner transformation recreates the phenomenon anew in every given moment.... God manifests his presence in
the perpetual demise and birth of the universe. (Soroush 1982, 65)

Second, and more importantly, by regarding Mulla Sadra as the
philosopher par excellence of Shi`ite theology, Soroush established
himself as part of a philosophical tradition whose main contemporary proponent was Ayatollah Khomeini. Whether Soroush shared
Khomeini's political interpretation of Mulla Sadra or not, the publication of *The Restless Universe* brought the philosophical virtuosity
of the young Soroush to the attention of the revolution's father. It
has been said that with the encouragement of Morteza Motahhari,
whose commentary on Mulla Sadra had influenced Soroush,
Ayatollah Khomeini read the book and marveled at the erudition of
its young author (Quchani 2004, 50).

During the two years that followed the publication of his first
major treatise, from 1978 to 1980, Soroush published numerous
essays and books, most of which were based on his lectures in the
United Kingdom. In these publications, he demonstrated more
clearly the extent to which Anglo-Saxon analytical philosophy and
the postpositivism of Karl Popper had permeated his Islamic philosophical worldview.[3] He found himself at home with the nonrevolu-
tionary, elitist core of the British political tradition, as well as its
liberal anti-Marxian propensities. Even at the height of the revolutionary movement in Iran, Soroush remained committed to his philosophical endeavors and academic rumination. If Ali Shari`ati's
political discourse combined with his passionate oratory could
inspire thousands of otherwise Marxist young Iranians to join the

revolution, in a world apart, with his soft-spoken words and monotonous delivery, Soroush saw himself, and was accepted by the post-revolutionary regime, as the messenger of persuasion.

With its anti-imperialist agenda and focus on social justice, the new regime situated itself as an alternative to Marxist-inspired national liberation movements. To justify this position, the Islamic Republic launched a two-pronged assault on Marxism: first, by hampering the activities of communist groups through a campaign of intimidation and suppression and, second, by positioning itself as a more authentic and legitimate anti-imperialist force. For the first part of their mission they organized *hezbollahi* mob groups, club-wielding thugs mobilized by the Revolutionary Guards. For the second front they relied on the emerging Muslim intellectuals such as Abdolkarim Soroush.

Soroush's philosophical investigations of Mulla Sadra, combined with his knowledge of history and philosophy of science, situated him as an authoritative intellectual. However, the revolutionary events of 1978 and the establishment of the Islamic Republic deterred him from his scholarly path, forcing him to leave the quiet of his mystical love of philosophy for the boorish world of strident ideology. Like many contemporary Muslim intellectuals, he believed that the construction of a vigorous and engaging Islamic philosophy and an alternative discourse of social change would eventually weaken the ideological attraction of Marxism in Iran. Whereas earlier Muslim critics of Marxism advanced their discourse within the context of a struggle against a common enemy, the monarchy and imperialism, Soroush's critique coincided with the strategy of the new regime to consolidate its power by eliminating its Marxist-Leninist and liberal opposition.

Soroush castigated Marxism, a la Popper, for advancing an irrefutable ideological view of history and society wrapped in pseudoscientific claims. Such an ideological conviction, Soroush reiterated, would inevitably render Marxism a deterministic totalitarian ideology (Soroush 1979a, 13). He argued that Marxists invented the idea of scientific philosophy or scientific socialism in order to justify their teleological view of history. "In [Marxists'] minds," he scolded, "there is no distinction between scientific truth claims and what is right or legitimate" (Soroush 1979d, 15).

In contrast to his nuanced treatment of Mulla Sadra, his engagement with Marxism was polemical and narrow in scope. Whereas, in the former, he pursued genuine philosophical investigations, in the case of Marxism, his argument was primarily shaped by political considerations and the state of the Iranian communist movement. Rather than a serious engagement, his critique was mostly shaped by a vulgar interpretation in which Stalinism appeared to be the only logical political manifestation of Marxist philosophy. Marxism seemed to be an uninterrupted continuum from Marx's ideas, communist utopia to Stalinist totalitarianism, operated as a *satanic ideology*.[4] Soroush called this ideology a "masked dogmatism"[5] that wrapped itself in the colorful sentiments of emancipation and freedom.

He wrote that the proponents of the satanic ideology divide societies into two groups: conscious, deliberate actors and unwitting masses. They "consider people to be entrapped in the claws of mysterious elements of history and condemn their rationality to the manipulation of their subconscious or class-based motivations" (Soroush 1980, 27). The bearers of dogmatic ideology bestow upon themselves mysterious powers, afforded to them by history, which enable them to lead the masses to their "true destiny." *Satanic ideology* (Marxism) draws its seductive powers, he warned, from "opening the arms at the expense of closing the mind, unleashing passion by imprisoning Reason." *Satanic ideology* substitutes the "clash of bodies," for "the encounters of minds." Masked dogmatism "would usher in the worship of power," it would "cast its opponents out of the scene and would legitimize itself based only on the power it holds" (Soroush 1980, 71).

The publication of Soroush's attacks on Marxism and its Islamist sympathizers, that is, the Organization of the People's Mujahedin, coincided with the postrevolutionary regime's *la Terreur* and state-building project. One of these efforts for the consolidation of power was the Cultural Revolution of 1980, the purpose of which was to cleanse the university of the undesirable students and faculty. In May 1980, in a well-planned project, *hezbollahi* mob groups, guided by the factions in the ruling Islamic Republic Party, ransacked the universities around the country and demanded their indefinite closing. During the skirmishes scores of students were killed or injured.

On June 12, 1980, after the bloody attacks of the earlier month, Ayatollah Khomeini issued a decree announcing the formation of the Cultural Revolution Council (CRC). He appointed a seven-member committee, the most junior member of which was Soroush, to carry out a systematic project to Islamize and reopen the universities. Admitting the failure of its initial phase, Khomeini reiterated that "no effective measures have been taken for the realization of the cultural revolution." He asked his appointees to draw up a new plan for the "restructuring of higher education based on Islamic culture" (Khomeini 1994, 177).

If the Cultural Revolution shut the doors of the universities, it opened a door through which Abdolkarim Soroush entered the postrevolutionary political landscape. Although he served in the CRC for less than three years, his short tenure continues to be controversial, especially among Iranian expatriate intellectuals. He was an anomaly in the CRC, having neither a significant history of political activism nor an affiliation with any of the factions in power.

Despite his obscurity at the time, soon Soroush lent significant weight and legitimacy to the CRC and thereby emerged as an influential intellectual of the new republic. Since his resignation in 1983, he has maintained that his role in the Council was to reopen the universities and has consistently distanced himself from its bloody inauguration and political context.

Nevertheless, it is well documented that Soroush rejoiced at the disgrace and impeachment of his intellectual rival President Bani Sadr and the arrest and execution of members of the Mujahedin and communist groups. He justified the reign of terror as Divine Will, which brought love and kindness to those who assented and agony to those who resisted. "I need to emphasize," he pointed out after more than one year of state-sponsored nightly executions,

> That God has consecrated the emergence and the establishment of the Islamic Republic. This divine blessing has descended upon us like the coming of springtime to an arid land and it is the duty of all peoples of this country to be content and grateful for the blooming of this spring. Like a tree, they ought to submit themselves to this breeze and wear the green garment of appreciation. Otherwise, God forbid, they will suffer retributions if they show no gratitude towards God's benevolence. (Soroush 1983, 5)

The Orwellian description that Soroush advanced in 1982 of the Islamic regime as a gentle, life-giving breeze could not be more in contradiction to the emerging totalitarian tendencies of the Iranian political apparatus. The young philosopher who condemned Marxism for its dogmatic core and Hegelian philosophy for its historicist negation of freedom found himself exulting in the disappearance of his philosophical rivals, through execution or exile. "We are pleased now," he exclaimed, "that the pain of having such an undesired president is over.... Like a healthy body that excretes its putrid parts, people have egested him" (Soroush 1983, 6–8).

Soroush's early intellectual project focused on demystifying Marxism. He criticized Marxism as a determinist, totalitarian ideology and, more importantly, advanced a vehement critique of the Muslims who had succumbed to the temptations of its emancipatory discourse. But during the late 1970s and early 1980s, Soroush remained oblivious to the fact that such a critique politically situated him on the side of the ruling factions whose measured encroachment into the state power would soon threaten the conditions of his own intellectual livelihood.

EPISTEMOLOGICAL CRITIQUE OF THE ISLAMIST TRUTH CLAIMS

From early 1988, a group of Muslim intellectuals began to write for and congregate around the editorial board of *Kayhān-e Farhangi,* a monthly journal of cultural and literary criticism, published by the daily newspaper *Kayhān.* From May 1988 to March 1990, in a four-part essay in *Kayhān-e Farhangi,* entitled "The Theoretical Contraction and Expansion of the Shari'ah," Soroush laid out the foundation of a theoretical, political, and social engagement with the emerging totalitarianism. While he framed his argument as a matter of the epistemological problems of religious knowledge, his readers had no trouble reading the implications of his thesis. With these short essays, Soroush inaugurated an intellectual movement the main premise of which was to salvage Islam from its *officially* sanctioned straitjacket. His daring words proved to be one of most important theoretical foundations of political reform in postrevolutionary Iran. He knew that his ideas could not remain limited to the pages of a journal of social criticism. He therefore congregated in the early 1990s with a number of key political, academic, and intellectual figures and journalists in a group known as the "Wednesday night circle."[6]

Soroush did not advocate a political platform. He left the issues of politics and policies out of these meetings. Rather he intended to develop a community in which a "thousand flowers could bloom." The Muslim students, whose credentials included invading the American Embassy in Tehran, had reentered the political scene bearing postgraduate degrees in the humanities and social sciences from British universities. Soroush had left an important mark on their education abroad. With an invitation from the Islamic Student Association of the United Kingdom, for six months in the mid-1990s, he delivered a series of lectures and held seminars on his theological position in seventeen British towns and cities (Jala'ipour 1999, 45). His formal and informal students emerged as the new voice of Islamism, ready to leave behind their Jacobin past and embark on the project of crafting an Islamic-democratic public sphere.

After Ayatollah Khomeini's death in June 1989, the Soroushians gradually lost their prominence at *Kayhān-e Farhangi*; the journal no longer welcomed their contributions. Soroush's circle therefore launched its own monthly journal called *Kiyān*. Although Soroush did not hold any official position at the paper, from the publication of its first issue it was conspicuously clear that the journal would express the views of these dissident intellectuals. *Kiyān*, which ran for more than ten years from 1991 until its closure by the order of Tehran's chief prosecutor in 2001, became one of the most contentious venues in which dissident Muslim, and at times secular, intellectuals could address their critics. Although it was not the only opposition journal permitted to circulate in these years, it occupied a distinct position among elite literary-political journals.

Ten years after the Cultural Revolution, a majority of those who were involved in its implementation now voiced their opposition to its totalitarian implications. Soroush, who stumbled onto the revolutionary scene and became the reluctant spokesperson for the CRC, was best situated to lead this movement—a movement of those who shared both the culpabilities of the past and the hope for the future.

The combination of his antitotalitarianism and his unwanted role in a totalitarian project to Islamize higher education pushed Soroush into a contradiction. This sociopolitical location contributed to the formation of his project, the central feature of which was rescuing the religion of Islam from its dominant ideological articulations. Soroush advanced his critique of ideological Islam vis-à-vis two tendencies in Iranian politics, both of which he chastised for their reductionist conceptions of Islam. The first, put forward by Ali Shari`ati, demoted Islam into a mere liberation theology and operated as the ideological frame of the Iranian revolution. The second, promoted by the ruling clerical *nomenklatura* with privileged access to its meaning, transformed Islam into a state ideology.

In a series of talks and articles, which were collected in the book *Farbeh-tar az eideolozhi* (Loftier Than Ideology), Soroush called into question Shari`ati's notion of Islam as ideology. Although formally composed as a critique of his philosophy, Soroush's underlying theme was his rejection of the ideological society established by the Islamic Republic. Rejecting Shari`ati's theory of permanent revolution, Soroush argued that although useful as a weapon to fight oppression, Islam as ideology and its prescribed establishment of an ideological society was a plague that must be eradicated in order to constitute a free religious society. Whereas Shari`ati defined ideology as a revolutionary rearticulation of culture, Soroush regarded it as an exclusionary truth claim, which not only distorts the reality of religion but also facilitates the establishment of totalitarianism (Soroush 1994, 135–154).

Soroush proposed that claiming the *Truth* has always been a part of all Islamic revivalist movements. These movements, he wrote, shared three basic elements. First, they campaigned against folk religious practices and rituals. Associated with *Wahhabism* and some trends of *Salafiyyah* movements, their aim was to create a homogenous and universal conception of Islam through strict and a literal reading of the Qur'an and the *Hadīth*. Second, they emphasized the hitherto neglected dimensions of Islam, especially in the realm of *fiqh* (jurisprudence). They offered alternative genealogies of Islamic praxis, as for example in the case of Shari'ati, the Islam of Abu Dharr replaced the Islam of Ibn Sina, an Islam of the political vanguard supplanted the Islam of the 'ālim (scholar). And finally, they appropriated selective Qur'anic verses that would justify the validity of their sociopolitical as well as scientific ideas. Many proponents of Islamic revival, for example, fallaciously locate the root of liberal democracy and electoral politics in the Islamic notion of *shura* or *ijmā'* (consultation; Soroush 1987, 368).

Whereas all Islamic revivalist movements had to separate what was permanently sacred from what was situational and changing in the Islamic text, Soroush distinguished religion as intended by God from humanity's mundane knowledge of it. "What remains constant is religion [itself] and what changes is religious knowledge" (Soroush 1995, 52). Humanity could not fathom God's true intentions. Therefore, those who ordain their ideology as the Divine commandment laid the foundation for totalitarianism. All possible interpretations of religion, both the so-called permanent and its historically contingent parts, are mundane and informed by sociocultural particularities. In effect, Soroush argued that *any* claim to the *Truth* of Islam transforms religion into an ideology—a falsified world picture.

Iranian predecessors of Soroush, Shari'ati and Motahhari, had already emphasized the social, cultural, and historical contingencies of religious knowledge. Shari'ati developed the idea in his sociology of Islam, and Motahhari in his critique of *qeshriyyat* (fanaticism). For example, Shari'ati wrote, "*Tawhid* descends from the sky and becomes earthly and enters into particular social relations in the context of which its meaning is constructed" (Shari'ati 1981, 140). Or in another place, Shari'ati retorted to a critic, "I shall emphasize that I am a sociologist of religion and I understand *tawhid* historically. I am not concerned with the Truth of the Book, or with the correct comprehension of the Qur'an, Muhammad or Ali. For me, the important matter is the social and historical *tawhid*, it has always been the most important issue" (Shari'ati 1981, 215).

Similarly, on the problem of the cultural and historical contingency of religious knowledge Motahhari argued, "If one compares *fatwas* of different *fuqahā* and at the same time considers their personal lives and states of mind, it becomes clear that the intellectual presuppositions of a *faqih* and his knowledge of the external world inform his *fatwas*. That is why the *fatwa* of an Arab has an Arab flavor and the *fatwa* of an 'Ajam [non-Arab, Persian] has an 'Ajam flavor" (Motahhari 1962 and 1978, 101). Motahhari often compared the Qur'an to nature, a phenomenon that becomes increasingly comprehensible with the passage of time (Motahhari 1988, 147–152). In contrast to the revivalists who considered pristine renditions of Islam to be more authentic than contemporary interpretations, Motahhari believed that "*future* generations will have a better grasp and a deeper appreciation of the Divine text" (Motahhari 1985, 134).

But neither Shari'ati nor Motahhari developed an epistemological pluralism in which, as Soroush intended, *all* truth claims become contingent. Soroush did not question the certainty of faith but highlighted its *ineffability*. In this light, he rejected the revivalist (reformist or revolutionary) distinction between eternal and ephemeral, text and context. These dichotomies presupposed the responsibility of the reformist to appropriate religion as intended by God in a modern formulation.

In contrast to revivalists' Islamic ideology, which interprets the finality of Islam as a sign of its exhaustive rigidity, Soroush contended that Islam's finality signifies its indeterminate fluidity. The finality of Islam means that every generation experiences revelation *anew*. "Thus," he remarks, "revelation incessantly permeates us, in the same way that it hailed the Arabs [during the time of the Prophet], as if the Prophet were chosen today. The secret of the finality of Islam lies in the perpetuity of the revelation" (Soroush 1994, 78). Accordingly, he reenvisioned the sharī'ah from a preconceived dogma into a continuously renewed and contested text.

By abandoning Islam as ideology, Soroush seeks to reclaim the enigma of religion. Rather than being a manifesto for action, he proposes that the *sharī'ah* is silent; it is given voice by its exponents. It is like history, which is given voice by the historian, or nature, the laws of which are constructed by the scientist. The *sharī'ah* does not put forward immutable answers to predicaments of all historical moments. That is not to suggest, he asserts, "the silence of the *sharī'ah* empties it of any meaning. Rather, its silence impedes any particular group from claiming access to its essence whereby they would prohibit and condemn competing understandings of religion" (Soroush 1995, 34). One should not regard the *sharī'ah* as an a priori knowledge. Religiosity demands an incessantly renewed exegesis. Accordingly, one cannot presuppose any particular meaning of the *sharī'ah* and then consider changes in its interpretation to be problematic (Soroush 1995, 186).

Various movements, Soroush observes, to make religion contemporary were based on a fallacy: one cannot *make* religion contemporary; any comprehension of religion is already shaped by contemporary concerns. "The modernity of religious knowledge is a description rather than a prescription" (Soroush 1995, 487). Human cognition is contingent on time and place. We comprehend only what religion *is* rather than what it *ought to* be. In other words, one grasps the social-temporal existence of religion, not its Divine-absolute essence (Soroush 1994, 199–231).

Soroush considers the religious text to be *hungry for* rather than *impregnated with* meaning. He believes that meaning is given to religion rather than extracted from it. "In every era," he writes, "the ʿulamaʾ interpolate new questions and devise new responses from the *sharīʿah*. . . . The *totality* of these questions and answers define the contemporaneous religious knowledge" (Soroush 1995, 442). He argued that the mistaken identification of religion with the knowledge of it emanates from either "fiqhi positivism or popular idealism." For the positivist, the real is the tangible, thus objectively comprehensible through its transmission by senses. In contrast, the idealist regards existential reality as the reflection of a priori ideas lodged in the mind. Thus Soroush refers to "*fiqhi* positivism" as a doctrine that highlights the primacy of jurisprudence (*fiqh*) in religion and equates jurisprudential knowledge of religion with religion itself (Soroush 1995, 342–344). It is only in the idealist's perception that subjectivity and existence were identical and inseparable. "The minimum condition for a realist epistemology is the distinction between the object and the knowledge of it. Therefore, our understanding of the *sharīʿah*, even if we consider it flawless, is distinct from the *sharīʿah* itself" (Soroush 1995, 341).

The official responses to Soroush's theological interventions were uncompromising. In December 1991, the Central Office of the Honorable Leader's Representatives in the Universities warned "the spread of thoughts which consider religion to be a dependent variable of other human sciences is dangerous and negates the legitimacy of the Islamic state" (cited in Soroush 1995, 501). On September 9, 1995, in an editorial in Tehran's state-run paper *Ettelā'āt,* the supreme leader, Ayatollah Khamenei, also cautioned Soroush not to criticize clergy's privileged social position and their interpretive authority. In the words of then Iranian minister of foreign affairs, Ali Akbar Velayati, the "Dr. Soroush issue" was a matter of "threat to our national harmony" and "Iranian national independence." After mob groups attacked Soroush during a lecture in Isfahan, Velayati warned him to cease "dragging [issues of religious authority] into the daily newspapers" (1995).

A vast array of government officials and seminarians uniformly attacked Soroush for calling foundational religious texts historically contingent and equally open to multiple interpretations. Two influential ayatollahs, Mesbah Yazdi (Yazdi 1999) and Naser Makarem Shirazi (Shirazi 1991), both outspoken critics of Ali Shari'ati, warned their disciples and state officials of the perils of Soroush's "relativization of religious knowledge" and especially dangerous attempt to emasculate the interpretive authority of the clergy in religious matters.

During the 1990s, Soroush's theory of contraction and expansion became the conceptual framework for debating the religious justification of the Islamic Republic. From the floor of the parliament to editorial pages, from seminary quarters to street corners in Tehran, friends and foes clashed over the question of the contingencies of religious knowledge. The former speaker of the *majlis,* Ali Akbar Nateq Nuri, called for an end to competing interpretations of Islam and warned that they will weaken Muslims' faith in their religion. In a speech delivered to the Revolutionary Guards, he warned his audience that "the enemies of the revolution are exploiting naive people with these complicated theories to undermine their faith in order to defeat the revolution.... We need, to utilize new technologies of communication such as the internet to generate certainty in defending the principles of Islam and the revolution" (*Asr-e Azadegan,* September 18, 1999, No. 7, p. 3). A day later, in one of his repeated attacks on pluralism, Ayatollah Mesbah Yazdi began his Friday prayer sermon with the declaration that "We need to shut the mouth of anybody who claims that he has a new interpretation of Islam.... The consequence of uttering words against the absolutes of Islam is nothing but burning in hell, we will throw these fashionable ideas into the dustbin of history.... We should cut out the tongue of those who speak of multiple interpretations of the Qur'an" (*Asr-e Azadegan,* September 18, 1999, No. 7, p. 2).

The significance of Soroush's intervention in the postrevolutionary period was that he expanded the exegetical authority to actors outside seminaries. As the many attacks on his person and his ideas demonstrate, what was at stake was the authority to produce religious knowledge, which Soroush expanded to civil actors without clerical religious training. The most influential authorities in the clerical establishment viewed Soroush's ideas as a political intervention, which, if realized, would lead inevitably to the secularization of the Islamic Republic. They were not wrong.

By the end of 1996 it became apparent that the Soroush's public presence would be tolerated by neither his clerical detractors nor the vigilante guardians of the "blood of the martyrs." Even after the election of his friend and ally Mohammad Khatami to the presidency in May 1997, he remained as the main target of the "pressure groups." The failure of his friends in power to engender a safe, sustainable public sphere forced Soroush to head off for a fellowship at Harvard in 2000. For the first time, Harvard fellowship, and thereafter Princeton and the Wissenschaftskolleg in Berlin offered Soroush the possibility of situating himself within a global network of

Muslim intellectuals. Before his departure for Cambridge, he published two of his most controversial books. Not only did the pressure fail to deter him from criticizing the orthodoxies of the Shi`ite clerical hierarchy, but also he continued to advance a radical religious pluralism that scandalized even some of those who had politically and theologically invested in his project.

HERMENEUTICS AND RELIGIOUS PLURALISM

Through his epistemological critique, Soroush concluded that (1) God revealed religion so it could enter the domains of human culture and subjectivity within which it is comprehended and observed. The moment religion enters human subjectivity inevitably it becomes particular, and historically-culturally specific. (2) Religious knowledge corresponds to other mundane forms of knowledge. It is related to and inspired by *non*-religious knowledge production. (3) Religious knowledge is also historically progressive. Its advancement depends on the evolution of scientific understanding of the physical world and ever-expanding notions of rights and mutual obligations in society such as civil liberties or the rights of women, and so on.

In his earlier work, Soroush defined the epistemological contingencies of religious knowledge in an ambiguous relation with the historical and cultural contingencies of the Divine text. Whereas he initially approached problems in attaining religious knowledge with logical and systematic reasoning, later he became increasingly concerned with religious hermeneutics. Whereas he originally understood the diversity of religious knowledge as a reflection of historical progression, in his hermeneutics, he underscored regional, ethnic, and linguistic differences in exegesis of the sacred texts. Whereas earlier he put forward epistemological questions about the limits and truthfulness of knowledge claims, later, in two important books, *Straight Paths* (1998) and *Expansion of the Prophetic Experience* (1999), he emphasizes the reflexivity and plurality of human understanding.

The political context of his earlier work forced him to promote a suprahistorical conception of reason against the onslaught of basic institutions of civil society. This is evident in his openly political writings in *Siyāsat-Nāmeh* (Political Letters), where he defines the goal of democracy as the establishment of procedures that guaranteed the free engagement of rational experts (Soroush 2000). He believed that public deliberation of the meaning and social implications of religion should take place in a secure arena for the exercise of public reason, as in John Rawls (1993), and within a public sphere that allows undistorted communication and deliberative politics, as in Jürgen Habermas (1996).

While his detractors continued their assault on paper and pavement, with the publication of *Straight Paths,* Soroush took a significantly greater step away from doctrinal renditions of Islam. As Said Amir Arjomand observes, in *Straight Paths,* which conspicuously pluralizes the key Qur'anic phrase, "Soroush totally disregarded legalistic Islam and drew heavily on the tradition of Gnostic mysticism (*'irfān*), especially in the poetry of his favorite Rumi (d. 1273), to establish the principle of religious pluralism" (Arjomand 2002, 723). Soroush had always referenced Rumi in his argument for plurality of paths to *Truth*; this time he radicalized his rendition of Rumi to establish the plurality of *Truth* itself. "From the standpoint of Rumi," Soroush asserts, "the problem is not that some people have failed to find the Truth, [and] thus remained misguided and deprived. Rather, people's bewilderment results from the multiplicity of truths and the diversity in their manifestation. We are in awe of and attracted to different constituents of this divine diversity" (Soroush 1998, 27).

In Iran, Soroush's ecumenicalism came on the heels of controversies over his promotion of tolerance for diverse interpretations of Islam. Soroush weds these two projects, in his most radical book, *The Expansion of Prophetic Experience*. Walking on the razor's edge between heresy and faith, he ponders the moment when the earthly Prophet encountered the Divine. Soroush regards the Prophet's life and character as absolutely central to the revelation of the Qur'an. "Rather than a mere book or a collection of narratives," he contends, "Islam represents a historical movement; it is the embodiment of a historical mission. Islam is the historical expansion of a *gradually realized* Prophetic experience. Pivotal to its meaning is the Prophet's persona.... The Qur'anic revelation was woven around the Prophet's life circumstances; it revolved around his internal and external life experiences" (Soroush 1999, 19).

By linking revelation to the biography of the Prophet, not only does he bring to light the historicity of the Qur'an and the contingencies of its verses, but he draws distinctions between Islam, Christianity, and Judaism without interrogating their inherent Truth. That is to say, by emphasizing the constitutive significance of the Prophet's life circumstances in shaping the Qur'anic text, he transfers the debate over theological incongruities of Abrahamic religions to the realm of history. Soroush's assertion on the significance of the Prophet's life in shaping the message of the Qur'an revives two foundational debates from the formative decades of Islam. The first concerned the indeterminacy and rationality of human action, and the second the eternity (*qadim*) of the Holy Text.

REASON AND RELIGION

Since the emergence of the earliest Islamic schools theology, rationalist philosophers thought that God's Justice (*'adl*) required believers to be responsible for their own actions. In order to accept the principle that a just God rewards salutary deeds and punishes the sinful, one must possess the freedom to determine one's own destiny. The rationalists considered it a violation of the principle of justice if God held people accountable for actions over which they had no power. Reason, the rationalist philosophers believed, was a constitutive faculty of humanity; its realization in action necessitated the recognition that life was essentially indeterminate. An important corollary of this principle was the link between Divine revelation and the actions of the Prophet. The Qur'an could have been different had the Prophet made different decisions in his social and political career. Soroush writes,

A person would come and ask the Prophet a question, someone brought an accusation against his wife, one would ignite the flames of war, the Jews or Christians made particular decisions, many accused the Prophet of lunacy ... they buried their sons and daughters alive, all these are reflected in the Qur'an and in the Prophet's words. Had the Prophet lived longer and faced more predicaments, those incidents would also have been reflected in the Qur'an. So, that is the meaning of the assertion that there could have been more written in the Qur'an. If Ayesha had not been accused of having an affair with another man, would the early verses of the *Sura Nur* have descended? If the war of *Ahzāb* had not occurred, would the *Sura al-Ahzāb* have been revealed? If there had been no Abu Lahab in Hijaz and he and his wife had not behaved with animus towards the Prophet, would the *Sura Abu Lahab* have appeared? These were all unnecessary events the occurrence of which did not have any historical significance. Now that they have indeed occurred, their mark is left in the Qur'an. (Soroush 1999, 20)

He argues that all religions are composed of two categories, '*arazi*, the contingent or accidental, and *zāti*, the substantial or essential. Accordingly, while they differ in their contingencies, all religions in their essence promote the same principles. "Religion," he reiterates, "does not have an Aristotelian nature, it only expresses God's *intentions*. These intentions define the essence of religion" (Soroush 1999, 80, emphasis added). Religious languages, the cultural and historical contexts of their revelations, particular juridical assertions, concrete teachings of everyday life, the wars they launch, and the peace treaties they forge are nonessential and contingent.

THE ETERNITY OF THE QUR'AN

Muslim theologians who rejected the idea of indeterminacy and subscribed to the determinist doctrine of predestination (*Jabriyya*) argued that the principle of eternity of the Qur'an exposed the fallacy of the hermeneutics of the Divine text. They rejected the rationalists' idea that God created (*Hadīth*) the Qur'an in relation to the Prophetic experience of Muhammad. Rather they argued that the Qur'an was eternal (*qadim*) and was revealed in its entirety in one instant to the Prophet. These theologians insisted that the Divine revelations speak eternal Truth without essential relation to the Prophet's biography or character. Not only did they argue that the Qur'an was uncreated and eternal, but more orthodox schools also went further to advocate that since speech was a Divine attribute, the verses in the Qur'an were spoken words of God.

Reviving an old debate, Soroush now stresses that the Prophet did not hear the *words* of God but had an inner experience of divinity, kindled by God, the meaning of which he was able to divulge to his contemporaries in words comprehensible to them. The language of Arabic, its cultural norms, economic and political doctrines, symbols of beauty, and all the other particulars in the Qur'an have nothing to do with the unattainable eternal Truth.

Soroush's detractors did not misjudge the political implications of his theses of religious pluralism. If the word of God, *Kalām Allah*, was not to be understood literally as Divine words but speechless mystic intuits known only to the Prophet, then no leader may justify his political authority as the exclusive and uncontested expression of the Divine Will. That would be tantamount politically to totalitarianism and religiously to blasphemy. "A politically sanctioned official rendition of Islam," Soroush declares, "is thus null and void" (Soroush 1999, 134).

CONCLUSION

Soroush has inaugurated one of the most important intellectual movements in contemporary Iran. He began his journey with an ideology critique first of Marxism and later of Islamism of pre- and postrevolutionary Iran. His hermeneutics and pluralist approach to Islam encouraged a new generation of intellectuals to moderate the Jacobin impulse of the postrevolutionary regime. They interpreted Soroush as calling for struggle for participatory democracy through the recognition of competing interpretations of Islam. For this generation, revolutionary Islamism, with its exclusivist truth claims, provided the ideological justification for totalitarianism. Rather than being an epistemological or cognitive matter, they understood hermeneutical Islam to be a deeply political issue.

Soroush advances his Islamic hermeneutics in response to theocratic tendencies in the Islamic Republic. Through this Islamic hermeneutics, unlike the ideological Islam of his predecessors,

Soroush intends to *de*-politicize Islam and to reinvigorate its enigmatic core. For Soroush, political Islam is as an inescapable ground for totalitarianism. Although Soroush does not deny the public significance of religion in the promotion of a just society, this significance, he insists, needs to be exercised outside the sphere of state power.

NOTES

1. His real name is Hossein Haj-Faraj-Dabagh, but he has always been known by his penname, Abdolkarim Soroush.
2. Mulla Sadra was a seventeenth-century Persian Gnostic philosopher. Many contemporary Muslim philosophers believe that he was one of the greatest exponents of metaphysical doctrines in Islam. Henry Corbin compared Mulla Sadra to a combination of St. Thomas Aquinas and Jakob Boehme within the Islamic context. According to S. H. Nasr, "Mulla Sadra's *Spiritual Journeys* [*al-asfar*] is the most monumental work of Islamic philosophy, in which rational arguments, illuminations received from spiritual realization and the tenets of revelation are harmonized in a whole which marks in a sense the summit of a thousand years of intellectual activity in the Islamic world" (Nasr 1992, 335–336). While the great ayatollahs and other teachers at the Shi'ite seminaries were generally experts in *fiqh,* Allameh Tabataba'i, revived Shi'i philosophical traditions, especially Mulla Sadra's illuminationist rationalism in the Qom seminary. Ayatollah Khomeini was another exponent of Gnostic philosophical traditions at Qom, where, in addition to Mulla Sadra, he also taught Ibn Arabi's Sufism.
3. Included in these publications were Soroush 1979a, 1979b, 1979c, 1979d, 1980.
4. *Satanic Ideology* was the title of book published in 1980. It contained a series of talks and articles against the perils of Marxism, which he delivered soon after the triumph of the revolution.
5. "Masked Dogmatism" was the title of the talk Soroush delivered in 1979 at the School of Economics at Tehran University, which was later published as a short monograph. *Satanic Ideology* was an expanded version of the same monograph.
6. Among them were influential figures of the reform movement such as Reza Tehrani, Mashallah Shamsolva'ezin, Morteza Mardiha, Majid Mohammadi, Mostafa Tajzadeh, Hamid Reza Jala'ipour, Mohsen Sazgara, Akbar Ganji, Ahmad Borqani, Mohammad Abtahi, Said Hajjarian, and even Mohammad Khatami, who later was elected as the president in 1997.

REFERENCES

Habermas, Jürgen. 1996. *Between Facts and Norms: Contribution to a Discourse Theory of Law and Democracy*. Cambridge, MA: MIT Press.

Jala'ipour, Hamid-Reza. 1999. *Pas az dovvom-e Khordād* [After the Second of Khordad)]. Tehran: Kavir.

Khomeini, Ayatollah Ruhollah. 1994. *Sahifeh-ye Nur: Majmu'e-ye rahnemudha-ye Imam Khomeini* [The Collected Declarations of Imam Khomeini]). Vol. 12. Tehran: The Organization of the Islamic Revolution's Cultural Documents.

Motahhari, Morteza. 1962. *Bahsi darbāre-ye marja'iyyat va rohaniyyat* [A Treatise on the Source of Imitation and the Clergy]. Tehran.

Motahhari, Morteza. 1978. *Motahhari's Dah goftār* [Ten Discourses]. Tehran: Hekmat.

Motahhari, Morteza. 1988. *Khātamiyat* [Finality]. Tehran: Sadra.

Motahhari, Morteza. 1985. *Shesh maqāleh* [Six Essays]. Tehran: Sadra.

Nasr, Seyyed Hossein. 1992. *Science and Civilization in Islam*. New York: Barnes & Noble Books.

Quchani, Mohammad. 2004. "Qabz va bast-e perātik-e Soroush" [The Practical Expansion and Constriction of Soroush]. *Sharq* (New Year Special Edition) 1383, pp. 50–51.

Rawls, John. 1993. *Political Liberalism*. New York: Columbia University Press.

Said, Amir Arjomand. 2002. Reform Movement in Contemporary Iran. *International Journal of Middle East Studies* 34: 4, pp. 719–734.

Shari'ati, Ali. 1981. *Islamshenāsi* [Islamology]. Vol. 1. Tehran: Entesharat-e Shari'ati.

Shirazi, Naser Makarem. 1991 *Javānān va moshkelāt-e fekri* [Youth and Problems of Mind]. Qom: Khorram.

Soroush, Abdolkarim. 1979a. *Tazād-e diālektiki* [Dialectical Contradiction]. Tehran: Serat.

Soroush, Abdolkarim. 1979b. *Danish va arzesh* [Knowledge and Value]. Tehran: Yaran.

Soroush, Abdolkarim. 1979c. *Falsafeh-ye tārikh* [Philosophy of History]. Tehran: Payam-e Azadi.

Soroush, Abdolkarim. 1979d. *'Elm chist? Falsafeh chist?* [What Is Science? What Is Philosophy?]. Tehran: Serat.

Soroush, Abdolkarim. 1980. *Eideolozhi-ye shaytani* [The Satanic Ideology]. Tehran: Serat.

Soroush, Abdolkarim. 1982. *Nahād-e nā-ārām-e jahān* [The Restless Nature of the Universe]. Tehran: Qalam.

Soroush, Abdolkarim. 1983. *Bani Sadr, Sāzmān-e Mojāhedin va Hegelism* [Bani Sadr, the Mojahedin, and Hegelianism]. Rome: Centro Culturale Islamic Europeo.

Soroush, Abdolkarim. 1987. *Tafarroj-e son': Goftārhā-ei dar Akhlāq va san'at va elm-e ensāni* [Essays on Human Sciences, Ethics, and Technology]. Tehran: Serat.

Soroush, Abdolkarim. 1994. *Farbeh-tar az eideolozhi* [Loftier Than Ideology]. Tehran: Serat.

Soroush, Abdolkarim. 1995. *Qabz va bast-e teorik-e shari'at* [The Theoretical Contraction and Expansion of the Shari'ah]. Tehran: Serat.

Soroush, Abdolkarim. 1998. *Serāt-hā-ye mostaqim* [Straight Paths]. Tehran: Serat, 27.

Soroush, Abdolkarim. 1999. *Bast-e tajrobeh-ye nabavi* [The Expansion of Prophetic Experience]. Tehran: Serat.

Soroush, Abdolkarim. 2000. *Siyāsat-Nāmeh* [Political Letters]. Vols. 1–2. Tehran: Serat.

Velayati, Ali Akbar. December 26, 1995. *Kayhan,* editorial. (Cited in Human Rights Watch Report, *Iran: Power Versus Choice,* March 1996, vol. 8–1 E). Available at: http://hrw.org/reports/1996/Iran.htm. Accessed 20 May 2013.

Yazdi, Mohammad Taqi Mesbah. 1999. *Tahājom-e farhangi* [Cultural Assault]. Qom: Imam Khomeini Teaching and Research Institute.

INDEX

Names starting with "al-" are alphabetized by the subsequent part of the name.

Divine Will, 241
"dual containment," 118

economic conditions and Ghannushi's
ideology, 164
ecumenicalism, 238
education
gender issues and, 151–152, 179
reformism of Khatami and, 205
effendiyya, 143
Egypt. *See also* Muslim Brotherhood
al-Banna and, 21
political parties and, 37–38
Qutb's ideology and, 81
Revolution of 1952, 179
Revolution of 2011, 181
Sudanese politics and, 143
electronic networking, 186–187
Enayat, Hamid, 106
Enlightenment, 94, 151
Ennahda, 170–171, 175
Enneifer, Ahmida, 162
epistemology, 219, 227–236, 241–242
equality and egalitarianism. *See also* women
and gender issues
democratization of *shura* and, 35–36
gender issues and, 167–168
Qutb's ideology and, 72
Shari`ati's ideology and, 91
Soroush's ideology and, 238
Esposito, John L., 173
Ettela'at, 133n33
European Council for Fatwa and Research
(ECFR), 185
existential philosophy, 90, 91
Expansion of the Prophetic Experience
(Soroush), 238
Expediency Council, 134n55

Fadaiyan-e Islam, 132n11
family law, 182
Fanon, Frantz, 91, 97, 102n2
faqih, 104, 108, 231. *See also* velayat-e faqih
Farabi, Abu Nasr al-, 204
Farbeh-tar az eideolozhi (Soroush), 229
fascism, 45
Fatima, daughter of the Prophet, 101n1

fatwas
Khomeini's ideology and, 121
Qaradawi's ideology and, 183,
185–186, 189, 196
Soroush's ideology and, 231
Fawzan, Salih al-, 198n44
Faza'il-i Balkh (Balkhi), 87
Feyziyeh Madreseh, 106, 109
Fifth Republic (France), 111
al-Fikr al-Jadid (magazine), 69
finality of Islam, 232
fiqh
"*fiqhi* positivism," 233
Khomeini's ideology and, 128
renewal of Islamic jurisprudence and,
189–191, 195
Shi`i Islam and, 242n2
Soroush's ideology and, 230
Fiqh al-Zakat (Qaradawi), 182–183
fitra, 27
France
Fifth Republic, 111
French existentialism, 93
French Revolution, 211
Ghannushi's ideology and, 162
headscarf controversy, 185
French Revolution, 211
fundamentalism, Islamic, 111, 144–145
fuqaha (Islamic jurists), 104, 108

Gaddafi, Muammar, 189
Garaudy, Roger, 169
Gellner, Ernest, 173
gender issues. *See* women and
gender issues
Ghamari-Tabrizi, Behrooz, 12, 219–244
Ghamidi, Javed Ahmed, 49, 59
Ghannushi, Rashid al-, 10, 11, 17,
159–176, 188
Gharbzadegi (Al-e Ahmad), 113
Ghazali, Abu Hamid al-, 168
Ghazali, Muhammad al-, 26, 164, 179
globalization and Turabi's ideology,
145–146
Gnosticism, 221, 237, 242n2
Golden Age of the Islamic Renaissance, 221
Gräf, Bettina, 11, 178–197

Khomeini, Ayatollah Ruhollah, 7,
    8, 104–138
  al-Banna and, 17
  background, 104–105
  constitutionalism and, 107–110
  death, 228
  exile, 110
  Ghannushi's ideology and, 166–167
  Gnosticism and, 242n2
  key quotes, 104
  Khatami and, 205
  legacy of, 9, 123–127
  Mawdudi's ideology and, 52
  rejection of the West, 9
  revolutionary sentiment and, 112–114
  Shari`ati's ideology and, 89, 101
  Soroush's ideology and, 222
  theocratic-populism of, 9
  vali-ye faqih concept and, 8, 116–123
Khomeini, Mostafa, 133n33
Kitab al Asrar (Sadra), 128
Kiyan, 228
kufr (disbelief), 32, 37, 50

law. See *shari`ah*
The Lawful and the Prohibited in Islam
    (Qaradawi), 179–180, 182
Lazard, Gilbert, 87
legal authority. See *shari`ah*
Leninism, 99
liberal democracy, 58, 230
liberation, personal, 94–95
liberation movements, 223
liberation theology, 220
Livingstone, Ken, 188
logic, 74. *See also* reason and rationality
London bombings, 192

Mahdavi, Mjotaba, 9, 104–138
Mahdi, Muhammad Ahmad al-, 143
Mahdism, 143–144
Mahsouli, Sadeq, 136n84
majlis, 118–119, 130
Maliki school of jurisprudence, 165
Manai, Ahmed, 162
al-Manar al-Jadid, 193
marriage, 190

martyrdom, 71, 192
Marxism, 91–92, 97–99, 125, 219–227, 241
Mashariqi thought, 167
Mashhur, Mustafa, 181
"Masked Dogmatism" (Soroush), 242n3
Massignon, Louis, 87
mass media, 186–187, 196
materialism, 152–153
al-Mawardi, 23, 40
Mawdudi, Sayyid Abu al-`Ala, 4–5, 7, 39,
    44–61, 161
  al-Banna and, 17, 39
  background, 44–46
  Ghannushi's ideology and, 164, 167
  intellectuals' disagreement with, 11
  Islam as a way of life and, 46–49
  Islamic state and, 5–6, 49–53
  Qutb's ideology and, 75, 77–78
  role of non-Muslims and, 54–56
  western modernity and, 56–58
May 23 Movement, 206
media, 186–187, 196
Messiri, Abd al-Wahhab al-, 173
metaphilosophy, 221
metaphysics, 242n2. *See also* Sufism
migrant workers, 69
Milestones (Qutb), 78
militancy, 191
military rulers. See *specific leaders and countries*
al-minhaj al-islami (Islamic way), 75, 77
Mirghani, Mohammed Osman al-, 143
modernity and modernization
  al-Banna and, 6
  Iranian Revolution and, 115
  Khatami's ideology and, 12, 216
  Mawdudi and, 6, 45
  Qaradawi and, 179, 195
  Turabi's ideology and, 144
  Western influence and, 56–58
Mo`in, Mostafa, 212
Mojahedin of the Islamic Revolution
    Organization, 134n52
monarchism, 108, 112, 114
Montazeri, Hossein-Ali, 121, 136n85
Montazeri, Mohammad, 204
Moore, Barrington, 125
Mosaddeq, Mohammad, 109, 132n12